SHATTERED STATES

SHATTERED STATES

Disorganized Attachment and Its Repair

THE JOHN BOWLBY MEMORIAL CONFERENCE MONOGRAPH 2007

Edited by

Judy Yellin and Kate White

KARNAC

First published in 2012 by
Karnac Books Ltd
118 Finchley Road, London NW3 5HT

British Library Cataloguing in Publication Data

A C.I.P. for this book is available from the British Library

ISBN 978 1 85575 831 5

Edited, designed and produced by The Studio Publishing Services Ltd
www.publishingservicesuk.co.uk
e-mail: studio@publishingservicesuk.co.uk

Printed in Great Britain

www.karnacbooks.com

CONTENTS

ACKNOWLEDGEMENTS

Thanks to the other members of the John Bowlby Memorial Conference 2007 Planning Group: Sarah Benamer, Judith Erskine, and Richard Bowlby for their creative work in producing yet another stimulating and ground-breaking conference which has enabled the emergence of this important publication. Also, many thanks to all the contributors to the conference whose profound, creative, and courageous work can now reach a much wider audience.

A special thank you to Oliver Rathbone for his continuing belief in the value of publishing these monographs and to his colleagues at Karnac Books for their patience and support in their production and publication.

Finally, thanks to our 14th John Bowlby Memorial Lecturer 2007, Judith Lewis Herman, whose moving presentation provided a context for the leading edge clinical discussions emerging out of this conference.

Judy Yellin and Kate White

Brett Kahr is Senior Clinical Research Fellow in Psychotherapy and Mental Health at the Centre for Child Mental Health in London, and Honorary Visiting Professor in the Department of Media, Culture and Language in the School of Arts at Roehampton University. He is also the Chair of the British Society of Couple Psychotherapists and Counsellors, the Professional Association of the Tavistock Centre for Couple Relationships at the Tavistock Institute of Medical Psychology. He has worked with the Bowlby Centre since 1991 as a registered member, training therapist, supervisor, and teacher, as well as Consultant in Psychology and Psychohistory. He has worked with people diagnosed with "schizophrenia" since 1979. He has written or edited six books including *D. W. Winnicott: A Biographical Portrait* (Karnac, 1996), which received the Gradiva Prize for Biography, and *Sex and the Psyche* (Allen Lane/Penguin Books, 2007). He maintains a private practice for individuals and couples in North London.

Bernice Laschinger had many years of experience in community mental health prior to becoming an attachment-based psychoanalytic psychotherapist. She is a member of The Bowlby Centre, where she is a training therapist and supervisor and has been very involved in the development of The Bowlby Centre's innovative training curriculum, particularly with the integration of the relational model of psycho-analysis into the course.

Judith Lewis Herman is Clinical Professor of Psychiatry at Harvard Medical School and Director of Training at the Victims of Violence Program at The Cambridge Hospital, Cambridge, Massachusetts. She is the author of two award-winning books: *Father–Daughter Incest* (Harvard University Press, 1981), and *Trauma and Recovery* (Basic Books, 1992). She has lectured widely on the subject of sexual and domestic violence. She is the recipient of the 1996 Lifetime Achieve-ment Award from the International Society for Traumatic Stress Studies and the 2000 Woman in Science Award from the American Medical Women's Association. In 2007 she was named a Distinguished Life Fellow of the American Psychiatric Association, and in 2011 she received the Lifetime Achievement Award from the Trauma Psychology division of the American Psychological Association.

Giovanni Liotti is a psychiatrist and psychotherapist and he currently teaches in the APC School of Psychotherapy and in the Post-graduate School of Clinical Psychology of the Salesian University, Rome, Italy. He is Founder and President of the Roman Association for Research on the Psychopathology of the Attachment System (ARPAS). His interest in the clinical applications of attachment theory and research dates back to 1975, and was first expressed in a book co-authored with V. F. Guidano, *Cognitive Processes and Emotional Disorders* (New York: Guilford Press, 1983). Since then, this interest has focused mainly on the links between dissociative psychopathology and disorganization of attachment, a theme explored in a number of journal papers and book chapters.

Kate White is a training therapist, supervisor, and teacher at The Bowlby Centre. Formerly senior lecturer at South Bank University in the Department of Nursing and Community Health Studies, she has used her extensive experience in adult education to contribute to the innovative psychotherapy curriculum developed at The Bowlby Centre. In addition to working as an individual psychotherapist, Kate runs workshops on the themes of attachment and trauma in clinical practice. Informed by her experience of growing up in South Africa, she has long been interested in the impact of race and culture on theory and on clinical practice.

Rachel Wingfield Schwartz is a former the Chair of The Bowlby Centre, where she is also a training supervisor and teacher. Rachel has a wide range of clinical experience in a variety of settings, including forensic settings, and has specialized in working with survivors of trauma and abuse, including sexual abuse, rape, domestic violence, war, state terror, torture, and organized abuse. She has a particular interest in concepts of diagnostic labelling, such as "unsuitability" and "untreatability" in relation to psychotherapy, and how they are used to distance us from working towards change with traumatized people. Rachel is also a psychotherapist with the Clinic for Dissociative Studies, which provides a cutting-edge approach to working with those labelled with personality disorders.

Judy Yellin trained at The Bowlby Centre. She works as a psychotherapist in private practice and is a member of the teaching staff on the The Bowlby Centre's psychotherapy training. She frequently teaches attachment theory and relational psychotherapy in other psychotherapy training organizations. She also has a legal background and, prior to training as a therapist, specialized as a solicitor in family law and public law in relation to child protection. Judy has a particular interest in questions of attachment, sexuality, and gender, and in working with lesbians, gay men, and transgendered clients from a relational perspective. She is an associate of Pink Therapy, an organization offering affirmative psychotherapy to sexual minority clients, as well as training for psychotherapists in working effectively with the LGBT communities. She is a founder member of The Relational School and a member of its Steering and Education Committees.

Introduction

Judy Yellin and Kate White

The fourteenth John Bowlby Memorial Conference, held in London in March 2007, stands out as a special conference in a special year. It coincided with the centenary of John Bowlby's birth, and the conference organizing committee were conscious, in particular, of a desire to celebrate the pioneering nature of his work, and the profoundly significant contribution it has made to the understanding, prevention, and healing of emotional suffering. It was with this in mind that we sought to choose a conference topic that would explore a fittingly groundbreaking area of clinical practice, and highlight the application of contemporary developments in attachment theory to new areas of clinical challenge. One such area is the understanding and treatment of the extreme states experienced in psychosis and major dissociative disorders by clients who have so often been regarded as unable to benefit from psychoanalytic psychotherapy.

Recent research in the fields of attachment and trauma is once more pointing to the contribution of early relational failures to extreme psychic suffering. "Disorganized" patterns of attachment, identified in children whose caregivers are simultaneously a source of fear and a source of comfort, have been linked to the development of both dissociative and so-called "borderline" disorders in adult life.

Research studies show childhood sexual or physical abuse in the history of the majority of psychiatric patients, and studies of people labelled as "schizophrenic" have found rates of such abuse as high as 69% for women and 59% for men. It has been found that those who have suffered "moderate child abuse" are eleven times more likely, and those who have suffered "severe child abuse" are forty-eight times more likely, to develop "pathology level psychosis". In addition, the role of emotional abuse and neglect in the aetiology of severe psychological suffering is being increasingly recognized. Recent studies of adult in-patients diagnosed as schizophrenic, for example, show rates of emotional abuse, physical neglect, and emotional neglect of 35%, 42%, and 73%, respectively. Symptoms of post-traumatic stress disorder have also been connected with schizophrenia. (For details of these and other studies, see Badouk Epstein, Schwartz, & Wingfield Schwartz, 2011; Benamer, 2010; Read & Gumley, 2008.)

Early interactions with significant others in which there are fundamental failures of empathy, attunement, recognition, and regulation of emotional states have been shown to cause both partial and global breakdown of any coherent attachment strategy. The child who repeatedly encounters either frightened or frightening behaviour from attachment figures and who cannot reliably predict their responses to approaches for soothing and comfort is presented, in Mary Main's words, with a situation of fear without solution.

In the face of such experiences, which are likely to include cumulative relational trauma in family settings, sexual, physical, and emotional abuse and neglect, as well as infanticidal threats, powerful dissociative defences might be employed, encapsulating overwhelming feelings of fear, rage, and shame which are then split off from the rest of the personality. "Shattered states", thus, characterize the human response to unmanageable helplessness and terror when facing the possibility of psychic or physical annihilation.

The conference aim was to bring together speakers able to extend our thinking and bring insights from attachment theory and psychoanalysis to the current debate about the links between the traumatic disorganization of attachment relationships and more severe mental and emotional distress (dissociative states, borderline experiences, and psychosis) as they emerge in clinical practice. The informative and provocative conference papers included in this collection address through theoretical presentations and clinical narratives the ways in which these extreme states are experienced emotionally and physically, and how they are expressed in the therapeutic encounter. They cover a diversity of themes, from a psychohistorical overview of psychosis and schizophrenia and its treatment, and the role of "infanticidal attachment" in the genesis of psychosis to the evidence for links between disorganized attachment and dissociation. They include the exploration of the central place of unregulated shame in the generation of post-traumatic states, and the clinical process of recovery and repair of such states in the context of an ongoing, long-term, attachment relationship.

The conference was privileged to open with a personal tribute and reminiscence of his father from Sir Richard Bowlby on the occasion of the centenary of his birth, which served as an enlivening and fitting prologue to the clinically rich and theoretically exciting series of papers reproduced in this volume.

Introducing the theme of psychosis and its relationship with psychoanalysis, Brett Kahr provides a sweeping historical overview of the variety of theories of schizophrenia. His paper "The infanticidal origins of psychosis: the role of trauma in schizophrenia" is a *tour de force*, drawing upon his extensive clinical experience of working with persons diagnosed as schizophrenic, and their treatment in psychiatric settings. In considering the role of trauma in the genesis of extreme states of mind, he introduces a new attachment category—infanticidal attachment—and suggests how conscious and unconscious death threats and wishes on the part of caregivers towards their children might play a significant causative role in the genesis of schizophrenia. This, is turn, can give rise to the "infanticidal transference" and its correlate, the "infanticidal countertransference", transference states to which therapists will need to pay special attention in their clinical encounters with clients who have been subject to this type of profoundly disorganizing attachment experience.

Giovanni Liotti is among the world's leading authorities on the concept of disorganized attachment and its clinical applications. His work combines cutting edge theoretical analysis with great depth of clinical understanding, synthesized in a highly creative and innovative approach to complex clinical problems. This makes his contribution indispensable to attachment-orientated therapists working with highly traumatized and dissociated client groups. His conference paper, "Disorganized attachment and therapeutic relationships with people in shattered states", provides a state-of-the-art piece marrying a review of current empirical research findings in the field of disorganized attachment with cogent hypotheses about how disorganized internal working models appear in the therapeutic relationship. Liotti's descriptions of the dilemmas posed to therapists by the evocation of the powerful contradictory transference–countertransference dynamics special to disorganized attachment patterns, and his suggestions for the fostering of co-operative therapist–client interactions, including parallel integrated treatments involving more than one therapist or therapeutic setting, make this paper an invaluable resource for all therapists seeking fresh approaches and more effective therapeutic tools than conventional frameworks have hitherto supplied.

It would be difficult to overstate the influence of our 2007 Bowlby lecturer, Judith Lewis Herman, upon therapists concerned with the long-term impact of trauma. She pioneered the recognition of the psychic impact of intrafamilial child sexual abuse with *Father–Daughter Incest* in 1981, breaking over eighty years of near silence post Freud about the reality of the sexual coercion of children. Her second book, *Trauma and Recovery*, documenting the experience of trauma shared by survivors of war, domestic and child abuse, and political terror, has been no less influential, informing generations of practitioners since its publication in 1992. Her paper in this volume, "Shattered shame states and their repair", extends the pioneering work of her own mother, Helen Bloch Lewis, on the under-theorized subject of shame and its role in attachment dynamics. Her account of the disorganizing and traumatic effect of toxic shame states, associated with rejection, ridicule, and coercive control, on the abused child's developing sense of self brings a powerful additional dimension to therapeutic work with trauma survivors. Shame is shown to be a precursor and predictor of post-traumatic stress disorder and dissociation, and a central issue in the treatment of survivors.

The realities of the clinical challenges encountered by therapists and their clients in working to heal "shattered states" are beautifully and powerfully evoked by Rachel Wingfield Schwartz's paper, "You can kill me with what you say: working with shattered states and the breakdown of inner and outer, self and other, from an attachment-based perspective". The paper highlights the distance still to travel in persuading our national health services of the value and efficacy of long-term, attachment-based psychotherapy for highly traumatized and dissociated clients. A difficult, often unsuccessful, struggle is involved in obtaining funding for such treatment, and this group of clients continues to be seen as unable to benefit from talking therapy. However, as Rachel Wingfield Schwartz's work shows, if clients are able to access long-term therapy that is informed by a sophisticated understanding of the impact of relational trauma on the development of the self, they and their therapists can work highly effectively together. She provides three clinical vignettes that illustrate both the difficulties of establishing a secure base in therapy with severely traumatized clients, and the astonishing human capacity for healing that is demonstrated when such clients are able to experience a reliable and secure attachment, often for the first time, within the therapeutic relationship.

The papers in this volume have in common a committed insistence upon placing human relationship at the centre of their accounts of extreme psychological suffering, both as the source of injury and, most hopefully, as the potential agent of repair. In this respect, they contribute fittingly in his centenary year to the continuation and extension of John Bowlby's pioneering work for the understanding, treatment, and relief of such suffering.

Brett Kahr describes asking Dr Bowlby on his first meeting with him a quarter of a century ago in Oxford whether he thought that his work on attachment theory might have relevance to an understanding of the aetiology of schizophrenia. At that time, Bowlby replied firmly in the negative. The subsequent development and growth of Bowlby's attachment model of human emotional development can now provide therapists with tools for understanding that suggest a very different conclusion. We hope that, as Giovanni Liotti comments of Bowlby in his piece on disorganized attachment and the therapeutic relationship with people in shattered states, "He would have appreciated the choice of this theme for a celebration".

References

Badouk Epstein, O., Schwartz, J., & Wingfield Schwartz, R. (2011). *Ritual Abuse and Mind Control: The Manipulation of Attachment Needs*. London: Karnac.

Benamer, S. (Ed.) (2010). *Telling Stories? Attachment-Based Approaches to the Treatment of Psychosis*. London: Karnac.

Read, J., & Gumley, A. (2008). Can attachment theory help explain the relationship between childhood adversity and psychosis? *Attachment*, 2(1): 1–35.

CHAPTER ONE

Attachment theory and The John Bowlby Memorial Lecture 2007: a short history

Bernice Laschinger

This year's Bowlby Memorial Conference marks the centenary of John Bowlby's birth in 1907. One of the outstanding psycho-analysts of the twentieth century, as a theory builder and reformer his societal impact and influence on social policy have been greater than that of any other. He has been described by Diamond and Blatt (1999, p. 669) as "the Dickens of psychoanalytic theory": he illuminated the human experiences of attachment and loss as vividly as Dickens represented those of poverty and deprivation.

The origins of Bowlby's work lay in his early work with children displaced through war or institutionalization. This led him to the conviction that at the heart of traumatic experience lay parental loss and prolonged separation from parents. His landmark report for the World Health Organisation in 1952, *Maternal Care and Mental Health*, enabled him to establish definitively the primary link between environmental trauma and the disturbed development of children

With these understandings, he entered the public arena to bring about change in the way childhood suffering was addressed by the adult world. Bowlby's work created a bridge over the chasm between individual and social experience and, hence, between the personal and the political.

There is congruence between the social and therapeutic perspectives of John Bowlby and those of this year's John Bowlby lecturer, Judith Herman. She, too, has directed her life's work to the "restoring of connections" between the private and public worlds in which traumatic experience takes place, but her focus has been on the traumatic experiences that take place in adulthood. She has shown the parallels between private terrors, such as rape and domestic violence, and public traumas, such as political terrorism. Her conceptual framework for psychotherapy with traumatized people points to the major importance of attachment in the empowerment of the survivor. She writes, "Recovery can take place only within the context of relationships; it cannot occur in isolation" (Herman, 1992, p. 333).

Bowlby had also sought to bridge "the chasm between clinician and researcher". His preparedness to leave the closed world of psychoanalysis of his time in order to make links with other disciplines, such as ethology and academic psychology, was vital in the building up of attachment theory. The documented and filmed sequence of children's responses to separation in terms of protest, detachment, and despair, as researched by James Robertson, provided evidence of separation anxiety. The impact of these ideas on the development of care of children in hospital has been enormous. The 2001 Bowlby Lecturer, Michael Rutter, discussed institutional care and the role of the state in promoting recovery from neglect and abuse. His lecture was a testament to the continuing relevance of Bowlby's thinking to contemporary social issues.

Although Bowlby joined the British Psychoanalytic Society in the 1930s and received his training from Joan Riviere and Melanie Klein, he became increasingly sceptical of their focus on the inner fantasy life of the child rather than real life experience, and tended towards what would now be termed a relational approach. Thus, in searching for a theory that could explain the anger and distress of separated young children, Bowlby turned to disciplines outside psychoanalysis, such as ethology. He became convinced of the relevance of animal, and particularly primate, behaviour to our understanding of the normal process of attachment. These relational concepts presented a serious challenge to the closed world of psychoanalysis in the 1940s, and earned Bowlby the hostility of his erstwhile colleagues for several decades.

The maintenance of physical proximity by a young animal to a preferred adult is found in a number of animal species. This suggested to Bowlby that attachment behaviour has a survival value, the most likely function of which is that of care and protection, particularly from predators. It is activated by conditions such as sickness, fear, and fatigue. Threat of loss leads to anxiety and anger, actual loss to anger and sorrow. When efforts to restore the bond fail, attachment behaviour might diminish, but will persist at an unconscious level and might become reactivated by reminders of the lost adult, or new experiences of loss.

Attachment theory's basic premise is that, from the beginning of life, the baby human has a primary need to establish an emotional bond with a caregiving adult. Attachment is seen as a source of human motivation as fundamental as those of food and sex. Bowlby (1979, p. 129) postulated that

> Attachment behaviour is any form of behaviour that results in a person attaining or maintaining proximity to some other preferred and differentiated individual . . . While especially evident during early childhood, attachment behaviour is held to characterise human beings from the cradle to the grave.

Attachment theory highlights the importance of mourning in relation to trauma and loss. An understanding of the relevance of this to therapeutic practice was a vital element in the foundation of The Bowlby Centre. The consequences of disturbed and unresolved mourning processes was a theme taken up by Colin Murray Parkes when he gave the first John Bowlby Memorial Lecture in 1993.

Mary Ainsworth, an American psychologist who became Bowlby's lifelong collaborator, established the interconnectedness between attachment behaviour, caregiving in the adult, and exploration in the child. While the child's need to explore and the need for proximity might seem contradictory, they are, in fact, complementary. It is the mother's provision of a secure base, to which the child can return after exploration, which enables the development of self-reliance and autonomy. Ainsworth developed the Strange Situation Test for studying individual differences in the attachment patterns of young children. She was able to correlate these to their mother's availability and responsiveness. Her work provided both attachment theory and psychoanalysis with empirical support for some basic premises. This provided the necessary link between attachment concepts and their application to individual experience in a clinical setting.

Over the past two decades the perspective of attachment theory has been greatly extended by the work of Mary Main, who was another Bowlby Lecturer. She developed the Adult Attachment Interview in order to study the unconscious processes that underlie the behavioural pattern of attachment identified by Mary Ainsworth. Further support came from the perspective of infant observation and developmental psychology developed by yet another Bowlby Lecturer, Daniel Stern. The Bowlby Lecturer for 2000, Allan Schore, presented important developments in the new field of neuro-psycho-analysis, describing emerging theories of how attachment experiences in early life shape the developing brain.

The links beween attachment theory and psychoanalysis have also been developed. Jo Klein, a great supporter of The Bowlby Centre and also a former contributor to the Bowlby Conference, has explored these links in psychotherapeutic practice. In particular, the 1998 Bowlby Lecturer, Stephen Mitchell, identified a paradigm shift away from drive theory within psychoanalysis. His proposed "relational matrix" links attachment theory to other relational psychoanalytic theories that find so much resonance in the current social and cultural climate. Within this area of convergence, between attachment research and developmental psychoanalysis, the 1999 Bowlby Lecturer, Peter Fonagy, has developed the concept of "mentalization", extending our understanding of the importance of the reflective function, particularly in adversity.

In similar vein, the work of Beatrice Beebe, the 2001 Bowlby Lecturer, represents another highly creative development in the unfolding relational narrative of the researcher–clinician dialogue. Her unique research has demonstrated how the parent–infant interaction creates a distinct system organized by mutual influence and regulation, which is reproduced in the adult therapeutic relationship.

In the movement to bring the body into the forefront of relational theory and practice, the 2003 Bowlby Lecturer, Susie Orbach, has been a leading pioneer. It was the publication of her ground-breaking books, *Fat is a Feminist Issue* and *Hunger Strike*, which introduced a powerful and influential approach to the study of the body in its social context. Over the past decade, one of her major interests has been the construction of sexuality and bodily experience in the therapeutic relationship.

The 2004 Bowlby Lecturer, Jody Messler Davies, has made major contributions to the development of the relational model. Her integration of trauma theory and relational psychoanalysis led to new understandings of the transference–countertranference as a vehicle for expressing traumatic experience (Davies & Frawley, 1994).

Kimberlyn Leary, Bowlby Lecturer in 2005, illuminated the impact of racism on the clinical process. The importance of her contribution lay in her understanding of the transformative potential inherent in the collision of two "racialized subjectivities" in the therapeutic process. She showed the possibility for reparation when both therapist and client break the silence surrounding their difference.

The 2006 John Bowlby Memorial Lecturer Bessel van der Kolk's contribution to the understanding of post trauma stress in terms of a developmental trauma disorder has been seminal. His 1987 book, *Psychological Trauma*, was the first to consider the impact of trauma on the entire person, integrating neurobiological, interpersonal, and social perspectives.

Within this tradition of great trauma theorists, the contribution of this year's Bowlby Lecturer, Judith Herman, a collaborator of Bessel van der Kolk, has been outstanding. As a teacher, researcher, and clinician, her life's work has been directed to survivors of trauma. Her landmark book, *Trauma and Recovery* (1992), is considered to have changed the way we think about trauma. Bridging the world of war veterans, prisoners of war, and survivors of domestic and sexual abuse, she has shown that psychological trauma can only be understood in a social context.

References

Bowlby, J. (1952). *Maternal Care and Mental Health* (2nd edn). World Health Organisation Monograph Series, No. 2. Geneva: World Health Organisation.

Bowlby, J. (1979). *The Making and Breaking of Affectional Bonds*. London: Tavistock.

Davies, J. M., & Frawley, M. G. (1994). *Treating the Adult Survivor of Childhood Sexual Abuse: A Psychoanalytic Perspective*. New York: Basic Books.

Diamond, D., & Blatt, S. J. (1999). Prologue to attachment research and psychoanalysis. *Psychoanalytic Inquiry*, 19(5): 424–447.

Herman, J. L. (1992). *Trauma and Recovery: The Aftermath of Violence From Domestic Abuse to Political Terror*. New York: Basic Books.

Van der Kolk, B. (1987). *Psychological Trauma*. Washington, DC: American Psychiatric Press.

CHAPTER TWO

The infanticidal origins of psychosis: the role of trauma in schizophrenia

Brett Kahr

"Mad let us grant him then, and now remains
That we find out the cause of this effect,
Or rather say, the cause of this defect,
For this effect defective comes by cause"

("Polonius", in Shakespeare, ca. 1601,
Act II, Scene ii: 100–104)

"Perhaps if one talked to him one would understand"

(Strachey, 1956, p. 25, Letter to Virginia Stephen
(later Virginia Woolf), 3rd January, 1909)

"Love in all its myriad forms still stands as the principal prescription for the treatment of schizophrenia. Affection and sympathy, tenderness and approval; these are the medicines of choice"

(Wexler, 1951, p. 157)

Taking tea with Dr John Bowlby

The late Dr John Bowlby, whose hundredth birthday we celebrate this evening, deserves the eternal gratitude of every citizen of our planet for his gargantuan contribution to the science of humankind. In a career which spanned over six decades, Bowlby succeeded in demonstrating, beyond all doubt, that mental health—our greatest prize—derives from consistent, reliable, and tender attachment relationships between infants and their caregivers, and that mental illness—our greatest tragedy—stems not necessarily from our genetic, biochemical, or neurophysiological endowments, but, rather, from parental attacks, abandonments, and impingements. Bowlby's paradigm, now known as attachment theory, deserves a place in the history of medicine, in the history of psychology, in the history of science, and in the history of humanity, as one of the greatest achievements, on a par, I wish to suggest, with the art of Leonardo da Vinci, the music of Wolfgang Amadeus Mozart, and the non-violent militarism of Mohandas Gandhi. For, in Bowlby's work, we find that the roots of depression and anxiety, neurosis and delinquency, alcoholism and anorexia, can all be traced to deficiencies and ruptures in the security of the earliest bond between a vulnerable infant and his or her primary caretakers.

Bowlby's work has touched millions, and he deserves our celebrations this weekend. I count myself deeply privileged that not only have I had the great pleasure of continuing to learn from his son Sir Richard Bowlby, from his daughter-in-law Lady Bowlby, with whom I work at the Centre for Child Mental Health here in London, and from his niece, the distinguished child psychotherapist Dr Juliet Hopkins, and from other members of the Bowlby clan, but that I also had the deep privilege of having known the late Dr Bowlby himself.

We first met on Monday, 20th February 1984, at approximately 3.00 p.m., in the Porter's Lodge at Corpus Christi College at the University of Oxford. The very fact that the day of the week, the date, and the time of our first meeting remain so emblazoned in my long-term memory indicates the impact of this encounter. As a young postgraduate student in psychology at that time, I had invited Dr Bowlby to the university to speak before the Oxford Psycho-Analytical Forum, a group that I had formed the previous year to provide public education on psychoanalytical topics as an antidote to the strong behaviourist and pharmacological climate so prevalent in British academia and health care at the time. Dr Bowlby graciously accepted my offer to deliver a lecture, and I shall never forget the sight of the vigorous septuagenarian psychiatrist and psychoanalyst striding through the gate of the courtyard about to have an Oxford tea with me, prior to his talk in the steely lecture theatre in the Department of Experimental Psychology. Although a mere stripling at the time, twenty-three years of age to be precise, I knew even then that I would, in all likelihood, never meet a more distinguished and influential mental health practitioner in my lifetime, and so, I memorized the moment.

At tea, in a café on Broad Street, only a stone's throw from the very spot where Queen Mary ("Bloody Mary") had burned several Protestant martyrs in the sixteenth century, Dr Bowlby reminisced generously about his early career, regaling me with stories of his student days at the University of Cambridge, his earliest encounters with the writings of Sigmund Freud, his reminiscences of pioneering figures of the 1920s' and 1930s' medico-psychological movement in the United Kingdom, as well as his clinical supervisions with Melanie Klein. Although he and I had only just met, he dared to be playful, and he performed the most charmingly wicked imitation of Mrs Klein, raising his voice by at least an octave in the process. Quippingly, he reminisced that Melanie Klein worshipped, quite narcissistically, at the shrine of "St Melanie", whereas Anna Freud worshipped, perhaps more humbly, at the shrine of "St Sigmund".

I told Dr Bowlby of my admiration for his work, and that I had found his trilogy of books on *Attachment and Loss* (Bowlby, 1969, 1973, 1980) of inestimable value in my fledgling work with depressed patients at the nearby psychiatric hospital. Midway through our conversation, I also spoke to Dr Bowlby of the clinical research work that I had begun to undertake on the psychodynamics of schizophrenia. He listened attentively, with the seriousness of a true scientist. To his credit, he admitted that he had very little experience of working with schizophrenic men and women, and he asked to know more. In a fumbling manner, I shared what little I knew at that point, and I became impressed that this aged Hercules of the mental health world actually had space in his mind for further inquisitiveness. At one point, I asked Dr Bowlby whether he thought that his own work on attachment theory might have relevance to an understanding of the aetiology of the schizophrenic psychoses. He looked at me across the tea table with thoughtfulness as he tucked into a scone with jam, and then, with resolution in his voice, he replied that attachment theory had *nothing* to contribute to schizophrenia. Daunted by the genius of Dr Bowlby, I nodded respectfully, and I refrained from saying anything more about this topic.

I then walked Dr Bowlby to the lecture theatre on Oxford's South Parks Road, introduced him to a packed audience which included my late and much-missed mentor, the literary psychiatrist Dr Anthony Storr, and then sat enthralled as Bowlby talked brilliantly about secrets in the family. That evening, I took him to supper with two other postgraduate students in psychology, and I know that Dr Bowlby enjoyed this very much; in fact, I believe Dr Bowlby even remarked on the futility of preaching to one's older colleagues, underscoring that one must, instead, cultivate the minds of the next generation. In the taxi en route to the railway station, Bowlby (1990) regaled me with details of his forthcoming psychobiography of Charles Darwin. That evening, I returned to my tiny student accommodation on the Iffley Road in a very heady state indeed (Kahr, 1984).

Over the remaining six years of his life, I had the privilege of further conversations and correspondence, ever amazed at the generosity of this Titan who, I know, had thousands of requests for his time from scholars, researchers, and clinicians from all over the world. I count myself fortunate to be one of the veritable army of mental health workers who had a personal experience of Dr Bowlby, and I know there will be many others here tonight who knew him infinitely longer and infinitely better, and who now find themselves much enriched by the experience.

In spite of my unwavering admiration for Dr Bowlby, I wish to argue, here tonight, that he might have made an error.

In the pages which follow, I propose to discuss the work that I have undertaken over the past twenty-five years or more, as well as the work of generations of mental health practitioners over the past one hundred years, which demonstrates that broken attachments, and, in particular, a type of attachment that I have come to refer to as the "infanticidal attachment", might play a pivotal role in the development of the schizophrenic psychoses. The error perpetrated by Dr Bowlby, through no fault of his own, might best be described as an error of undue scientific *modesty*, and I hope to demonstrate that

Bowlby's philosophy of mental health and mental illness might well have given us an important key—more important than he knew during his own lifetime—to the eradication of the most severe form of psychological illness known to humankind: schizophrenia.

The ravages of schizophrenia

Although every trained psychiatrist, psychologist, social worker, and psychiatric nurse will have an experience of working with individuals diagnosed as suffering from schizophrenia, I do know that many psychotherapists and counsellors—those professions which have become increasingly the backbone of the mental health industry— might not have such first-hand contact with the gross, overt psychoses, and, therefore, I wish to describe some of the characteristics of schizophrenia before proceeding to understand something more about its aetiology and treatment. Many mental health professionals regard schizophrenia as a psychiatric rarity, something encountered only by a tiny proportion of colleagues who still work in psychiatric hospitals, many of which have now closed down in this era of so-called "community care". It might be true that not all of us will encounter schizophrenic men and women in our private consulting rooms, but we must not forget that schizophrenia still constitutes one of the greatest health problems of all time. Recent epidemiological estimates of incidence and prevalence suggest that approximately 0.5–0.8% of the world's population struggles with schizophrenia at any time, and this would amount to roughly 60,000,000 individuals, virtually the same number of people as the population of Great Britain (e.g., Van Os & Kapur, 2009). Therefore, if we deported every man, woman, and child from British soil, and replaced them with the all the world's schizophrenics, the figure would be almost exactly the same, thus underscoring the sheer weightiness of schizophrenia as an international epidemic (cf. Cohen, 1988; Jones & Buckley, 2003; Taylor, 2006).

From a formal, phenomenological point of view, schizophrenia[1] can be described as the most severe manifestation of psychosis, characterized in many instances by so-called thought disorder, and, often, by the presence of hallucinations (whether auditory, visual, olfactory, gustatory, or tactile–haptic–kinaesthetic) and by the presence of delusions (whether grandiose, persecutory, or erotomaniacal). The perceptual and cognitive distortions so characteristic of schizophrenia will include thought broadcasting, thought insertion, impaired attention, impaired memory, impaired eye-tracking capacities, and impaired language (such as word salad, klang associations, echolalia, or impoverishment of speech). Patients frequently present, as well, with autistic withdrawal, catatonic waxy flexibility, ambivalent object relationships, loosened associations, and inappropriate affect. Investigators will often divide the common symptoms of schizophrenia into two categories: so-called "positive symptoms" such as hallucinations and delusions, characterized by the *presence* of abnormality (e.g., Benedetti, 1973; Cox, 1997; Crider, 1979; Strauss & Carpenter, 1981), and so-called "negative symptoms", such as flattened affect, impoverishment of speech, alogia, apathy, anhedonia, poor eye contact, inattentiveness, unchanging facial expressions, lack of vocal inflection, inappropriate affect, paucity of gestures, and physical anergia, all characterized by the *absence* of function (e.g., Gibson, 1966; Greden & Tandon, 1991; Peralta & Cuesta, 1996). Certain investigators have noted many physical abnormalities in these patients, such as abnormal distribution of bodily hair, abnormal size of the testes in men, cyanosis of the hands and feet, excessive sweating, increased salivation, and exaggerated tendon reflexes, as well as minor anatomical anomalies (e.g., Klingmann, 1946; cf. Murphy & Owen, 1996; Compton & Walker, 2009), not to mention unusual body shapes (e.g., Rees, 1957).

The schizophrenic illness infests every aspect of an individual's functioning, whether motoric (e.g., Malla, Norman, Aguilar, Carnahan, & Cortese, 1995; Morrens, Hulstijn & Sabbe, 2007) or perceptual and cognitive (e.g., Allen, Liddle, & Frith, 1993; Burch, 1995; Chapin, Rosenbaum, Fields, & Wightman, 1996; Chapman & McGhie, 1962; Chen & McKenna, 1996; Davidson, 1937; Harrow & Quinlan, 1985; Harvey & Walker, 1987; Kasanin, 1944; Liddle, 2001; Owens & Johnstone, 1980; Rickers-Ovsiankina, 1938; Rizzo, Danion, Van der Linden, & Grangé, 1996; Rochester & Martin, 1979; Saccuzzo & Braff, 1986; Salzinger, Portnoy, & Feldman, 1978; Schwartz, 1978). Such cognitive defects will include poor verbal learning, poor perceptual capacities, poor eye-tracking, greater distractibility, poor reaction time, poor abstract thinking, as well as a poorer sense of time estimation, overinclusiveness of thinking, and failure to reason abstractly. Patients will also display impairments in social and sexual functioning (e.g.,

Hoskins, 1943; Milne, Curson, Wilkie, & Pantelis, 1993). Further, we know that in regard to intimate contact, those who combat this condition will be much less likely to forge successful couple or sexual relationships (e.g., Sampson et al., 1964), will be less likely to bear children (a phenomenon known as schizophrenic subfecundity) (cf. Bundy, Stahl, & MacCabe, 2011; Kallmann & Rypins, 1938), and might even be more prone to erotomania (e.g., Phillips, West, & Wang, 1996). For those schizophrenic individuals who do have children, the offspring will often suffer. An important Israeli study has documented that the children of schizophrenic parents tend to have lower Wechsler IQ test performance scores, will have more difficult interpersonal relationships, will be more likely to suffer from overt psychopathology, will have more pronounced sibling rivalry, will be more likely to manifest a "primary habit disorder" such as enuresis, eating problems, sleeping problems, and crying spells, will be more likely to display physical aggression, will have poorer personal hygiene, will have sadder facial expressions, will have poorer nutrition and physical health, will have more difficulties in establishing a solid sexual orientation in later life, will be more likely to lie, will have a less obvious interest in creative pursuits, will show more evidence of impaired reality testing and thought disorder, and will have a greater number of psychosomatic complaints, as well as flattened affect, and depressive, obsessive, compulsive, and impulsive tendencies (Landau, Harth, Othnay, & Sharfhertz, 1972). Often, the children of schizophrenic patients will be taken into care, and, hence, will have to struggle additionally with the effects of parental separation and subsequent adoption.

Schizophrenic people will also be less likely to complete their education (Jones et al., 1993), will be less likely to sustain gainful employment (e.g., Marwaha et al., 2007), and will be less likely, in many cases, to maintain a reasonable standard of personal bodily hygiene (e.g., Brewer, Edwards, Anderson, Robinson, & Pantelis, 1996) or oro-dental hygiene (e.g., Klinge, 1979). They will also have poorer physical posture. Further, schizophrenic patients will also be at greater risk of co-morbidity for other psychiatric conditions, and for substance abuse (e.g., Smith & Hucker, 1994), as well as obsessive–compulsive disorder and post-traumatic stress disorder (e.g., Buckley, Miller, Lehrer, & Castle, 2009). They also suffer from horrific side-effects of their medication (e.g., Breggin, 1983, 1991; Waddington et al., 1995). The iatrogenically induced sequelae of pharmacological interventions include increased tumorigenicity (e.g., galactorrhoea, hyperprolactinaemia, and pituitary tumours), metabolic disturbances (including weight gain), haematologic symptoms (e.g., agranulocytosis and neutropoenia), gastrointestinal symptoms (including constipation), not to mention salivary symptoms such as sialorrhoea, as well as teratogenic effects (Carvajal, Arias, & Jimeno, 2009). Others have reported thyroid dysfunction in schizophrenic patients (e.g., Hoskins, 1946), and still others have documented the sexual dysfunctions, which result from prolonged use of medication (e.g., Wehring & Kelly, 2009). And those with schizophrenia often place an enormous burden of care on their relatives (e.g., Alanen, 1958; Mishler & Waxler, 1968; Dearth, Labenski, Mott, & Pellegrini, 1986; Scazfuca & Kuipers, 1996; cf. Walsh, 1985; Wyden, 1998).

For many years, researchers have known that those diagnosed with schizophrenia (or with "dementia praecox") will die at earlier ages (Malzberg, 1934); indeed, these individuals will be two to three times more likely to die sooner than the average member of the population (McGrath, Saha, Chant, & Welham, 2008). Tragically, they will also be more likely to commit suicide than members of the general population (e.g., Tsuang, Woolson, & Fleming, 1980). For those who do not take their own lives, the physical consequences of schizophrenia can, in fact, be quite marked, often as a result of neglect of bodily caretaking; thus, schizophrenic patients will be more likely to suffer from obesity (Cohn, 2009; Thakore, 2005; Thiels, 2005; Winkelman, 2001; cf. Justo, 2006), sleep apnoea (Winkelman, 2001), cardiovascular disease (Camm, 2003; Filik et al., 2006; Nielsen & Toft, 2009), and from respiratory disease (Hussar, 1966; Brenner & Cohen, 2009). According to the British cardiologist, Professor John Camm (2003), those schizophrenic individuals who take antipsychotic medications will be more likely to die from the effects of diabetes, hypercholesterolaemia, hypertriglyceridaemia, obesity, sinus node dysfunction, cardiomyopathy, myocarditis, and a host of other medical conditions (cf. Ray, Chung, Murray, Hall, & Stein, 2009; Tiihonen et al., 2009).

Additionally, schizophrenic patients will be much more likely to smoke (Itkin, Nemets, & Einat, 2001), and to have an increased risk of HIV infection (Seeman, Lang, & Rector, 1990; Stefan & Catalán, 1995), as well as hepatitis B and hepatitis C (Rosenberg et al., 2001). According to the distinguished sexual health epidemiologist Professor Ann Kurth (2007) at the University of Washington in Seattle, and more recently at New York University in New York City, schizophrenic patients who have become infected with HIV often have a poorer prognosis owing to their greater incapacity to take their antiviral medications at the appropriate times. Those struggling with schizophrenia also have an increased risk of developing diabetes mellitus (Type 2) (Juvonen et al., 2007), and have a higher incidence of colon cancer (Hippisley-Cox, Vinogradova, Coupland, & Parker, 2007).

The long-term effects of managing and enduring a schizophrenic illness will also have an impact upon the immune system. Research has confirmed that schizophrenic patients will struggle with the consequences of poor T-lymphocyte functioning (Theodoropoulou-Vaidaki, Alexopoulos, & Stefanis, 1988). Schizophrenic patients will be more likely than members of the general non-psychiatric population to die from sudden death (Barnes & Kerwin, 2003; Mortensen & Juel, 1993; Tsuang, Woolson, & Fleming, 1980), or from accidents and suicide (Brown, 1997); indeed, the most recent research has concluded that the mortality risk for schizophrenia could well be two to three times that of the general population (Casey & Hansen, 2009; Brown, Kim, Mitchell, & Inskip, 2010).

Although most psychotic patients do not commit serious forensic crimes, schizophrenic individuals may be more predisposed to violence than members of the general public (e.g., Humphreys, Johnstone, Macmillan, & Taylor, 1992; Walsh, Buchanan, & Fahy, 2002). Furthermore, other researchers have noted that schizophrenic patients do not have great insight into the meaning of their violent behaviour (Buckley et al., 2004).

The financial costs of caring for schizophrenic individuals must not be underestimated (Maynard, 1996; Moscarelli, Rupp, & Sartorius, 1996). One report has underscored that the price of nursing a person diagnosed with schizophrenia could well be six times as expensive as the costs of a case of myocardial infarction (Andrews et al., 1985). Contemporary authors have estimated that the yearly costs for schizophrenia in the United States alone have exceeded $62,700,000,000 (Wu et al., 2005; cf. Knapp, 1997; Lewis, McCrone, & Frangou, 2001; Rockland, 2010).

Having worked with psychotic, schizophrenic patients since 1979, I have become increasingly struck not only by the preponderance of hallucinations and delusions which characterize these patients, but perhaps, above all, by the sheer emotional *pain* experienced by these heroic strugglers. When I first stepped on to a psychogeriatric hospital ward as a fledgling psychology trainee, I found myself in shock at what I witnessed: elderly patients surrounded with puddles of urine, with saliva streaming down their chins, suffering from tardive dyskinesia, a tragic side-effect of the first generation of psychotropic medication, which attacks the extrapyramidal neuronal tracts and thereby causes patients to lose control over the motility of their tongues. Unable to speak with clarity, owing to this dreadful iatrogenically induced psychomotor symptom, it took time to learn that "Anthony", an elderly schizophrenic gentleman, had first entered hospital after carving the eyes out of all of the priceless paintings in a nearby stately home, because he thought the eyes could see into the depths of his anus. Similarly, it took time to learn that "Beatrice", an elderly schizophrenic woman had first entered hospital because she believed that every night eight million Chinese men would enter her bed and rape her. And it took time to learn that "Curtis", another elderly schizophrenic individual, had shot both his mother and his father, in the face, at point blank range, desperate to assuage the voices in his head that forced him—so he claimed—to kill his terrifying parents.

After several years of working with the long-stay psychogeriatric patients, I then had the opportunity to engage in psychotherapeutic work with young acute schizophrenic patients as well, most of whom had only recently experienced their first psychotic episodes. I shall never forget one of my first encounters with a teenage schizophrenic male whom I shall call "Damian", who, upon meeting me, extended his right hand for a shake. I noticed at once that he had only three fingers on his hand. He quickly explained that he had heard voices in his head that told him that he must take a meat cleaver from the butcher's shop in which he worked, and hack off each of his fingers, one by one. A work colleague restrained him from carrying out this internalized injunction fully, but tragically, Damian had already severed two fingers in the process. I shall also never forget my first conversation with a young schizophrenic woman called "Eliza". She found life so intolerable, tormented by images of severed penises flying around her head, as well as visions of buckets of blood being poured over her body that, quite understandably, she wished to die. During one of our psychotherapy sessions, she turned to me quite plaintively and told me that she wished desperately to drink the blood of a fellow hospital patient dying from AIDS. She moaned, in agonised tones, "If I could've cut him and sucked out his blood, I would've done." Only in this way, would she be freed from the terrors of her mind. Another teenage schizophrenic patient, whom I shall call "Flavia", pleaded with me in session to bash in her aching brain with a hammer, crying out, "If you really loved me, you would kill me." Yet another schizophrenic youngster, whom I shall call "Gertrude", explained that she found life so unbearable that she wanted to hang herself, but feared that even this would not stop the pain, and, there-fore, she would be forced not only to hang herself, but also to stab herself in the jugular, then shoot herself in the head, and then jump from a tall skyscraper. Only in this way would death be truly ensured. And finally, I recall "Herbert", a schizophrenic man who explained to me, "My heart is like a broken bottle . . . soaked in a bath of acid." The tormented, tortured poetry of the schizophrenic individual speaks volumes, underscoring our need as mental health professionals to understand the sources of such indescribable hurt.

Dr Murray Jackson, a psychiatrist and psychoanalyst who worked, quite famously, with hospitalized psychotic patients at the Maudsley Hospital in South London, bravely and helpfully filmed many of his psychotherapeutic sessions with schizophrenic patients, some of which I have had the privilege of viewing. In one of Jackson's films, he interviewed a woman suffering from extreme catatonic schizo-phrenia, who, in early childhood, had to endure the death of five of her six elder siblings, a set of bereavements reminiscent of the child-hood of Adolf Hitler. Understandably, this woman exclaimed, speak-ing perhaps on behalf of schizophrenic sufferers everywhere, "Hell can't be worse than this."

Dr Albert Honig (1972), an American osteopath who worked cre-atively with the gnarled bodies of schizophrenic patients, many of whom had spent decades in frozen, contorted postures, described schizophrenia, perhaps best of all, as "the awakening nightmare" (derived from the supratitle of Honig's neglected book *The Awakening Nightmare: A Breakthrough in Treating the Mentally Ill*). Imagine, in fact, your very worst nightmare. Recall the relief that you will have ex-perienced upon opening your eyes in the morning. Now imagine your very worst nightmare again. And then imagine that you never wake up. That experience—the awakening nightmare—might be the very best description that I have ever encountered which helps us to appreciate the deep, soul-destroying tragedy of schizophrenia.

Of course, in spite of the ravages of schizophrenia, I wish to remind us all that although a great many people do suffer lives of misery as a result of schizophrenia, many will recover, and even those who do not recover do not always regard their own lives as exercises in torment. Some recuperate so well, in fact, that they become mental health professionals. Several commentators have suspected that the pathbreaking American psychiatrist and psychoanalyst, Dr Harry Stack Sullivan, might have suffered from schizophrenia at some point during his early life, and that this intimate experience helped him to become a better psychotherapist to his own patients at the Sheppard and Enoch Pratt Hospital in Towson, Maryland, where he pioneered psychoanalytical treatments for the psychoses (Perry, 1982; cf. Sullivan, 1953; Kvarnes & Parloff, 1976). Similarly, Dr Fred Frese, a representative of the National Alliance for the Mentally Ill in the USA, had at one time struggled personally with schizophrenia, but has now become the Director of Psychology in the very institution where he had once been a patient (Alanen, González de Chávez, & Silver, 2006).

Indeed, I readily recall that one of the kindest people that I have ever met in my entire life suffered from schizophrenia for many years, afflicted by hallucinations and delusions, yet who, in spite of this debilitating mental illness, devoted her entire life to charitable works and to the care of others struggling with mental illness. This woman, for example, could never walk through the downtrodden streets of Soho, in Central London, without stopping in front of each homeless person curled up in a doorway and then offering them food, money, and conversation. I shall never forget her stories of asking each homeless mentally ill person what type of hamburger he or she would most enjoy, and then bounding into the McDonald's in Leicester Square, returning with a special order for her hungry fellow traveller. How many of us who have never suffered from schizophrenia turn a blind eye to the often overwhelming social suffering that we encounter on a daily basis?

My own position in relation to schizophrenia can be described in a relatively straightforward manner. I neither idealize nor revile, neither venerate nor pity, the person with schizophrenia. Instead, I try to recognize whatever suffering might be present in the individual as well as within his or her family, and offer help only when and where such help might be sought, required, or appreciated.

The aetiology of schizophrenia

What causes schizophrenia? Throughout the centuries, numerous writers and investigators have posited a veritable plethora of potential causes of schizophrenia (cf. Colbert, 1996; Foster, 2003). Our most remote historical ancestors had originally posited cosmological theories, explaining gross insanity as a result of the position of the moon (from which the term "lunacy" has derived). Others subscribed to a religious notion, having explained insanity as evidence of a plague or a curse sent by the gods; still others regarded what we would now call psychosis as a result of demonological forces (cf. Gilman, 1982). As ancient medicine became more sophisticated, distinguished Roman physicians, such as Claudius Galen, espoused the humoral hypothesis, explaining that madness must derive from an imbalance in the quantity of blood or bile. These early theories have formed the basis of later medico–pathological theories of aetiology, which sit uncomfortably beside those theories which have posited a purely psychogenic origin.

More recently, experts have engaged in extensive speculations as to the cause of schizophrenia. The late nineteenth-century German psychiatrist Dr Karl Ludwig Kahlbaum (1874) postulated that dementia praecox (the diagnostic precursor of schizophrenia) results from mental over-exertion. Dr Henry Maudsley (1868), whose surname now adorns the UK's most venerable traditional psychiatric hospital, argued that extreme madness stems, in certain cases, from masturbation (cf. Blandford, 1871; Hare, 1962). Other contemporaneous clinicians attributed the cause of extreme madness to corrupted breast milk, to narcotics, to skin disease, or to heart disease (Sueuer, 1996), or as a result of toxaemia (e.g., Noll, 2006a,b), or even as a consequence of whooping cough (Shuttleworth, 1904). The American neurologist and alienist Dr Morris Karpas (1908, p. 1062) regretted that, "It will be easily appreciated what a difficult task one undertakes to discuss the aetiology of a malady, the psychology and pathology of which are still obscure". Lamenting ignorance of the *"peculiar onset"* and the *"unexplainable behavior"* of the condition, Karpas (*ibid.*), summarized, nevertheless, much of late nineteenth-century and early twentieth-century literature on dementia praecox, noting the following possible causes: hereditary taint, toxins, parental intoxication, autointoxication (through hepatic impairment or renal dysfunction), meteorological factors such as high barometric pressure or dry days, fright, national-ity, modern civilization, lack of physical activity, poor education, insufficient food, lack of fresh air, masturbation, sexual abstemious-ness, marital discord, pregnancy, childbirth, head trauma, and many others to boot. Karpas even supposed that an inability to learn a trade constitutes a risk factor for dementia praecox, as does being Jewish, owing to the fact that throughout the centuries, Jews have suffered great persecution, leaving them with "a neurasthenoid constitution and a psychopathic predisposition" (ibid., p. 1067).

In 1918, Sir Robert Armstrong-Jones, one of the most influential psychiatric theoreticians and practitioners in the United Kingdom during the first quarter of the twentieth century, delivered four lectures on Physic to Gresham College in London, one of the most prestigious arenas in which to speak. Armstrong-Jones (1918) stated simply and categorically that insanity results from one of three causes: hereditary factors, venereal disease, or alcoholism. He gave no credence whatsoever to emotional, familial, psychological, societal, or traumatogenic factors.

To quote but one example of a more recent biopathological theory of dementia praecox (the late nineteenth-century to early twentieth-century term for schizophrenia), consider the research of Sir Frederick Walker Mott, a distinguished neuropathologist, a Fellow of the Royal Society, a Knight Commander of the Order of the British Empire, as well as a future president of the Royal Medico-Psychological Asso-ciation (the forerunner of the Royal College of Psychiatrists). Already renowned for his important work on the recognition of general paral-ysis of the insane as a manifestation of syphilis, Mott (1920) postulated that dementia praecox results from masturbation, and from a degen-eracy of the tubules in the testes of male patients. He did not attempt to provide a comparable explanation for female patients.

With great frankness, the late nineteenth-century–early twentieth-century psychiatric researcher Professor Emil Kraepelin (1913b, p. 224), the father of contemporary biological psychiatry, had to admit that, "The Causes of dementia praecox are at the present time still wrapped in impenetrable darkness". Kraepelin (ibid., p. 207) also described psychotic delusions as "nonsensical". In spite of the fact that so many authors conceded their ignorance about the origins of schizophrenia, countless psychopathologists have continued, none-theless, to proffer an extraordinary array of aetiological notions.

Questions of causation must not be dismissed as a mere academic indulgence, for the answer to this very conundrum determines only too clearly whether schizophrenic patients will be treated with surgery, electricity, pharmacotherapeutic agents, talking therapies, or with exorcism by a specialist priest.

Since the nineteenth century, theories of aetiology have tended to cluster into three principal categories:

- proto-biopathological theories, which regard schizophrenia as an exclusively medical condition, resulting from genetic inheritance, biochemical imbalance, neuroanatomical abnormality, or even viral infection (e.g., Lawrie, Weinberger, & Johnstone, 2004);
- proto-psychological theories, which regard schizophrenia as an exclusively psychological condition, resulting from trauma, and from disturbances within the parent–child matrix (e.g., Fliess, 1973; Karon & VandenBos, 1981);
- interactionist theories, also known as biopsychosocial or diathesis-stress theories, which acknowledge the importance of both biopathological factors and external social stressors as interactive aetiological agents (e.g., Lenzenweger & Dworkin, 1998; Williamson, 2006).[2]

Theories of biopathogenesis

Contemporary psychiatric and psychopathological investigators no longer regard schizophrenia as a result of demonic possession; rather, they understand schizophrenia as a genetically transmitted neurological disease. During the first half of the twentieth century, psychiatrists touted the genetic evidence with uncritical bombast. For instance, the somatically orientated physicians, Dr Willy Mayer-Gross, Dr Eliot Slater, and Dr Martin Roth (1954, p. 280), authors of *Clinical Psychiatry*, the most influential British psychiatric textbook for decades, pronounced, unhesitatingly, "It may now be regarded as established that hereditary factors play a predominant role in the causation of schizophrenic psychoses. The evidence is extensive, and is in the form of very thorough family and twin studies". Blithely, Mayer-Gross, Slater, and Roth (*ibid.*, p. 229) had noted, dismissively, that *"psychological factors,* in spite of a widespread belief in their influence, do not

frequently precipitate a schizophrenic illness or attack". Such confi-
dent rhetorical flourishes encouraged psychiatric researchers to ignore
the psychoanalytical studies on schizophrenia, and to focus, almost
monolithically, on genetic investigations, beginning with a monogenic
hypothesis—the notion that one gene will cause schizophrenia, rather
like Down's Syndrome or Huntington's Disease, which follow tradi-
tionally Mendelian patterns of inheritance (e.g., Kallmann, 1946;
Kallmann & Rypins, 1938).

Based on nearly a century of genetically and neuropathologically
orientated research on schizophrenia and its diagnostic precursor
"dementia praecox", investigators have had to abandon the crude
monogenic hypothesis, and have since come to espouse a more sophisticated polygenic hypothesis, positing that schizophrenia will be
caused by a combination of "susceptibility" genes, whose action
might or might not be triggered by environmental stressors, and
which might result in brain abnormalities, such as reduced volume in
the temporal lobes and the hippocampus, increased volumes in the
cerebellar ventricles and in the hippocampus, grey matter deficits, and
cellular disarray, as well as an excess of neurotransmitters such as
dopamine in the neuronal synapses (cf. Andreasen, 1984, 1986, 1994;
Antonova et al., 2005; Freeman, 1931; Frith & Johnstone, 2003; Grace,
2004; Green, Neuchterlein, & Satz, 1987; Harms et al., 2010; Henn &
Nasrallah, 1982; Hoskins, 1946; Lawrie, 2004; Lawrie & Abukmeil,
1998; Lawrie, Weinberger, & Johnstone, 2004; Lewis, Mimics, & Levitt,
2004; Matthysse & Kety, 1975; McDonald & Murray, 2004; Mednick,
Cannon, Barr, & Lyon, 1991; Norton & Owen, 2004; Rhinewine et al.,
2005; Schork, Greenwood, & Braff, 2007; Sharma & Chitnis, 2000;
Tsuang, 1993; Vyas, Patel, & Puri, 2011). Colleagues have even suggested head injury as an aetiological factor (e.g., Bartschinger & Maier,
1920), as well as nutritional causes of schizophrenia (e.g., Mahadik,
2004), or indeed, the use of cannabis (e.g., Murray et al., 2004), or even
influenza (e.g., Crow, 1994; Mispelbaum, 1891) and other infections
such as *Toxoplasma gondii* (Mortensen et al., 2007). Others have specu-
lated about the role of bromide intoxication in the causation of schizophrenia (Levin, 1946).

Such aetiological theories suggest either surgical or pharmacolog-
ical intervention (e.g., Crow, 1982; Crowe, 1994; Eccleston, 1986;
Patterson, Spohn, Bogia, & Hayes, 1986; Pettegrew & Minshew, 1994;
Roberts, 1991; Rosenthal, 1970; Shields, Heston, & Gottesman, 1975;

Slater, 1971; Slater & Cowie, 1971; Stern & Silbersweig, 1998; Stevens, 1982; Tandon & Greden, 1991; Weinberger, 1995). These treatments have proliferated enthusiastically, in spite of the trenchant critiques from the psychoanalytical community (e.g., Karon, 1996; Winnicott, 1943a,b,c, 1944a,b,c, 1945, 1947a,b, 1949a,b, 1951a,b,c, 1956; Wolman, 1973), from the anti-psychiatry movement (e.g., Cooper, 1978; Esterson, 1970; Jackson, 1990; Laing, 1960, 1964; Magaro, 1976; Sarbin & Mancuso, 1980; Silverman, 1983; Szasz, 1961, 1976, 2006), and from service users themselves (e.g., Andre, 2009; Barnes & Berke, 1971; Barnes & Scott, 1989; Burke, 1995; Chamberlin, 2004; Dorman, 2003; North, 1987; Vonnegut, 1975; Weisskopf-Joelsen, 1988).

Not only have our forefathers debated the causes of schizophrenic psychosis, but they have offered the most enormous number of treatment possibilities as well (e.g., Leigh, 1961; Zilboorg & Henry, 1941). In earlier times, mad people would be subjected to a procedure known as "trephination" or "trepanning", in which one or more holes would be bored into the skulls of the patients in order to release the putative evil spirits. Undoubtedly, many men and women would have died from such an attempted "treatment". In ancient times, mad people as well as disabled people would be murdered as a treatment of choice, often by being flung over the edges of cliffs, drowned at sea, or burned at the stake. The Roman physician Celsus, who flourished in the first century ACE, known popularly as the "Latin Hippocrates", and as the author of De medicina, advised fright as a cure for insanity, or, alternatively, immersion in total darkness. Remembered as the man who introduced the word "insania" into medical discourse, Celsus recommended actual tortures such as fetters, floggings, and starvation as appropriate remedies for psychotic delusional states. During the medieval period, madmen and madwomen would be forced to undergo exorcism (e.g., Youssef & Youssef, 1996; cf. Clarke, 1975). In Tudor times, some physicians even recommended that mad people should eat dead mice as a cure (Arnold, 2008).

In the eighteenth century, the German physician Dr Johann Christian Reil forced mad people to walk across a rickety bridge, or he would set them adrift in a leaky boat, and would even immerse his insane patients in a tub of live eels. Others would be lowered down a well. Another physician specializing in the treatment of lunatics, Dr Anton Ludwig Ernst Horn, devised a contraption known familiarly as "Horn's Bag", wrapping patients in burlap in order to restrict violent movements. Horn would also pile his patients on top of one another. Still further treatments, predicated upon gross brutality, consisted of beatings, chains, leg-locks, solitary confinement, and the application of freezing cold plunge baths (Guislan, 1826a,b). Also in the early eighteenth century, Dr Patrick Blair, author of an essay on "Some observations on the cure of mad persons by the fall of water", advised blindfolding mad people and pouring water directly on their heads, after he had stripped them of their clothing and tied them to a chair (cf. Blair, 1717). One patient, a mad woman who refused to undertake her housework, received bleedings, emetics, narcotics, as well as the water treatment, and Blair estimated that he had poured approximately fifteen tonnes of liquid on her face and body in an effort to eradicate her insanity (Hunter & Macalpine, 1963).

Still others used blistering, manacles, scarificators, cold baths, special diets, vomiting and emetics, bleeding, as well as blistering and cupping. And other doctors relied upon rotatory chairs (Cox, 1804; Guislan, 1826a,b), or ducking chairs, or upon special straitjackets, known as the "English camisole" (Zwelling, 1985, p. 15). Those who survived Dr Joseph Mason Cox's (1804) famous swinging chair, an ordinary Windsor chair suspended from a hook fixed into the ceiling, would frequently vomit and urinate upon themselves. Some doctors even attempted to drown their patients or would place them in coffins in the hope of shocking them from their catatonic states (Scull, 1993). And still other practitioners believed that one could diagnosis dementia praecox through a special blood test (Noll, 2006c).

Innumerable physicians would, of course, prescribe laxatives and purgatives (cf. Diethelm, 1939). Hippocrates himself advised the application of hellebore as a treatment for acute hallucinatory delirium. A reasonably enlightened mid-nineteenth century alienist such as Dr Thomas Kirkbride, for example, Superintendent of the Philadelphia Hospital for the Insane, employed a veritable pharmacopoeia in order to treat insanity, preferring morphine sulphate with antimony as a putative means of weakening the force of delusions. Kirkbride also deployed conium, a narcotic made from hemlock, administered with iron in order to aid the patient's digestion; additionally, he prescribed chloral hydrate, quinine, black henbane, and Dover's Powders—a mixture of ipecacuanha, opium, and potassium sulphate (Tomes, 1984). Other popular pharmacological treatments of the nineteenth century included morphine, bromide of ammonium, bromide of potassium (often resulting in bromide intoxication), hyoscyamine, digitalis, physostigma, cannabis, camphor, indica, amyl nitrate, ergot, pilocarpine, and paraldehyde (Fennell, 1996). By the late nineteenth century, specialists would treat dementia praecox with a motley assortment of ostensible treatments such as parathyroidin, lecithin, or even goat's serum. They would also advise castration of the testicles in schizophrenic men.

Professor Emil Kraepelin (1913b, p. 278) conceded his ignorance about the aetiology of dementia praecox, noting that, "As we do not know the actual causes of dementia praecox, we shall not be able at present to consider how to combat it". And yet, in spite of this admission, Kraepelin (1913a) had no hesitation in prescribing bed rest, supervision of food and sleep, prolonged baths, sedatives, moist warm packs, tube-feeding, evacuation of the bowels, and injections of sodium nucleinate.

In the earliest years of the twentieth century, physicians such as Professor Eugen Bleuler (1911), the Swiss psychiatrist who first coined the term "Schizophrenie", recommended such pharmacological agents as bromide, hyoscine, morphine, and somnifen. Others resorted to more extreme methods, such as Dr Theophile Raphael and Dr Sherman Gregg (1921) of Kalamazoo, Michigan, who injected dementia praecox patients with non-specific bacterial protein, or Dr Newdigate Owensby from the Bayview Insane Asylum in Georgia, in the American South, who advocated thyroid surgery for dementia praecox, based on a specious theory of hyperthyroidism in psychotic individuals (Noll, 2007; cf. Scull, 2005). Dr Charles Mercier (1916, p. 511), a venerated British alienist, claimed to cure paranoid mental disease by advising his patients to cut fat, butter, sugar, and tea from their diets, noting that a twenty-seven-year-old footman "completely recovered" from his delusion that the country had become infested with spies, simply by following Mercier's dietary recommendations. Dr Bayard Holmes (1918), Director of the Psychopathic Research Laboratory at the Cook County Hospital in Chicago, Illinois, prescribed appendicostomies (designed to irrigate the bowel) for his dementia praecox patients. In the 1920s, the Canadian physician Dr W. M. English (1929) relied on manganese chloride for the treatment of schizophrenia and manic–depressive illness as well. Others recommended sodium amytal (e.g., Bleckwenn, 1931), or histamine (e.g., Hill, 1938, 1940), or cardiazol (McCrae, 2006). Above all, however, the severely mentally ill would be completely neglected, left to languish in poverty and in disease-infested conditions (cf. Cutting, 1985; Jones, 1983; Roberts, 1967; Zilboorg & Henry, 1941).

More recent somatic treatments have included, in addition to pharmacotherapy, the practice of insulin coma therapy (Hill, 1940; Jones, 1940; Langfeldt, 1939; McConnell, 1945), psychosurgical procedures such as lobotomy or prefrontal leucotomy (Berrios, 1991, 1997; Burckhardt, 1891; Correia, 2006; Crossley, 1993; Damasio, 2000; El-Hai, 2005; Freeman & Watts, 1942; Gross, 1998; McGregor & Crumbie, 1941; Moniz, 1936; Partridge, 1950; Pressman, 1998; Raz, 2010; Shaw, 1889; Shutts, 1982; Stone, 2001; Tierney, 2000; Valenstein, 1986), electroconvulsive shock treatment (Berrios, 1996; Dynes, 1939; Fink, 1999; Freudenberg, 1941; Gilman, 2008b; Kalinowsky, 1939; Kalinowsky & Hoch, 1946; Kneeland & Warren, 2002; Passione, 2004, 2006; Power, 1942; Shorter & Healy, 2007; Stockings, 1945), using the so-called "shock-box" (Sargant, 1967, p. 82), electro-narcosis and electro-pyrexia treatments (Anonymous, 1949) or narco-analysis (Horsley, 1943), progesterone therapy (Billig & Bradley, 1946), and even haemodialysis (or blood transfusions), as well as treatment with smoking (Jacobsen et al., 2004), with diet (e.g., Berlet et al., 1966), or with vitamins (e.g., Cott, 1973; Hawkins & Pauling, 1973), or with acupuncture (e.g., Kane & Di Scipio, 1979), or with omega-3 fatty acids and yoga (e.g., Brown, Gerbarg, & Muskin, 2009), and even with aspirin tablets (Laan et al., 2010), to name just a few ostensible treatment options (cf. Dax, 1949; Braslow, 1997; Shorter, 1997), not to mention the multitudinous psychosocial and behavioural treatments ranging from token economy (e.g., McCreadie, Main, & Dunlop, 1978) to direct confrontation psychotherapy and psychoanalysis (e.g., Rosen, 1953), and from occupational therapy (e.g., Main, 1923) to re-education (e.g., Jones & Marder, 2008). Experts have resorted to religion as a treatment for schizophrenia (e.g., Davis, 1957), and researchers have even recommended nicotine and cigarette smoking as a means of improving visuospatial working in schizophrenia, for instance (Sacco et al., 2005).

Although I fully support every type of research programme in the effort to find a comprehensive cure for the suffering of the schizophrenic, including such fundamental, well-crafted, highly elaborate genetic, biochemical, and neuroanatomical research, this evidence, invariably presented in medical and scientific journals and textbooks with dogmatic prose, cannot be regarded as problem-free

(Altschule, 1970; Gilman, 2008a; Gould, 1981). Professor Edward Shorter (1997, p. 61), for example, a historian at the University of Toronto, Canada, who has undertaken no medical training or psycho-therapeutic training, asserts, nonetheless, with supreme confidence, "It is now clear that schizophrenia is a genetically influenced disease of brain development". Increasingly, authors present biopathological data in a completely selective, decontextualized manner, ignoring the century of psychoanalytically orientated research in this field.

Psychogenic aetiology of schizophrenia

Though compelling, the standard biomedical conception of schizo-phrenia as a brain disease best treated with pharmacotherapeutic sub-stances poses certain crucial problems. First of all, numerous investi-gators have offered trenchant methodological critiques of the validity of the genetic research into schizophrenia and its pharmacological treatment (e.g., Borges, 1995; Pam, 1995; Ross, 1995; cf. Breggin, 1983, 1991; Fisher & Greenberg, 1997; Moncrieff, 2008, 2011; Valenstein, 1998; Wiener, 1995). In particular, a group of British-based clinical psychologists, whom I have loosely identified as the British School of Critical Psychology, whose members include such considered authors as the late J. Richard Marshall (1984, 1990, 1995), as well as Professor Richard Bentall (1990, 2003, 2009), Professor Mary Boyle (1990), Dr Howard Jackson (1990), and Dr Lucy Johnstone (2006), have all offered trenchant methodological critiques of the scientific status of the genetic data or biopathological data, and their critiques stand alongside similar contributions from Dr Ronald Laing (1976, 1981) and Dr Joanna Moncrieff (2008, 2011) in the UK, Dr Susan Farber (1981), Professor Theodore Lidz and his colleagues (Lidz, 1983; Lidz & Blatt, 1983; Lidz, Blatt, & Cook, 1981), Professor Leon Kamin (1984), and Dr Jay Joseph (2003, 2004, 2006) from the United States, and Dr Bernard Cassou and his colleagues in France (Cassou, Schiff, & Stewart, 1980; cf. Carlier, 1980). Indeed, the genetic evidence, though increasingly refined and sophisticated, has received so many criticisms that even the more promising genetic linkage research has disappointed its most fervent proponents (cf. Double, 2006). According to Professor Patrick Sullivan, a physician and professor in the Departments of Genetics, Psychiatry, and Epidemiology at the University of North Carolina, and his colleagues, who have studied the so-called "candidate genes", "it would be a monumental advance for schizophrenia research if even *one* of these genes (or a gene network to which it belongs) proves to be involved in the etiology of schizophrenia" (Sullivan, Owen, O'Donovan, & Freedman, 2006, p. 51). He and his colleagues have had to conclude, reluctantly that, "It is not surprising that this proved to be an inflated hope" (*ibid.*).

With reference to the biochemical and neuroanatomical studies, many investigators have, of course, reported brain anomalies in non-hospitalized, non-medicated schizophrenic patients (e.g., Nasrallah, Schwarzkopf, Coffman, & Olson, 1991), but others have failed to repli-cate these findings, notably the infrequently cited work of Dr Terry Jernigan and her colleagues at the Stanford University School of Medi-cine in Palo Alto, California, whose research team had failed to con-firm the presence of ventricular enlargement in young individuals with schizophrenia. In a first study, Jernigan and her associates com-pared the computerized tomography scans of thirty individuals diag-nosed as suffering from schizophrenia with those of thirty-three "normal" people, and detected no significant differences in either ventricular or sulcal fluid volumes between the two groups (Jernigan, Zatz, Moses, & Berger, 1982). And in a further study, Jernigan and colleagues compared thirty-one schizophrenic individuals with thirty-two "normals", using computerized tomography scanning once again, and discovered no statistically significant differences between the groups on global hemicranial and ventricular volume differences in the brain (Jernigan, Zatz, Moses, & Cardellino, 1982). Even a commit-ted neuropsychiatrist such as Professor Nancy Andreasen (1986) has admitted that when neuroimagining studies report brain changes in schizophrenia, one cannot attribute causality to these findings, nor will these findings be specific to schizophrenia. Such brain changes as ventricular enlargement will be found in numerous other illnesses, and, therefore, cannot provide a totalistic explanation of the very specific psychopathology of schizophrenia (cf. Chua & McKenna, 2000). In fact, ventricular enlargement, a common finding in the biopathology literature, can also be found in "normal" subjects not suffering from any mental illness (e.g., Buckley, O'Callaghan, Larkin, & Waddington, 1992). Furthermore, none of the traditional psychiatric explanations of the ostensible neuropathology of schizophrenia con-siders the growing mountain of evidence of the ways in which psychological trauma has an impact upon neuronal structure and function (e.g., Bremner, 2002; Mazure & Druss, 1995; Wilkinson, 2010; cf. Blakemore, 1998), or the recent research on the neurobiology of post-traumatic stress disorder, which has demonstrated that combat veterans with no evidence of gross neurological disease upon entry into the United States army will often reveal abnormalities in the amygdala, medial prefrontal cortex, and hippocampus regions of the brain after discharge (Shin, Rauch, & Pitman, 2005), suggesting a very strong effect for the role of environmental trauma in the shaping of brain morphology (cf. Cozolino, 2006; Diamond, 1988). Ironically, the many studies of schizophrenic neuropathology might ultimately come to provide evidence of the way in which these patients will have experienced environmental, psychosocial traumata.

Related studies have revealed that those individuals who recall traumatic imagery will experience elevated cerebral blood flow in the anterior paralimbic region of the brain as well as in the orbitofrontal cortex and the anterior temporal pole (Shin et al., 1999), as well as exaggerated amygdala responsivity and diminished medial prefrontal cortex responsivity after viewing images of fearful faces (Shin et al., 2005). Indeed, modern investigators have demonstrated that when schizophrenic research participants undertake exercise, the hippocampal volume in their brains increases, as does their short-term memory, demonstrating yet again that brain changes often result directly from environmental stimuli (Pajonk et al., 2010).

Quite apart from the methodological difficulties inherent in theories of biopathogenesis, an increasingly large number of psychopathology researchers have begun to identify social and cultural factors that might have an aetiological role in the development of schizophrenia. Perhaps, rightly so, these psychological investigators have approached the role of social aetiology with a certain amount of caution, penning articles with tentative titles such as "Is there a role for social factors in a comprehensive developmental model for schizophrenia?" (Boydell, Van Os, & Murray, 2004), and "Can the social environment cause schizophrenia?" (Krabbendam & Van Os, 2004). Sometimes, these social factors interact with biological factors. For example, in a study designed by Dutch researchers Dr Jim van Os and Dr Jean-Paul Selten (1998), the authors undertook follow-ups of those individuals born in the Netherlands in May 1940, during the time of the German invasion. Assuming that the Hitlerian atrocities would prove to be stressful, Van Os and Selten examined the life trajectories of those foetuses still *in utero* during that critical period of world history. The authors discovered a slight statistically significant likelihood that foetuses *in utero* in May 1940, especially those in the first trimester of pregnancy, would develop schizophrenia in later life, thus arguing that intrauterine stressors contribute to schizophrenogenesis.

Other workers have identified migration (e.g., Littlewood & Lipsedge, 1982, 1988; McKenzie, Fearon, & Hutchinson, 2008; Malzberg & Lee, 1956; Sashidharan, 1993; Sugarman & Craufurd, 1994), or urbanicity (e.g., Freeman, 1994, 1998; Lewis, David, Andréasson, & Allebeck, 1992) as aetiological components, as indicated by an increased incidence of schizophrenia in those reared in city environments; and still others have focused on the causal role of ethnic discrimination (e.g., Metzl, 2009; Sharpley, Hutchinson, McKenzie, & Murray, 2001). Still others have identified seasonality, prenatal or obstetric complications (e.g., Eagles, Hunter, & Geddes, 1995; Geddes & Lawrie, 1995; Günther-Genta, Bovet, & Hohlfeld, 1994; Hultman, Öhman, Cnattingius, Wieselgren, & Lindström, 1997; Jones, Rantakallio, Hartikainen, Isohanni, & Sipila, 1998; McGrath, Welham, & Pemberton, 1995; McNeil & Kaij, 1978; Mednick, Cannon, & Barr, 1991), perinatal difficulties, influenza (e.g., Crow, 1994; Weiss, Winnik, & Assael, 1961), parental stress, social marginalization, and a host of other potentially impactful life events as causal factors (e.g., Bebbington et al., 1993; Hirsch et al., 1996; Morgan & Fisher, 2007; Obregia, Tomesco, & Dimolesco, 1936).

The biogenetic, neuroanatomical, and social interactional theories of schizophrenia, though certainly meritorious areas of scientific investigation whose pursuit I would encourage, suffer from another very compelling challenge: more than five hundred psychoanalysts and psychotherapists from around the world have published detailed case histories documenting the reversibility of chronic schizophrenia through the use of talking therapies.[3] Of course, practitioners of the nineteenth-century "Romantic Psychiatry" movement had, for many years, promoted non-biological treatments for extreme madness, referring to themselves as "Der psychische Arzt" ("the psychical physician") (Reil, 1803, p. 32), offering a "psychischen Curmethode" ("psychical method of cure") (*ibid.*, p. 31). These pioneers of psychological therapies anticipated the subsequent contributions of Professor Sigmund Freud and his psychoanalytical colleagues. As early as 1911,

Freud (1911a) wrote about the meaningfulness of deeply psychotic states. Shortly thereafter, the British psychiatrist (and future member of the British Psycho-Analytical Society) Dr Henry Devine (1914, p. 101) addressed the Section of Psychiatry of the Royal Society of Medicine in London on the sexual origins of delusional states, writing about the role of both "auto-erotic fancies" and wish-fulfilment in psychotic patients. Devine (*ibid.*, p. 89) noted further that "delusional formations fulfil a definite function", quite a prescient observation, in view of later psychoanalytical developments.

Psychoanalytical colleagues have treated schizophrenic men, women, adolescents, and children according to fairly classical methods, but have also utilized analytically informed group psychotherapy as well (e.g., Abrahams & Varon, 1953; Speers & Lansing, 1965; Stotsky & Zolik, 1965). Other psychoanalytical voices have approached treatment from a Kohutian standpoint (e.g., Magid, 1984), or from a Lacanian or post-Lacanian perspective (e.g., Kaufmant, 1989; Lacan, 1981; Ver Eecke, 2006), or even from an analytically informed art psychotherapy tradition (e.g., Killick, 1995). Still others have argued for the use of psychodynamic psychotherapy in conjunction with medication (e.g., Greenfield, 1985; Grinspoon, Ewalt, & Shader, 1972).

The list of all those who have worked psychoanalytically or psychotherapeutically during the second half of the twentieth century, and beyond, would be nearly inexhaustible, and still poses a powerful challenge to the hegemony of biological psychiatry. Nevertheless, the psychoanalytically suspicious dismiss this work as a collectivity of nothing more than single case studies or as merely anecdotal. Professor Emil Kraepelin (1913b, p. 250), for instance, disparaged psychoanalytical insights as "arbitrary assumptions and conjectures". Dr Willy Mayer-Gross and his colleagues excoriated psychoanalytical approaches to schizophrenia thus: "Prolonged psychotherapy, even in mild cases, can no longer be justified. *Psychoanalysis* is, indeed, *contraindicated* in any stage or type of schizophrenia" (Mayer-Gross, Slater, and Roth, 1954, p. 280). More recent professionals have proved far more castigating. Dr Stephen Lawrie (1999, p. 223), a psychiatrist in the Department of Psychiatry at the University of Edinburgh in Scotland, based at the Royal Edinburgh Hospital, has noted that in view of the paucity of randomized controlled trials for psychotherapeutic work with schizophrenic men and women, "Psychodynamic psychotherapy cannot therefore be recommended for schizophrenia."

In similar vein, Dr E. Fuller Torrey (1983, p. 124), a former staff member at the National Institute of Mental Health in the United States, and the author of the best-selling book *Surviving Schizophrenia: A Family Manual*, wrote that, "Insight-oriented psychotherapy, in which the therapist tries to make the patient aware of underlying unconscious processes, is now known to be not only useless in treating schizophrenia, but probably detrimental". This influential psychiatrist had further emphasized that, "To do insight-oriented psychotherapy on persons with schizophrenia is analogous to directing a flood into a town already ravaged by a tornado" (*ibid.*, p. 125). The American genetics researchers Professor Kenneth Kendler and Professor Carol Prescott (2006, p. 138) have cheerfully confessed, "we are not major fans of psychoanalytic theory", condemning the entire century-plus of Freudian research with one sweeping gesture.

In the United Kingdom, Dr John Cutting (1985, p. 205), an eminent emeritus consultant psychiatrist at the Bethlem Hospital and at the Maudsley Hospital, had written quite blithely that, "Psychoanalysis was never a serious proposition" (cf. Gottdiener, 2004). And Professor Peter Jones of Addenbrooke's Hospital in Cambridge, and Professor Stephen Marder of the West Los Angeles Veterans Administration Healthcare Center in California, authors of a definitive study of treatments for schizophrenia, published in the *Cambridge Textbook of Effective Treatments in Psychiatry*, have endorsed a host of psychosocial interventions such as psycho-education for individuals and families, cognitive therapy, compliance therapy, cognitive remediation, social skills training, vocational rehabilitation, and medication management. But they have dismissed psychodynamic methods as "*hocus pocus*", an historical oddity of the twentieth century (Jones & Marder, 2008, p. 470).

The campaign against psychoanalysis reached fever pitch in an editorial published in the journal *Psychological Medicine*, entitled "Psychodynamic treatment of schizophrenia: is there a future?". The authors, Dr Kim Mueser and Dr Howard Berenbaum, concluded that psychotherapy does not work for schizophrenia at all, and that it might even make patients more ill. Mueser and Berenbaum (1990, p. 260) concluded their report, "We have proposed a moratorium on the use of psychodynamic treatments for schizophrenia" (cf. Jones & Buckley, 2006).

In spite of these critical comments, psychologically orientated work has always had a strong position in the theorization of the causes of

extreme madness. Those less enamoured by biopathological explanations of madness had, of course, proffered their views about the potential psychogenesis of insanity for many centuries. The English alienist,
Dr Joseph Mason Cox (1804, p. 11), from Fishponds, near Bristol,
postulated that madness results from "Religion" and "Love", conclud-
ing that, "Religion and Love I have found among the most frequent
exciting causes of madness". He also suspected that madness might be
triggered by venereal indulgences, excessive heat, fever, intoxication,
sores, haemorrhages, head injuries, or even from parturition.

Consider, as well, the work of the great early nineteenth-century
French classificationist, Dr Jean-Étienne Dominique Esquirol, who
wrote his medical thesis, presented in 1805, on "Passions considered as
causes, symptoms, and therapeutic means of mental diseases". A con-
summate psychiatrist who played music to his mad patients, and who
knew about their passions at first hand, Esquirol (1832a,b) authored a
famous two-volume masterpiece *Des Maladies mentales considérées sous
les rapports médical, hygiénique et médico-légal*, published in Paris in 1838,
and generally considered one of the first textbooks in the field of
psychiatry. In his *chef d'oeuvre*, Esquirol noted that insanity, of the
sort that we would now diagnose as schizophrenia, could result from
either hereditary factors ("physiques") or from environmental factors
("morales") (Esquirol, 1838b, p. 235). The latter, exogenous causes of
madness might include: climatological changes, the abuse of wine or
spirits, head injuries, the abuse of drugs, masturbation, faulty education, relaxation of morals, social upheavals, disappointment in love,
passions (especially fear and dread), ambition, financial losses, family
problems, and conflicts between instincts and ethics, even moving into
a newly built house ("une maison nouvellement bâtie") (Esquirol,
1838b, p. 236). Unlike many psychiatric workers, past or present,
Esquirol actually lived in hospital with his patients, and, hence, he
came to know their stories more intimately, daring to wonder whether
factors such as disappointment in love might actually contribute to the
development of a psychotic reaction (Esquirol, 1838b).

By the late nineteenth century, the young neurologist Dr Sigmund
Freud (1895) had begun to write about the possible psychogenic
aetiological agents which might operate in the development of
psychotic states; and many generations of psychoanalysts have followed suit, each conceptualizing the origin of schizophrenic psychosis
in slightly different language. Freud, for instance, linked paranoid

schizophrenic illness to a suppression of homosexual impulses. By contrast, the early Viennese psychoanalyst Dr Annie Reich (1936), sometime wife of Dr Wilhelm Reich, believed that an excess of masturbation could contribute to the development of schizophrenia. In the United Kingdom, Dr Edward Glover (1968) described schizophrenia as a fixation at several points of early psychic development, whereas Dr Donald Winnicott (1953, 1963) had characterized schizophrenia as an environmental deficiency disease. And Dr Don Jackson (1957), an American psychiatrist and psychoanalyst, theorized that schizophrenia could be explained as a response to overwhelming anxiety, rejection, a flooding of the ego by the id, and as a consequence of the breakdown of repressive mechanisms. More recently, Mrs Eleanor Armstrong-Perlman (1995), a psychoanalytically orientated social worker and psychotherapist, formerly of the Tavistock Clinic in London, postulated that psychosis, in general, results from experiences of sacrifice within the family nexus, such as the sacrifice of sexuality. As Armstrong-Perlman (1995, p. 93) concluded, on the basis of her copious clinical experience over decades, "Psychosis can be provoked by a sacrifice that fails".

In 1926, in a projected book, Dr Harry Stack Sullivan, the pioneering American psychiatrist and psychoanalyst who treated hospitalized patients with psychotherapy at the Sheppard and Enoch Pratt Hospital in Maryland, averred that the social stigmatization against homosexuals, some of whom later become psychotic, may well be the main cause of schizophrenia (Wake, 2006). In fact, psychoanalysts have implicated virtually every psychological toxin from masturbation to homophobia as a possible aetiological factor in the development of schizophrenia. Unfortunately, in spite of numerous contributions from psychoanalytical writers on both the metapsychological theorization about schizophrenia and on its psychotherapeutic treatment, few have dared to formulate testable hypotheses concerning causation.

Sexual, physical, and familial abuse as aetiological factors

So, once again, we pose the question: what causes schizophrenia? And does trauma have a demonstrable aetiological role? Nowadays, after years of resistance, even orthodox biopsychological researchers admit that childhood trauma plays an important part in the aetiology of depression and anxiety (e.g., Hovens et al., 2010), but modern

researchers remain more sceptical about the role of childhood traumata in the genesis of the schizophrenic psychoses. The American
psychiatrist, psychoanalyst, and pioneer traumatologist Dr Henry
Krystal (1968c, p. 110) once commented that, "one problem has
remained impossible to solve—that is the problem of schizophrenia
and its relationship to trauma". More than forty years have elapsed
since Dr Krystal posed this challenge. Have we progressed at all in our
understanding of a traumatogenesis of the most severely crippling
and disabling of psychiatric illnesses?

As early as 1938, Dr John Rawlings Rees, a noted psychiatrist
working at the Tavistock Clinic in London, contributed expert testimony to the Central Criminal Court, involving a case of schizophrenia that developed in the immediate aftermath of a rape (Bourne,
1962). Five years later, in 1943, the American psychologist Dr Saul
Rosenzweig (1943) wrote about the potential role of sibling death as a
critical factor in the life of the schizophrenic (cf. Rosenzweig & Bray,
1943). And as early as 1956, the American psychiatrist and psychoanalyst Dr Charles Wahl (1956) published an important, though, once
again, virtually unknown study on the high frequency of early
parental deaths in the biographies of 568 male schizophrenics who
had served in the United States Navy, a study rather akin to that of Dr
John Bowlby's (1944a) and (1994b) work on the role of early abandonment and loss in the development of juvenile delinquency.

Even non-psychiatric physicians understood something about the
role of sexual trauma in the development of psychosis. Mr Aleck
Bourne (1962), for instance, a pre-eminent gynaecological surgeon,
reported a case of schizophrenia that unfolded after the rape of the
patient, confirming the observations of his psychiatric colleague Dr
John Rawlings Rees.

Of course, clinicians explored not only sexual trauma, but also
other types of intrafamilial impingement. During the 1960s, in the
immediate wake of both the social psychiatric movement, and the
antipsychiatric movement, clinicians on both sides of the Atlantic
Ocean began to write with increasing conviction about the potentially
pathogenic role of the nuclear family in the development of schizophrenia. In the UK, psychiatric practitioners such as Dr Ronald Laing
(1960), Dr Aaron Esterson (1970), Dr Dennis Scott (Scott & Ashworth,
1965, 1967, 1969), and Dr Ronald Welldon (1971) each explored the
role of family communication as a key ingredient in shaping both the

origin and form of schizophrenic reactions. The work of Ronald Laing and Aaron Esterson will be well known, that of Dennis Scott moderately so, but the legacy of Ronald Welldon will be little known, as this brilliant young psychiatrist died too soon, at the age of thirty-eight years (Welldon, 2006). His crucial, but relatively obscure paper on "The 'shadow-of-death' and its implications in four families, each with a hospitalized schizophrenic member", explores the role of strangulated grief and mourning as a compounding variable in the maintenance of a schizophrenogenic family. Welldon not only identified the crucial role of mourning for good mental health, but he has provided us with a role model of how much a clinician can learn about a family and its problems if one invests sufficient time and care to hear the story in full. As Welldon (1971, p. 298 n.) himself noted, "one of my colleagues expressed it succinctly at the time, 'What? Spend all that time with one crazy family—and nothing to show for it? *You must be mad*'".

Since the 1970s, pioneering psychiatrists such as Dr James Birley (e.g., Birley & Brown, 1970; Brown, Birley, & Wing, 1972) and Professor Julian Leff (e.g., Hirsch & Leff, 1975; Kuipers, Leff, & Lam, 1992; Leff, 2001, 2002, 2005; Vaughn & Leff, 1976, 1981) have explored the impact of stressful family environments on the likelihood of relapse and rehospitalisation in schizophrenia and other psychopathological constellations (e.g., Dohrenwend, Shrout, Link, Skodol, and Stueve, 1995), but few of these excellent researchers have dared to focus on sexual abuse or physical abuse as primary pathogens. Throughout the 1980s, however, researchers had begun to explore more systematically the role of child physical abuse (CPA) and child sexual abuse (CSA) as potential causative agents in the development of different varieties of mental illness or shattered states (e.g., Bryer, Nelson, Miller, & Krol, 1987).

In 1990, American Psychiatric Publishing, the publication arm of the American Psychiatric Association (arguably the most august psychiatric organization in the world), published a landmark textbook edited by the distinguished clinician and author Professor Richard Kluft (1990), entitled *Incest-Related Syndromes of Adult Psychopathology*. The seasoned contributors to this crucial volume included Dr Bennet Braun, Professor Jean Goodwin, Professor Judith Lewis Herman, Dr Richard Loewenstein, Dr Frank Putnam, Professor David Spiegel, and Professor Michael Stone, each a noted psychiatrist and traumatologist.

Drawing upon earlier work, such as the pathbreaking research of Professor Herman and her colleagues on incest and violence in the histories of patients struggling with a host of psychological conditions (e.g., Herman, Russell, & Trocki, 1986), the contributors to this volume provided a wealth of evidence demonstrating the aetiological role of early sexual abuse in the genesis not only of borderline personality disorder and dissociative identity disorder, but in many other types of shattered states as well. Indeed, in her comprehensive and scholarly review of the literature, psychiatrist Dr Diane Schetky (1990) summarized the findings, and reported that early child sexual abuse will serve as a contributory factor in: depression, low self-esteem, psychiatric hospitalization, substance abuse, self-abuse, somatization disorder, eroticization, learning difficulties, post-traumatic stress disorder, anxiety, dissociative disorders, conversion reactions, running away, prostitution, revictimization, impaired interpersonal relationships, and poor parenting. In spite of the brilliance of this paradigm-shifting work, not one of the authors had mentioned schizophrenia as a possible consequence of either child sexual abuse or child physical abuse, and the term "schizophrenia" does not even appear among the 289 separate principal entries in the fourteen-page Index. Of the contributors, only Professor Jean Goodwin (1990), a brilliant traumatologist in her own right, mentioned the term "psychosis", noting that psychotic patients might have suffered sexual abuse, but that, in all likelihood, the psychotic behaviour would have predated the abuse.

Any mention of child sexual abuse or child physical abuse in relation to schizophrenia had long seemed anathema, in spite of the fact that highly respected professionals such as Dr Robert Fliess (1973), Professor William Niederland (1974, 1984) and Professor Flora Rheta Schreiber (1983) had already published important book-length studies about schizophrenic patients (often quite famous) who had survived documentable physical abuse and documentable sexual abuse. As a result of his copious researches on the biography of the German jurist Daniel Paul Schreber, Niederland established definitively that Schreber's so-called delusions of being physically abused by God could, in fact, be traced back to the cruel, restrictive, orthopaedic contraptions that his father, the pedagogue Daniel Gottlieb Moritz Schreber, had forced his son to wear during much of his childhood. And through her study of the American multiple murderer Joseph Kallinger, also schizophrenic, and so diagnosed *inter alia* by the internationally renowned schizophrenia specialist Professor Silvano Arieti, Schreiber discovered that the young Joseph had experienced grotesque physical abuse and sexual abuse throughout his childhood from a variety of perpetrators, both intrafamilial and extrafamilial.

Professor William Niederland's work on Daniel Paul Schreber, and Professor Flora Rheta Schreiber's work on Joseph Kallinger, in particular, deserve special mention, because, although both authors boasted considerable psychoanalytical skill, neither drew upon work with *clinical* patients undergoing psychotherapy. Niederland based his findings on psychobiographical data about a long-deceased man, and Schreiber based her findings on behavioural science research interviews with Kallinger, during his long imprisonment in a high-security forensic institution. In each case, Niederland and Schreiber corroborated their suspicions about abuse as an aetiological factor by obtaining independent testimony from numerous confirmatory sources, including, in certain cases, eyewitness testimony, especially in the contemporaneous research of Schreiber, who found a neighbour who had witnessed Kallinger's adoptive mother Anna Kallinger beating her son with a hammer (cf. Kahr, 2002, 2011).

Fortified by my apprenticeship to both Professor Niederland and to Professor Schreiber (cf. Kahr, 2002), and by encouragement from Dr Alice Miller (1986), who believed, perhaps quite unfoundedly, that fully one hundred per cent of schizophrenics suffered from sexual abuse in childhood, I began to collate the small number of references within the clinical literature which offered case history reports of schizophrenic men and women who had experienced either physical or sexual abuse, especially those reported in the seminal textbook *Psychotherapy of Schizophrenia: The Treatment of Choice*, written by the fortitudinous psychologists Professor Bertram Karon and Dr Gary VandenBos (1981).

However, in spite of the growing ferment around these ideas in the classroom (e.g., Kahr, 1997) and at conferences and in brief communications (e.g., Kahr, 1993), and in periodicals (e.g., Greenfield, Strakowski, Tohen, Batson, & Kolbrener, 1994), no one had yet published a systematic review of the potential contribution of abuse in the aetiology of schizophrenic psychoses until the New Zealand psychologist Dr John Read, Director of the training programme in clinical psychology at the University of Auckland, had reviewed *not* the *psychoanalytical* case study literature, but, rather, the psychiatric and traumatological literatures, for evidence of studies which have controlled for a multitude of research variables which might offer data concerning causation, as opposed to correlation. In a series of articles both brave and brilliant, Read has not only explored the reluctance of mental health workers to enquire about abuse histories when speaking to psychotic patients, but he has also conducted a detailed meta-analysis, and has compiled systematically the results of the key studies published between 1997 and 2004, based on a combined sample size of over 30,000 individuals, which demonstrate a highly statistically significant increase in the likelihood of a schizophrenia diagnosis in those men and women who experienced reasonably documentable child physical abuse and child sexual abuse prior to the onset of psychosis (e.g., Kingdon et al., 2010; Read & Hammersley, 2005, 2006; Read, Goodman, Morrison, Ross, & Aderhold, 2004; Read, Rudegeair, & Farrelly, 2006). Read's vital work, and that of his collaborators, deserves infinitely greater examination and coverage than I can provide in this context.

But Read's work raises important questions, as any good piece of research would invariably do. One wonders, in particular, whether physical abuse and sexual abuse serve as the primary aetiological pathogens for schizophrenia, or whether, in fact, non-abused individuals who have suffered trauma might also become schizophrenic. Recent research from attachment theory investigators has identified the high rates of disorganized, traumatic attachments in parent–infant relationships in the life histories of those who later present as schizophrenic (Liotti & Gumley, 2008; Ross, 2000, 2008; Schäfer, Ross, & Read, 2008; Vermetten, Lanius, & Bremner, 2008; cf. Everett & Gallop, 2001; Kahr, 2007b,c; Osnato, 1930). This research represents an important watershed in understanding the psychosocial origins of schizophrenia.

Indeed, since the publication of the work of Dr John Read and others, much mainstream psychopathology research now explores the possible role of early sexual abuse or physical abuse as either causal agents, exacerbatory agents, or risk factors for the development of psychosis, borderline personality disorder, and other types of mental distress (e.g., Chen et al., 2010; Cohen, 2011; Lardinois, Lataster, Mengelers, Van Os, & Myin-Germeys, 2011).

But might there even be other forms of trauma less memorable and less visible than physical abuse or sexual abuse, or even disorganized attachments? In our attempt to answer some of these questions, we shall now turn to the Nazi Holocaust, as well as to a study of what I have come to refer to as "psychological infanticide", as potential sources of data about the origin of schizophrenia, and I shall review these two further bodies of literature which, to date, have never become properly recognized as relevant to mainstream research on schizophrenia.

Schizophrenia and the Holocaust

Introduction

In recent years, in the wake of the violent conflicts in Afghanistan and Iraq, for example, psychiatric researchers have documented that participation by soldiers in war activities increases the likelihood of suffering from post-traumatic stress disorder, alcohol abuse, and a variety of other common mental disorders. Dr Nicola Fear, of the Academic Centre for Defence Mental Health at King's College in the University of London, supervised a study of 9,990 regulars and reservists who fought in Iraq and Afghanistan, and discovered that as many as 19% of the participants in warfare suffered from common mental disorders (Fear et al., 2010). But can warfare produce specifically *psychotic* reactions as well?

Throughout the First World War and, subsequently, the Second World War, and shortly thereafter, numerous American and European psychiatrists wrote a stream of papers, now virtually eclipsed from memory, about the spate of new cases of schizophrenia and other psychoses which developed in military personnel, either as a result of direct combat, or even from enlistment, training, or furlough (e.g., Aldrich & Coffin, 1948a,b; Duval, 1944; Duval & Hoffman, 1941; Fox, 1944; Hitschman & Yarrell, 1943; Klow, 1943; Lebensohn, 1945; Malamud & Malamud, 1943; Paster, 1948; Prout, 1946; Rogues de Fursac, 1918; Rosen & Kiene, 1947; Stockings, 1945; Sutherland & Barnes, 1946; Sutton, 1940; Weiss, 1947a,b; Will, 1944; cf. Baird, 1941; Lewis & Engle, 1954). If the number of new schizophrenic patients rose as a result of reasonable treatment of Allied fighters who had not yet experienced combat, or who had returned on leave to Allied bases, one wonders how prisoners of war and internees in concentration camps would have fared.

I first became aware that the atrocities of the Nazi Holocaust might play an aetiological role in the development of traditional psychotic symptoms as far back as 1985, when I had the occasion to meet an Austrian-born woman who had spent time in the concentration camp at Auschwitz during the Second World War. She told me that during her internment in the camp, as a teenager, she would often glance at the enormous, hovering smoke stacks atop the infamous gas chambers. But, whenever she looked up at these smoke stacks, she claimed that she saw nothing at all. She knew that the building in question served as the execution centre, and yet, when she stared upwards in the direction of the smoke, she became temporarily "blind". This young girl, who, by the way, later became a distinguished mental health professional in her own right, experienced what psychopathologists refer to as a "negative hallucination", the refusal to perceive a piece of frightening external reality. Trauma, and, in particular, the fear of death, had prompted an otherwise mentally healthy teenage girl to experience an hallucinatory symptom.

Indeed, numerous authors have written about the psychologically toxic impact of Holocaust experiences. For example, in his comprehensive study of *Kristallnacht: Prelude to Destruction*, Sir Martin Gilbert (2006, p. 24), one of the most pre-eminent British historians of the twentieth century, reported that a Yiddish newspaper published in Paris described a number of cases of "insanity and suicide" among the group of more than 12,000 Polish-born Jews expelled from Germany on 18th October 1938 at the decree of Adolf Hitler. Upon reading of this outrage, Herschel Grynszpan, a young, seventeen-year-old German-born Jew of Polish ancestry, then resident in Paris, decided to exact revenge, and, on 7th November 1938, he assassinated Ernst vom Rath, the Third Secretary at the Germany Embassy in Paris, thus igniting the retributions of Kristallnacht, and the eventual Holocaust.

Bruno Bettelheim and the extreme situation

Of course, many distinguished professionals had already noted the psychotogenic effects of the Nazi concentration camps in a more systematic manner. In 1956, Professor Bruno Bettelheim, survivor of the concentration camps at Dachau and Buchenwald, published a classic essay on "Schizophrenia as a Reaction to Extreme Situations". Based on his personal observations in the camps, and on his later psychiatric experiences treating psychotic children, Bettelheim reported that some of the behaviour of inmates in concentration camps closely mirrored that of behaviour exhibited by long-standing schizophrenic patients. The symptoms characteristic of both groups included: delusions of persecution (as distinct from actual persecutions), catatonia, and infantile behaviour, in particular, as well as suicidality, melancholia, delinquency, anorexia, incontinence, and loss of memory. Bettelheim also noted that both groups of individuals displayed signs of hopelessness and of feeling at the mercy of others.

Bettelheim presented three cases of particular relevance. In the first case, Bettelheim reported about a boy, who, he implies, suffered from childhood schizophrenia. The boy's parents thought him feeble-minded, and they threatened to send him away, insisting that he should never have been born. Consequently, they deprived him of food. As Bettelheim (1956, p. 513) noted, "This added to his conviction that his parents wished to kill him through starvation". Bettelheim then presented a second case of a boy with delusions of persecution. Bettelheim noted that at the age of two years, this boy suffered a trauma while playing with his older brother and friends. The youngsters played a hanging game with the patient, imperilling the child's life, and, as a consequence, he had to be revived with artificial respiration. In the third case, also one of implied childhood schizophrenia, Bettelheim discussed the case of a small boy who had discovered his mother's infidelity. As a consequence, she threatened to kill him in order to keep his silence. In each of these three case descriptions, a preschizophrenic child had to survive either death wishes or a near-death experience.

Bettelheim has stressed the importance of children having re-birthing experiences in therapy, in order to overcome their early experiences of deadliness. One boy with whom Bettelheim had worked described himself as giving birth to himself, as though emerging from an imaginary egg. Bettelheim had earlier elaborated on the tendency to regression in an "'extreme' situation" (Bettelheim, 1943, p. 417), both in his classic article "Individual and Mass Behavior in Extreme Situations", and in his book, *The Empty Fortress: Infantile Autism and the Birth of the Self* (Bettelheim, 1967).

Reflecting on his 1956 article some twenty-three years later, Bettelheim commented that unless one has particular personal qualities as an investigator, one will be hard-pressed to detect the role of trauma in psychotic states. As Bettelheim (1979, p. 113) explained,

> Without my experience of being subjected to personality-disintegrating experiences in the camps, and of observing the reactions of others to these experiences, it would never have come to my awareness that there exists a parallel between these conditions and those which bring about the suffering of psychotic individuals.

William Niederland and massive psychic trauma

Professor William Niederland (1959a,b, 1963) will be known best for his work on the role of physical traumatization in the aetiology of the delusions of the famous German judge Daniel Paul Schreber (cf. Niederland, 1974, 1984), and also for his extensive writings on the treatment of the survivor of political terror (e.g., Niederland, 1961). Indeed, Niederland (1968a, p. 313) had introduced the term "survivor syndrome", also known as "Das Überlebenden-Syndrom", into both the psychiatric and psychoanalytical literature (cf. Niederland, 1980). He noted that the symptoms of surviving massive psychic trauma, such as the Nazi Holocaust, often include those resembling schizophrenic states, in particular:

- fully developed psychosis, or psychotic-like disturbances;
- delusional symptomatology, or semi-delusional symptomatology;
- paranoid formations;
- morbid brooding;
- complete inertia;
- stupor or agitation (often characteristic of catatonic schizophrenia).

At approximately the same time, Dr Leo Eitinger (1961, 1964), a psychiatrist in Oslo, Norway, worked with Holocaust survivors as well. He also noted the occurrence of psychotic states in survivors. Eitinger studied one hundred hospitalized psychotic patients, sixty-two of whom had received a diagnosis of schizophrenia. Of this sub-sample, thirty had ultimately developed schizophrenia as a direct result of their internment in a Nazi concentration camp.

Contemporaneously, Dr Henry Krystal, an American psychiatrist and psychoanalyst who had worked extensively with survivors of the Nazi Holocaust, hosted a series of clinical workshops held at Wayne State University in Detroit, Michigan, on the theme of "The Late Sequelae of Massive Psychic Trauma". The participants included distinguished clinicians such as Dr Gustav Bychowski, Dr John Dorsey, Dr Robert Jay Lifton, Dr William G. Niederland, Dr Editha Sterba, and Dr Richard Sterba. These conferences served as the basis of two landmark books, both, sadly, little known and grossly under-appreciated: the 1968 text *Massive Psychic Trauma* (Krystal, 1968a), and its successor, *Psychic Traumatization: Aftereffects in Individuals and Communities* (Krystal & Niederland, 1971). At the Wayne State University workshops, numerous investigators shared their experiences concerning the links between trauma, schizophrenia, and the Holocaust, underscoring the role of the Nazi incarcerations as potential aetiological factors in the development of schizophrenic psychosis.

Niederland (1968b, p. 64) shared his observations that the Holocaust survivors presented as having a "'Living-dead' existence", or a "'Walking corpse' existence". Niederland (*ibid.*, p. 65) also commented that they could be described as having a "'Shuffling corpse' existence" as a result of their experiences in the camps. Dr Joost Meerloo (1968) observed the presence of paranoid delusions among Holocaust survivors, and Dr Gustav Bychowski (1968a), a Polish refugee disciple of Sigmund Freud, presented a case of a woman who developed paranoid schizophrenia after witnessing the murder of her entire family, including the savage killing of her little sister, for whom the patient had cared, and whose head had been smashed against a wall in front of the patient's eyes. This traumatically bereaved woman subsequently developed not only visual hallucinations, imagining that she saw her murdered brother, but also delusions, believing that people in the street looked at her with pity. Bychowski (1968b) noted that Freud's one-time physician, Dr Max Schur, an internist who later became a psychoanalyst, had also worked with comparable cases of Holocaust-induced psychosis.

Even Professor Dr Ulrich Venzlaff (1968), a distinguished psychiatrist from Göttingen, in Germany (and keynote speaker at one of Krystal's workshops), steeped not in psychoanalysis and traumatology, but, rather, in the biopathology of schizophrenia, had to admit, nonetheless, that trauma plays a crucial aetiological role. Reporting on three of his own cases, all survivors of the concentration camp at Auschwitz, Venzlaff identified internment as the principal causal factor in these cases of camp-induced schizophrenia. None of the patients had demonstrated any evidence of either a hereditary taint or a premorbid psychotic history, and from a temporal perspective, all developed schizophrenia as an *immediate* result of their incarceration. After presenting his detailed clinical material, Venzlaff (*ibid.*, p. 118) opined,

> Although we are dealing with small patient populations which provide no statistical significance, these impressions are of scientific interest because they contradict earlier opinions and thereby provide us with an incentive to examine each case with special care.[4]

In the 1971 companion volume, Dr Edgar Trautman (1971), an Attending Psychiatrist at the Gracie Square Hospital in New York City, reported that he had identified twenty-four paranoid schizophrenic patients in his sample of 1,000 Holocaust survivors, indicating a rate of 2.4%, roughly three to four times the amount of schizophrenia that one would expect to encounter in the general population. This figure would perhaps have been higher had the Nazis not executed those individuals who became overtly psychotic while in the concentration camps. Therefore, this data provides powerful evidence for the schizophrenogenic impact of the concentration camps themselves. Dr Klaus Hoppe (1971), then Director of Research at the Hacker Clinic and Foundation in Beverly Hills, California, reported a case of clinical schizophrenia that developed in the wake of a concentration camp experience, as did Dr Magdalene Nemeth (1971), a psychiatrist who worked at the famous Ypsilanti State Hospital in Ypsilanti, Michigan. Nemeth explored the case of "Benjamin", a Polish barber interned in the coalmines of Jaworzno and also in Auschwitz, who developed a profound psychosis as a result of his experiences of torment. Nemeth (1971, p. 139) observed that, in order to survive, Benjamin had to become a "Kadavergehorscham" (a Nazi phrase which can be translated as "obedient like a cadaver"), a phrase reminiscent of Professor Leonard Shengold's (1989, p. 2) use of the term "soul murder", and Professor Robert Jay Lifton's (1967, p. iii) concept of "Death in Life", based on his work with the survivors of Hiroshima (cf. Lifton, 1968).

Methodological conundra

The combined clinical researches of Bruno Bettelheim, William Niederland, Ulrich Venzlaff, and others provide compelling evidence that a strong association exists not only between the clinical phenomenology of the "survivor syndrome" and that of clinical schizophrenia, but also between the experience of imprisonment in a Nazi concentration camp and the subsequent development of schizophrenia. The larger-scale work of Leo Eitinger and Edgar Trautman, in particular, based on a combined sample of 1,100 patients, offers even stronger data about the greatly increased incidence of schizophrenia among a Holocaust sample than among the general population.

Nevertheless, in attempting to establish a causal link between the concentration camp and schizophrenia, one must ask a crucial methodological question: if the virtually indescribable cruelty of the Nazi death camps exerted such a psychotogenic experience, why did more survivors, or indeed *all* survivors not become schizophrenic either during or after their incarceration? First of all, many of the overtly schizophrenic individuals in pre-Nazi Austria, Germany, Poland, and elsewhere, ultimately perished during the extermination experiments performed upon the mentally ill, and, therefore, never even had an experience in the camps (e.g., Kral, 1951; Krystal, 1968b). Furthermore, those who became psychotic shortly after their arrivals in the camps would be among the first to be murdered, and, therefore, did not survive in the final tally (Nemeth, 1971); in other words, the camps might well have produced many more schizophrenics than lived to tell the tale. Thus, if the Nazis had not killed the many Eastern European psychotics prior to transportation, and if those who did become incarcerated and then quickly developed psychosis had survived, the incidence and prevalence rates of schizophrenia among Holocaust survivors would be even higher, thus offering compelling evidence that one cannot dismiss the role of Nazi-induced traumatogenesis in the aetiology of the schizophrenic psychoses.

Psychological infanticide as an aetiological substrate

Tragically, schizophrenic patients have suffered not only from gross physical abuse, and from gross sexual abuse, and from stressors

within the family, and, in certain instances from extreme psychological traumatization such as the Nazi concentration camps, but, perhaps, from at least one other highly toxic aetiological agent as well.
Shortly after I had begun to work with schizophrenic patients in
hospital, I became increasingly aware of the sheer amount of stories
that I had heard about early experiences of *death threats*, from parents.
As I listened to these tales of horror, I learned that virtually all of my
schizophrenic patients had experienced what I have come to refer to
as "premature morbidization", an early exposure to death, to deadliness, and, in particular, to threats of death, usually at the hands of
caretakers. Fortified by Dr Donald Winnicott's (1949a) important work
on "Hate in the Counter-Transference", in which he carefully delin-
eated the many ways in which even ordinary, healthy parents will
hate their children, unthinkingly singing nursery rhymes tinged with
themes of infant death such as "Rockabye Baby", and subsequently,
by Lloyd deMause's (1974) ground-breaking work on the ubiquity of
the actual infanticide of babies in the ancient world, I learnt only too
clearly about the ways in which mothers and fathers transmit death-
related messages to their children, sometimes consciously, but often
unconsciously (cf. Kahr, 1994).

I first began to appreciate the possible connection between murderous parental wishes and psychiatric illness after reading the 1967
Thomas William Salmon Memorial Lectures on schizophrenia, delivered at the New York Academy of Medicine by the pioneering American psychoanalyst Professor Theodore Lidz of the Yale University
School of Medicine, one of the leading researchers on the psychogenesis of schizophrenia, whose work focused predominantly on the disturbed patterns of communication and the disturbed patterns of
misalliances within the families of schizophrenic patients (Lidz, Fleck,
& Cornelison, 1965). In a chilling case report, Professor Lidz described
his work with an overtly delusional young woman, a university-aged
student who suffered from clinical schizophrenia. Lidz (1973, pp. 99–
100) reported on a meeting with the patient and her family:

> The mother did all the talking, while the father, a wealthy art dealer,
> remained silent. When I directed remarks to him, I gained a response
> from his wife. When I purposefully turned my back on her and asked
> the father a question, the mother intruded before he completed a
> sentence. It was difficult to learn much about the patient for the

mother talked about herself, her Pilgrim ancestry, and her ambitions as a writer. When I finally interrupted and asked about the daughter's college career and her interests, I learned that the girl's whole life revolved about becoming a novelist; she had a passion for Virginia Woolf. Her mother hoped her daughter would follow in the footsteps of her idol. I hesitated before commenting, "But Virginia Woolf had psychotic episodes and committed suicide." The mother did not hesitate when she replied, "It would be worth it."

Six weeks later, while making rounds of the in-patient rooms, Professor Lidz noticed a brace of novels by Virginia Woolf newly despatched by the patient's mother. The patient explained to Lidz, "Mother sent them—she has a thing about Virginia Woolf" (quoted in Lidz, 1973, p. 100). Eventually, Lidz discharged the patient, who returned home to continue her treatment on the West Coast of America, where her parents lived. Heartbreakingly, Professor Lidz subsequently discovered that the patient eventually killed herself, just as Woolf had done, thereby enacting her mother's all too powerful injunction.

Although this vignette from Lidz's casebook appeared in print as long ago as 1973, based on his 1967 lecture, I have never seen this story cited in the clinical literature, except by myself (cf. Kahr, 2001), in spite of the fact that this clinical tale, penned by a well-known, internationally eminent psychiatric writer, has been available for many decades. Although one might dismiss this example of a patient whose mother wished her dead as but one brief illustration that defies replication (after all, how many schizophrenic patients believe themselves to be Virginia Woolf?), Lidz's report does, I propose, actually provide evidence of a more widespread phenomenon, for I would regard this interaction between the patient and her mother as a profound instance of the role of both conscious and unconscious parental death wishes in the aetiology of the schizophrenic illness, the very type of threat that would prompt patients to kill themselves, or, as Dr Ronald Laing (1960, p. 48) and others have noted, to experience "petrification" and become catatonic.

As my sensitivity to the murderous subtext of interactions between psychotic patients and their families became increasingly acute, I eventually came to realize that large numbers of the patients with whom I had worked both wanted and needed to tell me important stories of near-death experiences, death threats, and other types of premature morbidization. Indeed, I began to conceptualize these episodes as instances of what I have come to call "psychological infanticide", the transmission of a death wish, either directly or indirectly, from caretaker to child. Psychoanalysts, as well as psychopathologists, have, of course, appreciated the fact that many parents have harboured hateful feelings towards their children (e.g., Ferenczi, 1929; Myrhman, Rantakallio, Isohanni, Jones, & Partanen, 1996; Rosen, 1953; Winnicott, 1949a), but few have examined the impact on a child of being not only unwanted, but also of being wished *dead*.

As my thinking developed, I published a short, preliminary communication on this topic entitled "Ancient Infanticide and Modern Schizophrenia: The Clinical Uses of Psychohistorical Research" (Kahr, 1993), in which I reviewed data on both the history of actual infanticide in the ancient world, as well as the ways in which this phenomenon has become transmuted into *psychological* infanticide, so prevalent in the psychiatric population.

In this brief communication, I identified three principal subtypes of psychological infanticide, experiences which would leave the pre-schizophrenic child feeling persecuted, terrorized, tormented, and, in many cases, delusionally dead or completely catatonic. I described these principal subtypes as:

1. *Actual parental death threats*, in which a parent, through deeds or words, either attempts to kill a child, unsuccessfully, or threatens to do so.
2. *The replacement child syndrome*, in which the pre-schizophrenic child enters the world in the immediate aftermath of the death of an elder sibling, and then, the replacement child ultimately comes to realize that he or she can never satisfy the grieving, bereaved parents, and so becomes mad in the process.
3. *Aborted abortions*, whereby a parent, usually a mother, informs her child directly that she had planned to have an abortion, but that for some unpreventable, external reason, the abortion could not be carried out.

I shall now provide a more detailed description of the three principal subtypes of psychological infanticide.

With respect to actual parental death attempts or death threats, I have encountered numerous instances of near-death experiences perpetrated by parents towards children who would eventually be

formally diagnosed with schizophrenia. These include parents shouting "I wish you were dead", parents chasing their children with
knives or other dangerous implements, parents locking children in
darkened cupboards for more than twenty-four hours, thereby
depriving the child of food or sufficient oxygen, or depriving the child
of necessary medical attention. One schizophrenic woman, whom I
shall call "Jemma", told me that during her childhood, her Orthodox
Jewish parents would always refuse to telephone for medical assistance on the Sabbath (Friday night after sunset, and all day Saturday
until sunset), as the use of the telephone would be considered a con-
travention of Jewish law. I can think of few rabbis who would endorse
this as a feasible interpretation of Judaism, but Jemma's parents often
allowed both her and her brother to suffer without accessing necessary medical care. Both children, in fact, became schizophrenic in
adult life, and the brother ultimately committed suicide.

As for the *replacement child syndrome*, it staggers me how many psy-
chiatrically compromised individuals have had to endure the experience of succeeding a dead elder brother or sister into the world. Both
Vincent van Gogh and Peter Sellers, two rather different personalities,
yet both highly distressed, troubled, and deeply self-destructive (Van
Gogh psychotically so), entered the world in the wake of a dead sibling. In the case of Van Gogh, he replaced an elder brother called,
unsurprisingly, "Vincent". Of course, not all replacement children
become schizophrenic by any means, but I encountered a number of
cases of schizophrenic patients who had come into the world as
replacement children, and whose parents, crucially, had not even
begun to mourn the loss of the earlier child. In my clinical work, I had
never met a patient more ill than "Karina", a sixty-five-year-old
woman who had received a diagnosis of schizophrenia at the age of
nineteen. Karina spent all day walking up and down the corridors of
the psychiatric hospital wailing in an uncontrollable manner, begging
to die. She had done this for years, and, eventually, the staff became
numb to her rantings, and no one would work with her. When I sat
down with Karina and attempted to learn something about her history,
I soon discovered that her mother had had a depressive breakdown
only days after Karina's birth. When I asked Karina why she imagined
her mother had become ill, Karina replied, "She never got over the
other Karina." Naturally, I looked perplexed, but I soon came to understand that *exactly* nine months before Karina's birth, her elder sister

had died from diphtheria at the age of ten years. Her name? Karina. Apparently, the elder Karina had beautiful blue eyes and wavy blonde hair. My patient, the replacement Karina, had muddy brown eyes and kinky black hair. Whenever she compared herself to her deceased sister, Karina the younger felt deeply bodily inadequate. She constantly wondered why her parents had given her the same name as her dead sister, exactly as Vincent van Gogh's parents had done by naming him after his dead brother. Of course, the younger Karina could never compete with the cherished, idealized, unmourned older Karina, and, hence, my patient soon sensed that her parents had wished her dead, and often told her so.

More recently, I have encountered another variant of the replacement child syndrome in my work with distressed patients. "Lorenzo", a middle-aged man, confessed to me that, during his teenage years, he found himself embroiled in a conversation with his mother and with his twin brother "Mauro" about what would happen if their home should ever catch fire. Apparently, the mother stated earnestly that if their home should go up in flames, she would save her husband first, and only then would she endeavour to save her twin sons. Lorenzo and Mauro, both of whom nearly died from drug overdoses in adolescence, expressed their consternation, whereupon their mother exclaimed, "Well, I can always become pregnant again with more children, but I can't replace my husband." The boys became quite mortified, chillingly aware of the infanticidal undercurrent in their mother's mind.

With reference to the category of psychological infanticide known as "Aborted abortions", I recall a schizophrenic gentleman called "Norbert". During my first assessment interview with Norbert, I soon learnt that his mother had experienced a traumatic delivery of her son. When I asked Norbert what he knew about his own birth, he said, "Oh, apparently, I ripped my mother open." I then asked for clarification, whereupon Norbert replied, "Yes, that's right, all my life my mother kept telling me how I ripped her body open, and that she regrets not having aborted me." Another schizophrenic man, called "Otto", explained that his mother had also told him of her plans to have him aborted, but that their general medical practitioner, a fervent practising Catholic, refused to authorize such a procedure.

Of course, none of these experiences—whether being threatened with death, whether being a replacement child, or whether being an aborted abortion—provides complete evidence of traumatogenesis, at least not sufficiently so that one could comfortably attribute the aetiology of schizophrenia to one or more of these sub-categories of psychological infanticide. In fact, we all know of many people whose parents threatened them, of many replacement children, and of many aborted abortions, who did not become schizophrenically psychotic in any way.

Nevertheless, as I began to encounter more and more schizophrenic patients, first as an assessor, next as a psychotherapist in both individual and group contexts, and next as a clinical supervisor of the work of younger colleagues, I collected many more examples of these infanticidal interactions. I also discovered at least two other subtypes of psychologically infanticidal experiences which appeared and reappeared with increasing regularity in the life history stories of schizophrenic men and women, experiences which rarely appeared in the narratives of those who did not struggle with schizophrenia: instances of the murder of the patient's pets during early childhood, as well as the experience of having one's co-twin die in the third trimester of pregnancy, while still *in utero*.

The murder of pets occurs with great frequency in the childhood histories of pre-schizophrenic patients. I know of at least five schizophrenic patients who reported memories of parents burning their teddy bears in a dramatic manner, throwing their childhood dolls and toys away, and, in the more extreme cases, killing an actual pet, sometimes in the presence of the child, and sometimes not. Most horrifyingly, I recall the case of "Petrina", a twenty-something schizophrenic patient whose mother wrenched her favourite childhood transitional object from her hands shortly after Petrina's sixth birthday, explaining in a sneering tone, "Big girls like you shouldn't play with teddies", and then proceeded to tear the bear's head off in front of Petrina's eyes. Dr Valerie Sinason (2001), pioneering psychoanalyst, child psychotherapist, and traumatologist, has identified a similar phenomenon in her chillingly revealing essay on "Children Who Kill Their Teddy Bears", based on her work with patients suffering from all manner of psychiatric illnesses, including dissociative identity disorder. In Sinason's work with an eight-year-old mute, psychotic, and handicapped boy called "Steven", she observed him engaging in a repetitive ritual of drowning a toy teddy bear in the clinic sink during child psychotherapy sessions. On one occasion, Steven rifled through the dressing-up cupboard and emerged in adult, female clothing, resembling an older woman. Steven announced, quite eerily, that he had become a "mummy", and that he wanted to kill the teddy-baby. Steven intoned, "Kill, kill, kill", and "I'm my mummy" (quoted in Sinason, 2001, p. 45), revealing, only too clearly, the ways in which the child will often identify with the murderous mother, and repeat inexorably the death wishes and death threats absorbed during the pre-Oedipal period of development. Such early childhood experiences might not occur exclusively in the backgrounds of the pre-schizophrenic child, but might ultimately prove pathogenic, in fact, in a number of different psychopathological syndromes.

But the murder of pets can also occur in quite concrete form. "Quincy", a borderline psychotic patient, told me that his sadistic father had forced him to watch the family veterinarian inject their sick dog with a lethal shot. Aged nine years old at the time, Quincy later recalled the horror of the incident only too clearly, and confessed that he had never felt safe in the world since that time.

Death of a twin in utero might also feature as a potentially toxic agent in the development of adult schizophrenia. During my working life, I have encountered three floridly schizophrenic patients whose co-twins had died, *in utero*, during the third trimester of pregnancy. "Reed", a forty-something schizophrenic man, told me that his twin brother had died, shortly before his birth. A conversation with a family member confirmed the truth of Reed's assertion. Deeply tormented by hallucinations of being murdered by a giant hand, Reed could not sleep at night unless he could go to bed, on his hospital ward, clutching an enormous teddy bear, approximately five feet in height, to which he clung with symbiotic rigour. A tall, fully grown man, Reed would intone, before bedtime, "This is my brother." Episodically, Reed would lapse into deep catatonic states, pretending to be dead, and claiming that someone had sucked all of the blood from his body. I suspect that, from an unconscious point of view, Reed entered into a state of identification with his dead twin brother, and used the tall, five-foot teddy bear as a desperate means of enlivening himself, and shielding himself from the trauma of having had as his very first object relation a dead co-twin.

I have now identified five different, though interrelated, varieties of premature morbidization which one will encounter all too frequently in the biographies of men and women who eventually receive a psychiatric diagnosis of schizophrenia. All of these individuals have survived in a bodily sense (none became the victim of forensic infanticide), but all have suffered from what I have identified as *psychological infanticide*, having become recipients of one or more variants of parental death threats, or having been born with dead co-twins, which can, unconsciously, be blamed on mother. At any rate, all of these youngsters had experienced premature morbidization. As a result of becoming a victim of psychological infanticide, the young child in question will internalize a state of deadliness, which I have come to call the "infanticidal introject", which functions rather like a cancerous tumour in the mind, and which will remain toxic unless defused by a psychotherapeutic process or some other form of healing (Kahr, 2007b,c).

Those people who have internalized an infanticidal introject through psychological infanticide and other types of premature morbidization will, in my experience, develop a disorganized state of mind in relation to attachment, and, in particular, one which I wish to identify specifically as an "infanticidal attachment". To date, I have never met a schizophrenic patient with a secure attachment, and I have, by now, met many hundreds, and supervised or consulted to the treatment of many hundreds more.

Although I shall not attempt to discuss the ways in which one might begin to work psychoanalytically or psychotherapeutically with the psychologically infanticided schizophrenic patient, I do wish to remark that the dynamics of someone who has grown up with infanticidal attachments will invariably be relived in the treatment situation, and clinicians ought to become increasingly vigilant to the possibility of what I have come to call an "infanticidal transference", and its correlate, the "infanticidal countertransference". I can recall patients who, upon first meeting me, instantly thought that I had plans to kill them. One hospitalized patient, whom I had not met previously, ran into my consulting room at the beginning of our first session and, before I could even introduce myself by name, catapulted himself out of the window, fearful of being killed. Fortunately, the patient landed on a ledge and did not harm himself. Another hospitalized patient ran into my room and, before I could greet this person, hid himself under a table, cowering in fear of being murdered. Yet another schizophrenic patient, with whom I worked in a music therapy group, used to fantasize that I wanted her dead, when, in fact, I often regarded her as one of my favourite patients, as the others all suffered from catatonia and only this particular person would sing out loud! Still others will threaten the life of the psychotherapist as a desperately creative attempt to protect themselves from the even more terrifying fear of being killed by the clinician. For those who work with such patients, an infanticidal countertransference will be inevitable, and therapists of all backgrounds regularly report fantasies of hurling these understandably demanding and frightening individuals out of the window, which both represents the objective burden of working with such people (Winnicott, 1949a) and is also an unconscious communication of a deadly quality within the original intrafamilial environment.

Other mental health professionals have, of course, written about the possible aetiological role of the death threat in the backgrounds of psychotic individuals. Professor Bruno Bettelheim (1956), for example, reported several cases of psychotic boys who had suffered either death threats or near-death experiences, as I have already indicated. But, as yet, no clinician has attempted to theorize the relationship between infanticidal experiences and schizophrenic symptoms in a more systematic matter. In an era dominated by biopharmacotherapeutic approaches to mental illness, one can readily understand our reluctance as psychotherapeutic practitioners to share these arguably unpopular clinical observations.

I shall now present some more detailed clinical material: first a very short case vignette, and next, a fuller case history, illuminating, I trust, the ways in which the infanticidal introject might feature in the developmental history of the patient who eventually receives a formal diagnosis of schizophrenia. Clinical material obtained in the psychoanalytical situation, though based on small numbers of individuals, provides, nevertheless, a rich, intricate narrative of biographical detail that would not ordinarily emerge in a more traditional empirical psychopathological research investigation, and, therefore, has potentially great value for workers in the mental health field.

Clinical material

The case of Vita

During more than thirty years of work in the psychological profession, I have met few patients more distressed and crazed than "Vita".

Indeed, one of my senior colleagues, who knew Vita very well, described her as a veritable "museum of psychopathology", because she displayed so many symptoms, including auditory hallucinations, delusions of being murdered, anorexia nervosa, bulimia, multiple suicide attempts, self-cutting of the face, arms, legs, and genitals with a razor blade, burning of the skin, sexual promiscuity, profound sexual identity confusion (alternating nightly between male and female sex partners), drug abuse, alcohol abuse, chronic smoking of cigarettes, trichotillomania (hair-pulling), and others too numerous to mention. Although the large range of symptomatology might lead a traumatologist to suppose that Vita might better be diagnosed as a case of complex post-traumatic stress disorder, one must realize that she met all the formal *Diagnostic and Statistical Manual of Mental Disorders* requirements for a diagnosis of schizophrenia (American Psychiatric Association, 1994), and had, in fact, received this diagnosis from one of the world's leading experts in the field of psychiatric diagnosis, one of the many, many psychiatrists who had evaluated Vita over the years (all of whom agreed on the schizophrenia diagnosis). I shall not dwell upon the full details of Vita's history, except to report that she suffered from gross early abandonment, as, one month after her birth, Vita's mother became ill with lymphoma from which she eventually recovered, but which necessitated that she spend a full year in hospital so that she could receive very primitive chemotherapy. Vita's father attempted to look after the newborn baby, rather unsuccessfully. The father, a paedophile, abused Vita sexually, and, eventually, he participated in a child pornography ring and used Vita as one of the so-called "models". She believed that this abuse took place between the ages of eight and eleven. Unsurprisingly, Vita became a psychiatric in-patient at the age of twelve, and lived in many adolescent units, heavily medicated, and deeply despondent.

Vita had become a patient at the institution where I worked only a short while after I had already announced to colleagues that I would be leaving in one year's time to take up another post; therefore, I never had the opportunity to provide ongoing psychotherapy for her. I did, however, have the occasion to offer time-limited family work to Vita and her parents. The consultant psychiatrist in charge of Vita's case asked me to meet with the family, as Vita had begun to express a delusion that her parents wanted her dead, and so, as a result, she began to acquire large carving knives, stolen from local shops, the hospital kitchen, or from other sources unknown to staff, and Vita threatened to use these knives to stab her parents to death. On more than one occasion, colleagues and I had to confiscate these knives and attempt to convince Vita that murder would not be the best of ideas. At this time, Vita began using razor blades, and would make light tracings on her belly, often drawing blood.

One afternoon, Vita's rather frightening parents did not arrive for the family session, and I met with Vita alone. She told me that she had just remembered an episode that had occurred sometime during her childhood. Vita could not recall her exact age, possibly five, or six, or even seven years. It seems that Vita had a favourite transitional object, a teddy bear called "Harry". Vita loved Harry greatly, and she carried him everywhere. At one point, Vita became distressed because one of the old-fashioned wire coils inside of Harry's tummy became loose, and it began to protrude through the fabric of the soft toy. Vita brought Harry to her mother, who, according to Vita, feigned sympathy, and announced mockingly, "Oh, dear, poor Harry, he is very ill, isn't he? It looks as though we shall have to operate", whereupon the mother then took Vita and Harry into the kitchen, seized a large carving knife, and sliced open the teddy bear's stomach from sternum to abdomen. Vita began to scream hysterically at the sight of her mother mutilating her bear, and eventually, the mother taped the wire coil back inside, and sewed Harry together again. Vita shook demonstrably as she told me this tale.

Some weeks later, Vita's mother arrived by herself for a family therapy session. Vita could not attend, as she had elected to go to the cinema with the nurses and some of the other patients, and father, too, did not attend, as he had a cold. Mother felt very uncomfortable meeting one to one, as did I, but somehow, we survived the meeting. I asked her whether she might be able to tell me something of her own background, because I realized that I knew little about her history prior to Vita's birth, and prior to her own quite awful struggle with lymphoma and her subsequently successful treatment with chemotherapy.

Grudgingly, the mother offered only some skimpy details. I tried to facilitate the conversation by asking a raft of clarificatory questions. "What did your mother do?" I wondered. "Oh, just a housewife," replied Vita's mother. "And what about your father?" I asked. "Ah, yes, he was a doctor, in the country," she answered. And then, Vita's mother began to look away, and she turned her eyes towards the ceiling, as if concentrating very hard upon some newly formed thought or newly retrieved memory. "It's funny," she said, "I haven't thought about this in decades, but I suddenly remember that my father was not only a doctor, he was *my* doctor too, even though he wasn't a paediatrician." I looked quizzical as Vita's mother continued with her unexpected free associative recitation. She then explained that once, during her childhood, she could not recall her age at the time, she suffered from crippling appendix pains, and her father diagnosed a burst appendix, and knew that an immediate appendectomy would be needed. Unfortunately, the family were holidaying on a remote Scottish island at the time, far away from the mainland, and so could not access medical help in time. I worked with Vita in the early 1980s, at which time the mother must have been already sixty years old; therefore, I quickly estimated that this appendix crisis would have occurred in the 1930s, when being stranded on a remote Scottish island, with no mobile telephones or medicopters, would indeed have constituted a grave emergency. In the absence of any other qualified practitioner, the father announced, "We shall have to operate." With no anaesthetic other than chloroform available, and no operating theatre, Vita's grandfather actually performed surgery upon the tummy of Vita's mother, and, quite miraculously, she neither died nor developed an infection in the process.

I shall restrain myself from discussing more of the details of Vita's case in this limited context, but, rather, I wish only to underscore at this juncture the role of intergenerational trauma as a possible aetiological component in the development of Vita's symptomatology, and of her fear of being murdered. One might imagine that having her own mother hospitalized with lymphoma for the first year of Vita's life would, in and of itself, create a serious risk for a disorganized attachment in later life, but when one combines the abandonment by the mother with the sexual abuse perpetrated first by father, and then by father's child pornography accomplices, one wonders why Vita did not become schizophrenic much sooner, or, indeed, commit suicide. But then, when one considers the impact of mother committing an act of psychological infanticide on the teddy bear, Harry, and, through identification, on Vita herself, one begins to wonder whether schizophrenia, especially paranoid schizophrenia, becomes the inevitable outcome of such a set of childhood intrusions.

I have called this patient "Vita" as a testament to her desperate struggle to cling to life in the face of so much traumatic reliving across the generations, from grandfather to mother to the knife-wielding part of Vita herself. Heart-wrenchingly, I learnt that years after I had left the psychiatric hospital, Vita did indeed kill herself, although the nurse who told me about Vita's death did not know whether Vita used a knife, as I suspect she might have done. But, whatever the cause of her death, I have a strong suspicion that her mother's unanaesthetized surgery became replayed on Vita's teddy bear decades later, and that Vita became understandably fearful of being murdered by her mother. Then, when mother failed to protect her from the grotesque abuses of father and his confederates, murder, suicide, or madness became Vita's only options for survival. In the end, though she tried to kill her parents and become a murderess, she succumbed instead to madness and suicide, unaided by the literally hundreds of staff members across different hospitals and clinics who had tried to rescue her.

The case of Steven Froggit

I began to work psychotherapeutically with "Steven Froggit" approximately twenty-nine years ago. When I first discussed the possibility that I might one day wish to write about his story in a disguised, confidential manner, he seemed very pleased, and earnestly hoped that his life might help us to understand something about the causes and treatments of schizophrenia. I explained that I would, of course, not use his real name, and I wondered whether he might wish to suggest a name that suited him. Without batting an eyelid, my patient replied, "I want you to call me 'John Smith', the most common name in the English language." I explained that such a common name would certainly help to disguise his identity, but I also mused whether his choice of such a potentially unremarkable moniker indicated, in any way, his low sense of self-esteem, and his feeling that he might not be memorable, either to me or to others. After some further discussion, the patient replied, "Ah, Brett, I see your point, in that case, I would like you to call me 'Steven Froggit'."

I first met Steven Froggit on the ward of a provincial psychiatric hospital in a remote part of the British countryside. Steven, a chronic schizophrenic person in his early forties, had already spent more than twenty years as an in-patient on a long-stay ward, heavily medicated

with Chlorpromazine. Steven presented with a mixed picture diag-
nostically, alternating between classic manifestations of both catatonic
schizophrenia and paranoid schizophrenia. During his lengthy periods of catatonia, he would lie in bed all day and all night, with his
eyes, facial muscles, and limbs completely frozen, unable to move
even a centimetre. Sometimes, he would hide completely beneath the
bedclothes, resembling a cadaver in a mortuary. But during his
equally lengthy periods of *paranoia persecutoria*, he displayed all the
most classic Schneiderian first-rank symptoms of schizophrenic psychosis: persecutory delusions of being raped by Martians, delusions of
being bayoneted in the anus by marauding soldiers, delusions of
having his thoughts transmitted on the evening news by the British
Broadcasting Corporation, and others too numerous to mention.
Physically, he sweated profusely, and he would wash and change his
clothing only when the nurses forcibly managed to submerge him in
a bath. He would put up such resistance that, on most occasions, the
nurses lost all hope and allowed Steven to languish in a state of poor
personal hygiene. He also used snuff. He would regularly inhale a
large amount of snuff, sneeze with hurricane force, and emit copious
amounts of saliva and mucous which would remain stuck to his
ample beard and moustache, and he would then wipe the residual
brown snuff all over his clothing. As he would often remark, "I live in
a pig sty, and therefore, I am a pig."

In addition to his marked schizophrenic symptomatology, Steven
also perpetrated regular acts of violence on the ward. A large man,
over six feet tall, with a bulky, square frame, Steven had on more than
one occasion tried to murder the consultant psychiatrist, usually by
attempted strangulation, and would have to be restrained by four
male psychiatric nurses. On other occasions, he would take one of
those heavy-duty, industrial combination ashtray–dustbins and hurl it
through the window of the day room, inflicting much physical
damage and terrifying his fellow patients in the process.

Before I had arrived on the ward as a young trainee, Steven had
received regular courses of electroconvulsive shock treatment, as well
as an ongoing prescription of Chlorpromazine and other antipsychotic
medications, not to mention many aborted attempts at occupational
therapy. In a pharmacologically dominated institution, no one had
ever attempted to offer psychotherapy, however rudimentary, and the
ward employed not a single professional with psychotherapeutic

training or interest. The enlightened consultant psychiatrist respected my own fledgling interest in psychoanalysis, and he allowed me to explore this by beginning to work with Steven psychotherapeutically, under regular, helpful, clinical supervision, and, thus, we began three years of intensive psychotherapeutic work at a frequency of three sessions weekly. I had already begun my own experience of psychoanalysis at this time, and, though still a student and, therefore, not yet qualified, I knew enough about the boundaries of professionalism and about the nature of psychotherapeutic work that, with a good supervisor in place, I might perhaps manage the experience in some way.

I had already met Steven, of course, on the ward where I worked, although I had no extensive contact with him. But when the consultant psychiatrist asked him whether he might wish to have some regular private conversations with me, Steven seemed quite eager. He told the psychiatrist, "I like Brett. Private conversations would be good."

On the evening before our first session—the very first session of psychotherapy that I had ever facilitated in my career—I had a dream. The Nazis had captured me and sent me to a concentration camp, and then placed me in the gas chambers. The poison gas quickly filled the chamber, but somehow, I survived. Then I had a second dream that night. I found myself swallowing a packet of razor blades. And yet, somehow, I survived. As I rushed to work that morning, I did not dare to allow myself the time or space to think about the meaning of these extraordinary, highly uncharacteristic dreams, but I saw the consultant psychiatrist in the corridor, and I felt strangely compelled to share my dreams with him. He chortled out loud, and interpreted, "Here you are, about to take on the most dangerous patient on the ward in individual psychotherapy. In order for this to work, you will have to believe that you have the omnipotence to survive the Nazis." I, too, laughed at the grandiosity of my dreams. Perhaps one does need a naïve type of courage in order to work with such an ill and potentially unpromising psychotherapy patient. But, perhaps the dreams also represented something about what I may already have perceived about the internal world of Steven Froggit, a world of Nazis, Zyklon-B gas, and razor blades—a world that I might have intuited quite unconsciously, but could not yet understand.

Steven and I began to work. As the institution had not a single private room on the wards (all the patients lived in one great big, barn-like dormitory), I had arranged to use a tiny study room in the hospital's medical library. To my surprise and delight, Steven arrived, escorted by the nurses, in time for his first psychotherapy session . . . and mine. I sat silently. Within moments of sitting down on the chair, Steven stood up, and then turned his chair upside down so that the four legs stood in the air. He then proceeded to lower himself, laughing giddily, on to one of the protruding legs, pretending to hump it. To be frank, I cannot remember what I said in response to this arguably unusual start, or whether I said anything at all. Did he have an anxiety that such close contact with a younger male had evoked a fearful homoerotic transference? Did he want to communicate something to me about the upside-down nature of his internal world? Or did he wish, perhaps quite unconsciously, to offer some communication of early anal abuse? The possibilities seemed legion. I suppose that, in the absence of knowing, I would, in all likelihood, have sat quietly, unskilled in the art of interpreting quickly.

Eventually, Steven returned the seat to its upright position, and he began to talk, just as an ordinary psychotherapy patient might do. And as our three-times weekly sessions began to unfold, I learnt much more about the hallucinatory and delusional aspects of his internal world, many of which he had never verbalized before to other members of staff. Gradually, he and I began to develop a much more intimate knowledge of his symptom picture.

I learnt, for example, that in addition to his fears of being bayoneted in the anus by soldiers, and of being raped by Martians, and of having his private sexual thoughts broadcast by the BBC on the nightly news, Steven Froggit also heard voices which told him that he would one day come to be the cause of World War III. Additionally, he explained that a famous German general from the Second World War wished him dead, and had organized a plot to murder Steven. Similarly, he told me that he thought the television set on the ward spoke to him, and he claimed that every night, the BBC emitted a secret message which said, in German, "Das BBC ist ein Scheisser." Furthermore, he told me about a troop of secret agents, known as the "Me-ins" and the "We-ins", who plotted his death, and he also described a team of Tae-Kwon-Do experts who, if they discovered him, would thrash him to pieces. Death loomed everywhere in his material. He also informed me that one of the colleges of the University of Cambridge wished him dead, and that only by destroying the television on the ward would he be able to stop his persecutors. Steven had, by this point, smashed up the ward telelvision on more than several occasions.

I attempted, as best I could, to develop a more coherent picture of Steven Froggit's hallucinatory and delusional material, and, as I had not yet developed much interpretative finesse, I asked clarificatory questions in a quiet and contained style. I tried, in particular, to learn more about the phenomenology of each of his symptoms. As an example, let us examine his delusion of being bayoneted in the anus by a group of soldiers. I asked him, quite simply, to tell me more about this piece of material. Steven replied in a most helpful manner, and eventually, the imagery became richer and more detailed. I learnt, for example, that the marauding soldiers who shoved their bayonets up his rectum did not appear from nowhere. In fact, these soldiers would all congregate at Liverpool Street Station in London, board the train to the tiny village near the psychiatric hospital where he lived and I worked, and would then enter the ward secretly at night. Upon arriving on the ward, the soldiers, all uniformed, would cast a magic spell over all the nurses and patients, freezing them, and only then would they proceed to Steven's bed and, one by one, insert their deadly bayonets inside his anal aperture. I found his recitation of this psychological experience—a delusional experience, of course—quite shocking, and I tried, empathically, to imagine what one might feel like going to sleep every night in anticipation of such a cruel anal attack. I doubt very much that I did have the ability to really understand how dreadful such an experience could be. But, like a good trainee, I listened silently, compassionately, and dutifully to the material, and then brought it to my supervisor for discussion.

In 1982, very few British mental health professionals knew much about sexual abuse; therefore, my supervisor, a skilled clinician in his own right who had, in fact, trained with Miss Anna Freud, never mentioned the possibility of sexual abuse. I did have this thought in my mind, but did not quite know what to do with it. After all, the Cleveland child abuse scandal would not reach the national newspapers until 1987, and even if sexual abuse did feature in Steven Froggit's history, surely, I thought, it had no relation to such a severe illness as schizophrenia. After all, most victims of child sexual abuse did not ever become schizophrenic, so how could abuse and psychosis even have a connection?

In spite of the inability of both my supervisor and I to conceptualize Steven's material in terms of abuse and trauma, I persevered with the work. I tried again and again to follow Freud's dictum about the importance of detail in reconstructive work, and I wondered with Steven again and again as to why the evil soldiers would board the train at Liverpool Street Station as opposed to Euston Station, or even Victoria Station, for that matter? Steven laughed at my inquisitiveness, but did not provide any further biographical data that might help our understanding. Nevertheless, to my great surprise, Steven continued to attend, quite promptly in fact, his three weekly sessions of psychotherapy. Although I would describe our work more as supportive psychotherapy than as a more polished version of psychoanalytic psychotherapy, I suspect that he felt contained by the experience, and, to my great delight, he became less menacing on the ward, less incoherent, less likely to bombard the nurses with explosive recitations of delusional material, and, as a result, the consultant psychiatrist dared to reduce his medication.

I tried, of course, to learn more about Steven's early years, but he would not talk about it, other than telling me that he had a cold, cold mother, whom he nicknamed, privately, "The Ice Queen", and a lovely father. He also had an older sister who had attended university. He, on the other hand, had failed his eleven-plus examination, and did not apply to college. He knew that I had to be a graduate pursuing further university studies, and he took a great interest in my academic credentials and plans.

The work continued apace, and I did everything in my power to learn as much as I could about the psychotherapy of the psychoses, and I read every book, monograph, and article in the psychoanalytical literature, and attended every conference that I could find, both here and abroad. My vicarious supervisions with Harold Searles, with Bertram Karon, with William Niederland, and with other distinguished psychoanalysts, helped me, I suppose, much more than my own supervisions with a kindly, benign, and encouraging psychiatrist. I knew from my academic studies that many of the great psychoanalytical workers had managed to trace specific schizophrenic hallucinations and delusions back to early experiences of trauma, and I wondered whether I would be able to do the very same.

As someone with a long-standing passion for archival history, I wondered whether I might help my work with Steven Froggit by researching his history in a more thorough manner, and so I went to the nurses' station and read through his hospital case file, which contained hundreds of pages of notes, mostly a log of relatively recent reports about his violent incidents on the ward, his penchant for smashing the television set, his attempt to strangle the consultant, his medication regime, his baths or lack thereof—all very useful and very interesting, but not of great help in learning more about his past. During one lunch hour, a congenial nurse, bemused by my diligent reading and re-reading of Steven's files, suggested that I might wish to apply to the hospital archives to obtain Steven's earliest hospital records from the 1960s.

My heart leapt with fear and anticipation. The hospital archives? No one had ever told me that such a building existed on the sprawling grounds of our backwater institution. With compass and map, I trekked nearly half a mile across a muddy field, and eventually found my way to a tiny hut known as "Hospital Records". It seemed to me that not a single member of staff either knew of its existence or had ever visited this place, and the greying clerk inside seemed stunned by my arrival, as if to say, "We don't get many visitors in these here parts." After introducing myself as a postgraduate trainee, the dusty clerk disappeared into a back room, and, half an hour later, returned with two enormous boxes of Steven Froggit's earliest case notes from the 1960s, which contained all the documentation about his first decades of hospitalization. I received special permission to take the boxes away, and, as though researching the life of Dr Donald Winnicott in the archives of the Wellcome Library for the History and Understanding of Medicine, I began poring through old letters and files, and I began to do what I could to reconstruct Steven Froggit's biography.

Of course, in our next session, I told him about the discovery of these papers, and he seemed delighted, and together, we pored over the findings. The files began with the initial referral letter from Steven's general practitioner to the local psychiatrist, now deceased, who had first evaluated Steven as a troubled seventeen-year-old: "Dear Dr X., I am writing to you about one of my patients, Master Steven Froggit, a seventeen-year-old boy who has begun to show signs of paranoid ideation. Master Froggit believes that his next-door neighbour, a young soldier in the Army, wants to have homosexual contact with him. I believe this to be a delusion, and your evaluation of this patient would be much welcomed."

I asked Steven what he could remember about this soldier who lived next door. He seemed reluctant to speak, but eventually, he reminisced and explained that this soldier had caused him to become schizophrenic. I enquired whether the soldier had ever made sexual overtures to Steven. He shook his head emphatically, claiming that the soldier had never touched him, but Steven felt quite convinced that the young man wanted to do so, in spite of being married, and in spite of having several children.

We continued to search through the case notes. The deceased psychiatrist who first interviewed Steven had also noted having met with Steven's parents, but could not talk to Steven's elder sister, as she had already left home to study at the University of Cambridge. I suddenly remembered that once, and only once, Steven had mentioned that one of the colleges at the University of Cambridge had wished him dead. I regarded this communication as a subsidiary delusion, and not as one of his primary, nightly delusions such as the frequently mentioned one about the soldiers with bayonets. Naïvely, I asked Steven to remind me which college at Cambridge wanted him dead. "That would be Girton College," he replied. "And which college did your sister attend?" "That would be Girton College," he replied. My heart began to race, as I suddenly came to realize that these buried case notes from twenty years ago, hidden beneath the rubble of the hospital archives, might contain the many secrets of Steven's hidden biography.

Together, we commenced an examination of the possible links between his sister's attendance at Girton College of the University of Cambridge and his so-called delusional idea that the entire College wished him dead. Steven laughed heartily at this connection, and said, "Perhaps my sister wished me dead, and not the College. Perhaps I wished her dead too." We then embarked upon a series of very spirited conversations about Steven's shame at not having passed his eleven-plus exams, a failure which barred him, quite cruelly, from the possibility of university study, and which would have contributed greatly to the development of a scarred, vulnerable, and fragile sense of selfhood. He also spoke about his feelings of envy and competition towards his sister for having succeeded academically, and, likewise, of his feelings towards me, whom he regarded as a very clever person. In fact, he kept wondering aloud what my IQ might be.

These discussions of his school years facilitated the emergence of a series of memories of being bullied at school, including one very painful episode from the age of ten, when the other boys pinned him down, and "debagged" him, in other words, they removed his trousers and underwear, causing great humiliation and a loathing of his body. For the first time in sessions, Steven shed a small tear. Gradually, I could begin to witness ordinary pain, linked to ordinary trauma, which lurked beneath the carapace of a seemingly bizarre psychotic exterior.

Our joint archival and psychotherapeutic investigations continued to unfurl, and the process of reading through case notes fostered the verbalization of other memories. One day, quite bravely, Steven told me about what he remembered as his first sexual experience. At the age of twelve, he found himself in the attic of his parent's home, rummaging through old clothing. And there, in a cupboard, he stumbled upon his father's military uniform from the Second World War. His father had served in the British army, and he fought the Germans on German soil. Although he could not understand why, something compelled him to remove all of his clothing, and to dress himself up in his father's uniform. This aroused him greatly, and he began to masturbate for the first time, climaxing inside his father's clothes.

This new knowledge about Mr Froggit Senior's involvement in all matters militaristic and German made me begin to wonder about the soldiers who congregated nightly at Liverpool Street Station, and who would then travel to the psychiatric hospital and attack Steven anally with their bayonets. I also began to think about his delusion that a famous German general from the Second World War had plans to kill him. I reminded Steven that a voice in his head would often proclaim, in German, "Das BBC ist ein Scheisser." Could these references to all matters German be in any way related to his father? "Well done, Sherlock," Steven said, with great humour and great affection. I had a sense that Steven knew much more about the connections between his early experiences and his symptomatology than he would often reveal, but that he wanted to test my reliability, my fidelity, and my compassion towards him before he would dare to reveal any more.

Sometimes, we would read documentation together in sessions, but I could not restrain my archival, psychobiographical curiosity, and I often read Steven's notes, again and again, on my own, desperately searching for potentially helpful clues. And then, one day, I felt as though I had discovered the Rosetta Stone of Steven's archaeologically submerged childhood history. While leafing through further documentation, I found a note, written by Steven's father, Mr Froggit, in scrawled handwriting, to Steven's psychiatrist, expressing his concerns about Steven's violent temper during a recent weekend visit home. Mr. Froggit had penned this missive on British Broadcasting Corporation letterhead.

I had always assumed that Mr Froggit worked in agriculture, or so Steven had led me to believe, but, upon further discussions with Steven, I learnt that for a short period of time, his father did indeed work in London, for the BBC, in a research capacity, and that he would take the train every morning from the Froggit home in the wilds of the British countryside and journey to the capital, and then repeat the journey back home at the end of the day. My pulse began to quicken as I realized the potential significance of this biographical discovery. To which station in London did Mr Froggit travel, and from which station did he return? Steven could not remember the details of his father's journey during his tenure at the BBC, but a careful perusal of train timetables soon revealed that, just as I had suspected, Mr Froggit's train from an obscure rural village brought him into London's Liverpool Street Station, and each night, this former soldier, who had once fought the Germans in his military uniform, would depart from Liverpool Street Station, and return home to spend the evening with his wife, his daughter, and with his son Steven Froggit.

Steven delighted in my detective work, as we began, jointly, to hypothesize that his paranoid fear of the BBC revealing his sexual secrets on the television each night might, in some way, relate to his father's employment there, and that, likewise, his fear of soldiers congregating at Liverpool Street Station before coming to the hospital to insert their bayonets into his rectum might have something to do with sexual activities in relation to his father, the man whose army uniform provided Steven with his earliest memory of a masturbatory orgasm.

Could we now begin to explain the delusional notion of the BBC broadcasting his thoughts, and the private auditory hallucinations that "Das BBC ist ein Scheisser", and the fear of being murdered by a German general, as well as the delusion of the bayonet-carrying soldiers meeting at Liverpool Street Station, as symptoms which might relate to actual biographical details, what Freud (1937d, p. 268) had earlier referred to as the "kernel of truth" in the psychotic delusion? And what of the young, married soldier with children who lived next door to the Froggits? Did this man indeed make sexual overtures towards Steven, or did Steven, a potentially anally abused young boy, homoerotically taunted and humiliated by his schoolmates during the debagging ceremony, actually project his own homosexual ideation into the soldier? Did the soldier next door remind Steven, in a transferential manner, of the Second World War soldier, Mr Froggit Senior, who lived in the same house, and whose tantalizing military uniform hung in the attic as a source of excitation?

And what of Steven's mother? Thus far, I knew only that Steven had described her as very, very cold, and that he had chosen the phrase "The Ice Queen" as her nickname. He spoke about her so rarely, and as such a frozen person, that I had no idea what might lurk beneath the ice.

After eighteen months of three-times weekly psychotherapy, Steven had made such strides that the consultant psychiatrist felt sufficiently happy with his demeanour and with his growing lucidity that he removed Steven from all of his Chlorpromazine medication. Still an in-patient on a back ward, Steven told me that he now felt less of a zombie, less likely to perpetrate acts of aggression, and, indeed, less mad. He began to attend the hospital gardening group, and he allowed the nurses to work with him on improving his personal hygiene. He looked increasingly well scrubbed when he arrived at the hospital Medical Library for his regular sessions.

But then, Steven's father, Mr Froggit, died from a very rapidly metastasizing cancer, and Steven plunged into a state of catatonic despair. He took to his bed, and he became completely catatonic, acting rather like a corpse. No amount of medication, no amount of coaxing from the nurses, and no amount of cajoling from the psychiatrist could rouse Steven Froggit from his bed. He lay in fear, in terror. I, too, became deeply despondent, fearing that he and I had lost all of the ground that we had gained psychotherapeutically. My kindly clinical supervisor explained that, in his experience, a regression following the death of a parent need not cause us to lose hope; indeed, he would be surprised if Steven did not respond in this way to the death of his father.

In consultation with the psychiatrist, we decided that instead of cancelling Steven's sessions, I would sit by his bed, in a nearby chair, announce my presence in a quiet voice, and simply be there, in the hope that eventually he might emerge from his frozen, mute state. And indeed, I did so. I would arrive at the appointed hour, sit in a chair, and explain, "Hello Steven, it's Brett Kahr ... Brett ... and I have come for our session time. If you don't mind, I would like to sit here on the chair, and be available in case you want to talk." He said nothing. Indeed, on most occasions, he had the sheets pulled over his head, like a cadaver in a morgue. Sometimes, I would whisper, very quietly, "You must be very scared right now. But I will sit with you. I know you're very scared." I made very simple comments, completely devoid of psychoanalytical brilliance. I tried to be ordinary and to convey a sense of safety. After seven or eight sessions like this, Steven actually peered out from the top of the sheets, only for a few seconds, but he did meet my gaze.

After two or three months of these bedside catatonic sessions, Steven eventually emerged completely, and we resumed our sessions in the Medical Library, and Steven managed to talk about his sadness at the death of his father, and about his deep regret that he did not have a chance to say goodbye. He cried. Within a matter of weeks, Steven became restored to his pre-bereavement state, and the consultant psychiatrist began to discuss the possibility of transferring Steven from in-patient status to out-patient status, encouraging him to think about moving to a psychiatric halfway house in the community, attached to the hospital. Since his first hospitalization at the age of seventeen, Steven had only ever lived on the long-stay psychiatric ward, and he had done so for over twenty years. Would he now be able to manage a transition to the community?

After much discussion and much preparation, this dangerous, hallucinated, deluded, schizophrenic gentleman packed his bags and took up residence in the community, with no medication in his bloodstream at all. He continued to attend his three-times weekly psychotherapy sessions, and he managed to work alongside the occupational therapists in a daily gardening group. What had happened to his schizophrenia?

My work with Steven continued to raise questions. By this point, I had already discovered the work of the brilliant London psychoanalyst Dr Brendan MacCarthy (1988, 2005) who had begun to deliver papers on the sexual abuse of infants and young children, and on the collusion within the family. I already knew of the work of my mentor Lloyd deMause (1974), founder of the Institute for Psychohistory in New

York City, and editor of the landmark publication on *The History of Childhood*. And, of course, I had read Professor Judith Lewis Herman's groundbreaking book on *Father–Daughter Incest* (Herman & Hirschman, 1981). Did I have sufficient evidence to suspect that Steven must have endured early sexual abuse, either from his father or from his next-door neighbour? I continued to hold the tension and the uncertainty, as any good mental health professional must endeavour to do.

Gradually, Steven Froggit and I had developed a sufficiently robust therapeutic alliance that we could now begin to explore the pre-Oedipal material more fully, in particular, his relationship to his mother. Before long, I learnt that his mother did not always act "The Ice Queen". In her more raw moments, she would hit Steven, scream at him, and administer regular enemas into his bottom in order to facilitate the emptying of his bowels. Furthermore, Steven remembered that she used to threaten his life, lamenting the fact that she ever gave birth to children.

We also discovered one final, very revealing letter, buried in the box of archival notes in medical records. Two years after his first hospitalization, Steven received permission from his consultant psychiatrist to spend a weekend at his parents' home, since he had behaved so well of late. After six hours at home, he became increasingly hallucinated, increasingly deluded, and he started to shout that his mother planned to poison him. In desperation, Mrs Froggit telephoned the psychiatrist, who arranged for an immediate domiciliary visit so that Steven could be returned to the psychiatric hospital. Upon arriving, the psychiatrist found the front door to the Froggit house ajar, and so he let himself in, whereupon he stumbled into the kitchen, and observed Mrs Froggit chasing nineteen-year-old Steven in circles, clutching a very large carving knife. According to the psychiatrist's note, recorded historically in the case file, Mrs Froggit kept shouting, quite simply, "I will kill him. I will kill him."

Mercifully, Steven returned to the hospital.

Steven and I worked for one more year. He attended psychotherapy as regularly as any neurotic businesswoman or househusband from North London that I ever had the privilege of treating. He spoke with increasing lucidity, increasing playfulness, and increasing trust. Of course, we engaged with the negative transference. On one occasion, I arrived, most uncharacteristically, three minutes late for his session.

In twenty-five years of psychotherapeutic practice, I have only ever arrived late on two occasions. Once in 1993, I came five minutes late to a session with an escorted, brain-damaged, handicapped patient who had no wristwatch. I did so owing to the fact that I became inexorably delayed in a dreadful traffic jam, in spite of having left ample time to arrive for the session. I rectified the situation by apologizing to the patient and to her escort, and I extended the session by five minutes so that my patient could have a full fifty-minute session. And, just this once, I arrived late for one of Steven's sessions, albeit for a much less impressive reason. The consultant psychiatrist for whom I worked had a secretary with whom I had begun a flirtation, which later became an affair, and on this particular occasion, I became so engrossed in our flirtation that I allowed myself to lose track of the time, and then had to run across the hospital grounds, arriving nonetheless three minutes late for Steven. Of course, I did not tell him the reason for my tardiness, and I apologized, but no doubt he could sense that on this particular occasion I had flushed cheeks and a distracted mind. Within seconds, he announced, "The Me-Ins and the We-Ins have come back into the room. They want me dead."

I felt mortified as I realized that my lateness had unwittingly stimulated persecutory anxiety, and had re-evoked some of the paranoid ideation that I had not observed in Steven for quite some time, owing to the probable increasing success of our psychotherapy. By this time, I had become somewhat more psychotherapeutically sophisticated, and I ventured an interpretation: "I'm aware that you haven't been troubled by the Me-Ins and the We-Ins for some time, and I'm wondering why they've suddenly returned to your mind. I suppose that because I've come late, and kept you waiting, that you may have felt killed off by me, and that you've been wondering whether you can trust me now." To my horror, Steven absorbed my words, and then, for the first time, ran out of the consulting room. Fortunately, he returned five minutes later, sat down in the chair, and winked, "Shrewd, Brett, very shrewd."

With my heart in my stomach, I commented that perhaps he felt so killed off by me that he might have wanted to kill me in return, and that by running out of the consulting room at that moment, he succeeded, very cleverly, in protecting both of us from his murderous fury. Once again, Steven smiled and declaimed, "Shrewd, Brett, very shrewd." The paranoid ideation became contained, and Steven returned to his ordinary mode of functioning as an out-patient.

After three years of work, Steven no longer reported any evidence of psychotic delusions. He committed no violent acts. He maintained a menial, but nonetheless regular, job as a gardening assistant. He needed no psychotropic medication. He continued to live in a staff-assisted community halfway house. And he spent much of his time listening to records, especially German military music.

I, too, had aged, and after three years, I received a postgraduate fellowship in psychology, overseas, which I decided that I would accept, to work, unsurprisingly, on schizophrenia. I knew that I had to inform Steven that I would be leaving the hospital and, indeed, the country in six months' time. Steven struggled with my announcement, and asked me directly where I would be going. Instead of interpreting, I told him the name of the university to which I would be attached. He asked me what sort of IQ one needed in order to have a fellowship at this particular university. I said that he must have a strong wish to come with me, and feared that because of his experiences with the eleven-plus that he might not be able to come, and I wondered whether he would feel left behind once again by the sister who attended Girton College at the University of Cambridge. I wondered whether Yale University in America would also become a persecutor for him. He laughed, "I don't think so. No, I don't think so."

In our final session, Steven asked whether we could go to the hospital canteen and drink beer together. I explained that it would be important to celebrate our work together, but that perhaps we could do it in another way, rather than numbing the pain of separation by the use of alcohol. Again, he chortled, "Shrewd, Brett, very shrewd," a phrase that had now acquired the status of a standing joke. Steven asked me whether I would write to him, and I told him that I would. He also asked me whether I would visit him upon my return to England, and, indeed, I told him that I would. I sent him two or three letters from America, but received no reply. And upon my return to England one year later, I did visit him. The psychiatric halfway house had since closed due to budget cuts, and Steven returned to living in hospital as an in-patient, really the only proper home that he had ever known. But in spite of his move back, he had sustained the gains that he had made in his three years of psychotherapy, and I continued to receive favourable reports about him from the consultant psychiatrist who generously allowed me the opportunity to work with Steven in the first place, in spite of my extreme youth and inexperience.

My psychotherapeutic adventure with Steven has, of course, raised infinitely more questions than it has answered. Did Steven experience anal abuse by his father? Did he experience anal abuse from the soldier who lived next door? Did his fear of being bayoneted rectally stem from the administration of enemas by his mother? Could he have suffered abuse from all of these sources? In spite of exploring these questions with Steven on multiple occasions, I never succeeded in discovering the "correct" answer. Instead, I tried to function as someone who treated both his mind and his body with respect and dignity, and I think that, in doing so, I managed to offer at least something of what Dr Franz Alexander (1946, p. 66), the pioneering psychoanalyst from Berlin, would have called a "corrective emotional experience".

I began working with Steven in 1982, and it has taken me fully twenty-six years to put his case into words. Since 1982, I have published five books, dozens of papers, and literally hundreds of short communications, so, it seems clear that I do not have a writer's block. Why has it taken me so long to convey something of Steven's story in words? Inevitably, the fear of breaching confidentiality has preoccupied me, as it must do with every mental health professional. But I have disguised the location of Steven's psychiatric hospital so well, and all of the staff who knew Steven have since either died or retired, that identification would prove virtually impossible. I suppose my primary reluctance to have written about Steven before has stemmed from my fear that sexual trauma and infanticidal trauma might actually feature in the aetiology of the schizophrenic psychosis. After all, in 1984, even Dr Bowlby had told me that he doubted whether his work on disrupted attachments would have any relevance to the aetiology of schizophrenia. And then newer work on the neuroanatomical aspects of schizophrenia began to appear in the psychiatric literature, and I found myself wondering whether I had anything of value to convey.

But now, the literature on sexual abuse in schizophrenic patients has mushroomed, as have the critiques of the so-called genetic basis and the so-called neurological basis of schizophrenia, at least enough to allow one to wonder whether environmental factors might well play a role. Above all, in 1982, I knew of only one Steven Froggit, only one patient whose mother chased him around the kitchen clutching a carving knife shouting, in the presence of a witness, "I will kill him. I will kill him." Since 1982, I have met more than one hundred further Steven Froggits, many of whom reported memories of similar infanticidal communications in a more direct manner.

I remember, among others, "Ira", a young man who left home at the age of eighteen years in order to go into the army. On his first weekend leave back home, Ira searched in vain for his dog—his best friend from childhood. Upon asking about the dog's whereabouts, Ira's father explained, "Oh, I shot him." Ira buckled at the knees as the father continued to speak. "Oh yes," said his father, "on the day you left, your mother and I thought, well, Ira doesn't need the dog anymore, and *we* didn't want him, so we shot him." Two days later, Ira began to hear voices for the first time. The voices told him that he must kill himself. And so Ira took the father's gun, and placed it beneath his chin, aiming upwards at a 45° angle. Ira fired. Miraculously, although the bullet destroyed Ira's jaw, he survived. Admitted ultimately to a local psychiatric hospital, he received a diagnosis of schizophrenia.

Parental death wishes towards children cause more damage than even traumatologists might wish to admit. In 1909, Sigmund Freud published the immortal case of "Little Hans". As readers may recall, Freud (1909b, p. 122) argued, famously, that, "a thing which has not been understood inevitably reappears; like an unlaid ghost it cannot rest until the mystery has been solved and the spell broken". I suspect that, in the case of Steven Froggit, many of the psychiatric professionals who worked with him over the years understood virtually nothing of his life, of his communications, of the secret meaning of his symptoms. And, therefore, the details of his possible early traumas continued to re-emerge, constituting a full-scale return of the repressed.

Before I conclude my presentation in a more general sense, I wish to revisit two tiny features of my work with Steven Froggit, both of which I mentioned at the very outset of this case history, and both of which might have some import for our better understanding of the aetiology and the treatment of schizophrenia. First, I wish to remind us of the two dreams that I had on the eve of my initial psychotherapy session with Steven. In the first dream, I imagined that the Nazis had captured me, subjected me to poisonous gas, and that I had, nonetheless, survived. In the second dream, I swallowed a packet of razor blades, and yet, I survived. How can one analyse a dream from more than a quarter century ago, with no associations? Perhaps it would be folly to do so, but I suspect that the dreams contained evidence of the necessary "chutzpah" required of the psychotherapist—whether a neophyte or an old-timer—in order to work successfully with such a potentially mad and potentially traumatized individual. But I suspect that the dreams also conveyed only too clearly Steven's close struggles with death, his own experience of having felt infanticided, either by a mother, by a father, or indeed by a very murderous parental couple in his mind—a parental couple who, as we know, consisted of a father who knew the Nazis, and a mother who, I can now reveal, grew up in Germany.

I suspect that Steven became a victim of what I have come to call psychological infanticide, and that he struggled with an infanticidal attachment, a form of disorganized attachment too little understood, for much of his life. This infanticidal introject, this infanticidal attachment, manifested itself in the infanticidal transference, demonstrated by his fear that, by arriving three minutes late for a session, I had killed him off. And I suspect that my dreams of being murdered might be evidence of what I now regard as the infanticidal countertransference, my own fear of being murdered by Nazis and razor blades, and yet, somehow, surviving.

I also wish to comment upon the names that Steven had chosen for himself. When I first discussed the possibility that I might one day wish to share his story with colleagues in order to be of potential help to other men and women struggling with schizophrenia, Steven asked that I call him "John Smith, the most common name in the English language". When I queried whether he really wanted me to call him "John Smith", he changed his mind, and from the depths of his unconscious concocted the highly fictitious name of "Steven Froggit". At the time, I had no idea that "Steven Froggit" had any significance at all, and I do not pretend that nearly thirty years of reflection has in any way assisted a deeper understanding of this choice of name, but I did learn that as a little boy, Steven Froggit had a brother who died in infancy, the year before Steven's birth. His name—*Steven*. Furthermore, when I queried the meaning of "Froggit", Steven explained, "Don't you know? Froggit is the technical term for a special kind of braiding on an army uniform."

Perhaps Steven had one or more genes that had predisposed him to develop a schizophrenic psychosis; perhaps he had a surfeit of the neurotransmitter dopamine swirling between his neuronal synapses; perhaps he had an enlargement of his cerebellar ventricles. Perhaps not. Perhaps any history of sexual abuse, or any vestige of psychological infanticide might have been a sheer coincidence. Perhaps not.

Whatever the ultimate cause or causes of Steven Froggit's well-delineated schizophrenic psychosis, I trust that my case report will have provided sufficient evidence of the potential psychological reversibility of psychosis, a reversibility which might permit one to question whether the roots of psychosis lie in permanent damage to the brain, or in adverse experiences from early childhood. Whatever the ultimate cause or causes, I hope that we will also give pause to consider as well that if such supportive psychotherapeutic work can be facilitated by a young trainee, think of the potential that might be achieved by senior, more experienced, better qualified practitioners.

Conclusion

Schizophrenia damages lives. Schizophrenic patients with whom I have worked over the years have sliced the nipples from their breasts, have enucleated their eyeballs, have punched their pregnant partners in the stomach, have defecated in public places, have ingested their own used sanitary towels, have smashed up buildings, and have believed themselves to be rapists, paedophiles, and murderers even when they have committed no crime of any kind. Others have died because staff members did not take their symptoms seriously, as in the case of a young schizophrenic man I knew who complained of pains in his throat. The nursing staff dismissed his ache as a somatic delusion. In fact, he experienced an oesophageal ulcer, and the entire ward watched in horror as he bled to death before our very eyes. Another patient summed up the nature of schizophrenia only too chillingly. He told me that, "Living in my family, one has to walk on eggshells. Only the eggshells all have razor blades inside them."

In order to learn about the sources of misery in the lives of schizophrenic people, we must first listen to their stories and endeavour to discover exactly what causes them to believe that they walk on eggshells with razorblades. Sadly, many mental health professionals still find the schizophrenic psychotic too disturbed, too bizarre, and, indeed, in some cases, not sufficiently interesting. Professor Emil Kraepelin (1913b, p. 200), the nineteenth century progenitor of biological psychiatry, regarded his schizophrenic patients as "silly", and as "repellent" (*ibid.*, p. 282), describing them as "very dirty" (*ibid.*, p. 139), and "like a dog" (*ibid.*, p. 46). Continuing with the theme of the patients as animals, Kraepelin (*ibid.* p. 45) noted further that, "Frequently the patients simply thrust their hands into their plate, fall upon the common dish, hurriedly stuff their mouths as full as possible and swallow their food down almost without chewing", not pausing to consider the impact of long-term institutionalization on "table manners" (cf. Laing, 1960). Kraepelin (1913b, p. 49) found his patients suffering from dementia praecox to be "more or less inaccessible". In similar fashion, Dr William Brown (1920, p. 86), a prominent medical psychologist who flourished in the 1920s and 1930s, referred to cases of dementia praecox and paranoia as "incurable".

More recently, Dr Russell Reid (1990, p. 159), for instance, a psychiatrist who has devoted his career to the treatment of transsexual men and women, even proclaimed in print that, "My life would be dull and boring if I were dealing with just schizophrenics". Although few modern psychiatric workers would describe their patients as "pigs", as the nineteenth century Professor Kraepelin (1913a) had done, Dr Reid's more contemporaneous attitude still typifies that of many mental health workers who regard the schizophrenic as dull and boring, not worthy of relating their stories.

In 1930, "An Ex-patient" (1930, p. 364) wrote an article in *The British Journal of Medical Psychology*, lamenting that,

> The advance of psychology has changed the treatment of neurosis, it may be asked why it has influenced the general treatment of insanity so little, except in a few outstanding hospitals. Is it because the neurotic can complain, while the psychotic cannot?

With psychiatrists such as Kraepelin and Reid framing the twentieth century, one can certainly understand why "mental" patients have remained unheard, unappreciated, unvalidated (cf. Sullivan, 1944).

I wish to propose that of all the stories that one might encounter in the psychiatric sphere, those of the schizophrenic might well be the most dramatic; and yet, because of the patient's constant experiences of being misunderstood or threatened throughout childhood, the schizophrenic will not always relate his or her story in the most straightforward manner. Sometimes, the schizophrenic will cry that, "The *Sinep* of the *Senoj* is out to get me." It took me quite some time to decipher that "Sinep" signifies "Penis" spelled backwards, and that "Senoj" signifies "Jones", also spelled backwards. When a patient exclaims that "The Sinep of the Senoj is out to get me", he has found a contorted means of telling me that a neighbour called "Mr Jones" had assaulted him with his penis.

Although orthodox psychiatric theoreticians and researchers have devoted decades to the documentation of the genetic, biochemical, and neuroanatomical bases of schizophrenia, and have argued for biopathogenesis with such vigour that one would be frightened to offer a contradiction, we now have a sufficiently large body of evidence from the fields of social psychiatry, traumatology, war studies, and Holocaust studies to suggest that other aetiological factors might play a significant, if not primary, role in the aetiology of schizophrenia. Additionally, on the basis of my own clinical and supervisory work over the last quarter of a century, I have come to appreciate the role of infanticidal threats and other experiences of premature morbidization in the development of the schizophrenic psychoses. I have come to regard episodes of psychological infanticide as ubiquitous in the life histories of psychotic patients, and, although I do not propose that an instance of psychological infanticide will, in and of itself, cause schizophrenia, I wish to suggest that such factors might well prove to be necessary agents, if not sufficient ones, in the development of such psychoses. Psychological infanticidal experiences contribute to the development of an infanticidal attachment, a newly identified variant of disorganized attachment, rather akin to a heretofore undiagnosed version of *infantile post-traumatic stress disorder*.

Back in 1911, Professor Sigmund Freud wondered whether his theory of the psychodynamics of schizophrenia had any merit. Towards the conclusion of his essay on the famous case of Daniel Paul Schreber, Freud (1911, p. 68) mused, "Es bleibt der Zukunft überlassen zu entscheiden, ob in der Theorie mehr Wahn enthalten ist, als ich möchte, oder in dem Wahn mehr Wahrheit, als andere heute glaublich finden". ["It remains for the future to decide whether there is more delusion in my theory than I should like to admit, or whether there is more truth in Schreber's delusion than other people are as yet prepared to believe" (Freud, 1911c, p. 79). It seems useful to remind ourselves of this observation.

The human brain contains approximately 10,000,000,000,000 neurones, with approximately 1000 connections between each neurone (Klempan, Muglia, & Kennedy, 2004). In view of our relative ignorance of both the human brain, and the human mind (Kahr, 2007a), we ought to proceed, perhaps, with modesty and caution in our theorization. Whether schizophrenia ultimately proves to be a state of mind that results from aberrant genes, from cerebral neuropathology, from child sexual abuse, from emigration and racism, from urban overcrowding, from war, masturbation, overwork, the grippe (all theories advanced with conviction during the past one hundred years), or from early infanticidal trauma, our successors in future generations must decide. But whatever the ultimate origin (or origins) of schizophrenia, we cannot deny the landslide of evidence documenting the psychotherapeutic reversibility of schizophrenia (e.g., Menninger, 1922; Paskind & Brown, 1940), especially in the case reports of those clinicians who have worked with psychosis from both an attachment-based and trauma-based frame of reference, which regards the hallucinatory and delusional symptomatology not as *de facto* evidence of brain disease, but, rather, as tortured poetical transformations of actual, early experiences of abuse and pain, often within the intrafamilial environment.

Recently, while researching the (Edward) John (Mostyn) Bowlby (1907–1990) Collection at the Wellcome Library for the History and Understanding of Medicine in London, I happened to have the good fortune to stumble upon the tiny, pencil-written notebooks that Bowlby used to revise and summarize his medical knowledge, in preparation for his final examinations at University College Hospital as a young medical student. The notebooks bear no date, but, as Bowlby qualified in 1933, one can, nonetheless, date these archival treasures with a high degree of reliability to roughly that time. In his notebook on psychiatric topics, Bowlby wrote up a synopsis of what he had learnt about dementia praecox. He jotted down that most cases begin between the ages of fifteen and thirty-five years, and that dementia praecox will have an insidious onset. He also observed that in addition to the obvious symptoms such as hallucinations and delusions, impulsive behaviour, changeable behaviour, meaningless laughter, convulsions, mannerisms, antics, and grimaces, patients will also display physical abnormalities such as lowered blood pressure, cyanosis, and oedema. They will often be gloomy, solitary, and introverted, and could be characterized as having "NO EMOTIONS" (written thus in capital letters). Bowlby mentioned absolutely nothing about treatment, as psychiatrists of that period had very little to offer in that regard (Bowlby, n.d.).

In view of the fact that Bowlby had learnt about dementia praecox at such a point in time, and from such a classical medical model, it seems unsurprising that he might have found it difficult to engage with schizophrenic patients, or, in later years, to imagine that his own psychoanalytical and attachment theories might relate in any useful way to this group of individuals.

Dr John Bowlby may well have underestimated the importance of his work for an understanding of schizophrenia, that most severe form of mental illness. Had he lived to his hundredth birthday, and learnt what we have learnt in the past twenty years, I suspect that he might well have revised his own opinion.

Acknowledgements

Many kind and helpful colleagues have offered support and encouragement during the writing and research for this paper, and I wish to thank, in particular, Sir Richard Bowlby, and Xenia, Lady Bowlby, and also Graeme Galton, Professor Judith Lewis Herman, Dr Oliver James, David Leevers, Kate Pearce, Dr Geoffrey Pullen, Oliver Rathbone, Sue Richardson, Jennifer Riddell, Adah Sachs, James Sainsbury, Dr Joseph Schwartz, Lucy Shirley, Dr Valerie Sinason, Henry Strick van Linschoten, Susan Vas Dias, Dr Estela Welldon, Rachel Wingfield Schwartz, Judy Yellin, and, most especially, Kate White for her great wisdom and patience, and for her unparalleled support in all respects. I wish to dedicate this paper to Dr Valerie Sinason, friend, mentor, and humanitarian—a constant source of hope and inspiration.

Notes

1. The illness presents in many different subtypes, and these include: simple schizophrenia (also known as dementia simplex or schizophrenia

simplex), catatonic schizophrenia, hebephrenic schizophrenia, paranoid schizophrenia, non-paranoid schizophrenia, acute schizophrenia, chronic schizophrenia, process schizophrenia, reactive schizophrenia, early-onset schizophrenia, late-onset schizophrenia, latent schizophrenia, residual schizophrenia, disorganized schizophrenia, productive schizophrenia, non-productive schizophrenia, ambulatory schizophrenia, infantile schizophrenia, childhood schizophrenia, juvenile schizophrenia, paediatric schizophrenia, adolescent schizophrenia, child and adolescent schizophrenia, juvenile onset schizophrenia, *Pfropfschizophrenie*, Pfropfhebephrenia, pseudoneurotic schizophrenia, catastrophic schizophrenia, coenaesthetic schizophrenia, compensation schizophrenia, schizophrenia deliriosa, induced schizophrenia, mixed schizophrenia, postemotive schizophrenia, primary schizophrenia, secondary schizophrenia, *recidives in* schizophrenia, restitutional symptoms schizophrenia, reversible schizophrenia, familial schizophrenia, sporadic schizophrenia, schizophrenosis, toxic schizophrenia, transitory schizophrenia, treatment-resistant schizophrenia, unspecified schizophrenia, chronic undifferentiated schizophrenia, good premorbid schizophrenia, poor premorbid schizophrenia, sluggish schizophrenia, dormant schizophrenia, late-life schizophrenia, secondary schizophrenia, dissociative schizophrenia, preschizophrenia, schizocaria, psychogenic psychosis, psychogenetic psychosis, paranoia persecutoria, paraphrenia, paraphrenia confabulans, paraphrenia expansiva, paraphrenia phantastica, paraphrenia systematica, dementia hebephrenia, dementia paranoides, dementia sejunctiva, amblynoia, amblythymia, demenza primitiva, dysphrenia, paratonia progressiva, dementia dissociativa, dissecans, sejunctiva, delirium schizophrenoides, adolescent psychosis, alcoholic psychosis, anxiety psychosis, dissociative psychosis, exhaustion psychosis, furlough psychosis, gestational psychosis, juvenile psychosis, malignant psychosis, menstrual psychosis, menstrual insanity, liberation psychosis, post-liberation psychosis, protest psychosis, symptomatic psychosis, traumatic psychosis, emotional psychosis, experimental psychosis, larval psychosis, adolescent insanity, dementia praecox, acute dementia praecox, dementia praecocissima, juvenile dementia, insanity of puberty, agitated dementia, circular dementia, confusional speech dementia, drivelling dementia, dull dementia, manneristic dementia, negativistic dementia, paranoid dementia, paranoid dementia gravis, paranoid dementia mitis, periodic dementia, silly dementia, stuporous dementia, tension insanity, as well as other variants such as schizoaffective disorder, schizothymia, schizotaxia, schizophasia, schizohomosexuality, and schizotypal disorder. This extraordinary profusion of nomenclature indicates something about the confusion among psychopathologists, most of whom approach this problem from highly divergent points of view.

2. I have not included any discussion of still further possible theories of schizophrenia, those neither biopathological nor psychological , such as the mystical–occult approach to schizophrenia (e.g., Lux, 1976) or the Christian approach (e.g., Adams, 1976). No doubt one can find many other conceptualizations of schizophrenia in the contemporary literature as well.

3. Those who have written significantly on the psychoanalytical treatment and reversibility of schizophrenia include: Karl Abraham, Alfred Adler, Franz Alexander, Clifford Allen, Silvano Arieti, Jacob Arlow, Robert Bak, Mary Barkas, Thomas Beaton, Leopold Bellak, Lauretta Bender, Owen Berkeley-Hill, Bruno Bettelheim, Edward Bibring, Ludwig Binswanger, Wilfred Bion, Poul Bjerre, Eugen Bleuler, Manfred Bleuler, Lionel Blitzsten, Leonard Blumgart, Gerda Boigon, Mauricy Bornsztajn, Medard Boss, John Bowlby, Bryce Boyer, Charles Brenner, Abraham Brill, Hilde Bruch, Ruth Mack Brunswick, Dexter Bullard, Sr., Dexter Bullard, Jr, Gustav Bychowski, Denis Carroll, Mary Chadwick, Joseph Chassell, José de Matos Sobral Cid, Leon Pierce Clark, Robert Cohen, Franz Cohn, Isador Coriat, Helene Deutsch, Henry Devine, Frederick Dillon, Lucile Dooley, John Edelstein, Kurt Eissler, Rudolf Ekstein, Reginald Ellery, Erik Erikson, Ronald Fairbairn, Dudley Ward Fay, Paul Federn, Dorian Feigenbaum, Sándor Feldmann, Otto Fenichel, Antonio Ferreira, Sándor Ferenczi, Robert Fliess, Walter Fokschaner, Thomas Freeman, Thomas French, Sigmund Freud, Frieda Fromm-Reichmann, Angel Garma, Robert Gillespie, William Gillespie, Peter Giovacchini, Edward Glover, Bernard Glueck, Thomas Good, Scheina Grebelskaja, Phyllis Greenacre, Roy Grinker, Sr., Martin Grotjahn, Ernest Hadley, Noel Harris, Heinz Hartmann, Ives Hendrick, Lewis Hill, Leland Hinsie, Eduard Hitsch-mann, August Hoch, István Hollós, Louis Horn, Susan Isaacs, Otto Isakower, Mary Isham, Edith Jacobson, Ludwig Jekels, Smith Ely Jelliffe, Allan Sigfrid Johansson, Ernest Jones, Carl Gustav Jung, Bernard Kamm, Abram Kardiner, Jacob Kasanin, Maurits Katan, Ralph Kaufman, Edward Kempf, Arthur Kilholz, Melanie Klein, Robert Knight, Lawrence Kubie, René Laforgue, Karl Landauer, Nolan Lewis, Theodore Lidz, John MacCurdy, Alphonse Maeder, Margaret Mahler, Karl Menninger, Adolf Meyer, Marion Milner, Sophie Morgenstern, F.P. Müller, Sacha Nacht, William Niederland, Hermann Nunberg, Clarence Oberndorf, Johan van Ophuijsen, Gisela Pankow, Ping-Nie Pao, Sylvia Payne, Lionel Penrose, Oskar Pfister, Hannah Ries, Enrique Pichon-Rivière, William Pious,

Irmarita Putnam, Annie Reich, John Rickman, Franz Riklin, J.M. Rombouts, John Rosen, Herbert Rosenfeld, Saul Rosenzweig, Paul Schilder, Melitta Schmideberg, Max Schur, Gertrud Schwing, Clifford Scott, Harold Searles, Marguerite Sechehaye, Hanna Segal, Elvin Semrad, Sara Sheiner, Herbert Silberer, Ernst Simmel, Martti Siirala, Joseph Smith, Maurice Hamblin Smith, Sabina Spielrein, August Stärcke, Wilhelm Stekel, Karin Stephen, Editha Sterba, Arnold Stocker, Leo Stone, Harry Stack Sullivan, Alberta Szalita-Pemow, Veikko Tähkä, Viktor Tausk, Elizabeth Ter-Ogannessien, Charles Tidd, Johannes Hermanus van der Hoop, Robert Waelder, Edith Weigert-Vowinckel, Benjamin Weininger, Edoardo Weiss, Milton Wexler, William Alanson White, Otto Allen Will, Donald Winnicott, Henry Yellowlees, David Young, Gregory Zilboorg, and Earl Zinn, to name but a few from the first generations of psycho-analytical practitioners (cf., e.g., Maeder, 1910; Bjerre, 1911; Spielrein, 1911; Grebelskaja, 1912; Beaton, 1920; Devine, 1920, 1929, 1933; Forsyth, 1920; Fay, 1922; Brill, 1929; Allen, 1935; Schwing, 1940; Ellery, 1941; Rosenfeld, 1947, 1949, 1950, 1952; Segal, 1950, 1956, 1975, 1994; Eissler, 1951; Federn, 1952; Schultz-Hencke, 1952; Sechehaye, 1956; Freeman, 1962, 1975; Searles, 1963; Semrad, 1966; Boyer, 1967a, 1967b; Boyer and Giovacchini, 1967; Gunderson & Mosher, 1975; Whitehorn and Betz, 1975; Kvarnes & Parloff, 1976; Strean, 1976; Bruch, 1978; Pao, 1979; Arieti, 1980; Racamier, 1980; Stone, 1983, 1991a,b; Feinsilver, 1986; Silver, 1989; Strean & Freeman, 1990; Nagel, 1991; Rosenfeld, 1992; Oldham & Bone, 1994; Reilly, 1997; Leclaire, 1999; Benedetti, 2006; Müller, 2006; Pankow, 2006; Alanen, González de Chávez, Silver, & Martindale, 2009).

4.   Professor Dr med. Ulrich Venzlaff had also studied the psychological symptomatology afflicting those Jews who managed to avoid internment in the concentration camps, and who had spent the war in hiding. In an earlier study, he observed:

> Since 1956 I have been of the opinion that especially the extreme psychic stresses to which the persecuted were subjected, often over a period of many years, represent an exceptionally pathogenic factor, which is of definite significance for the origin of the late and long-lasting mental sequelae. [Venzlaff, 1964, p. 178]

References

Abrahams, J., & Varon, E. (1953). *Maternal Dependency and Schizophrenia: Mothers and Daughters in a Therapeutic Group. A Group-Analytic Study.* New York: International Universities Press.

Adams, J. E. (1976). The Christian approach to schizophrenia. In: P. A. Magaro (Ed.), *The Construction of Madness: Emerging Conceptions and Interventions into the Psychotic Process* (pp. 133–150). Oxford: Pergamon Press.

Alanen, Y. O. (1958). *The Mothers of Schizophrenic Patients: A Study of the Personality and the Mother–Child Relationship of 100 Mothers and the Significance of These Factors in the Pathogenesis of Schizophrenia, in Comparison with Heredity.* Copenhagen: Ejnar Munksgaard.

Alanen, Y. O., González de Chávez, M., & Silver, A.-L. S. (2006). Introduction. In: Y. O. Alanen, A.-L. S. Silver & M. González de Chávez (Eds.), *Fifty Years of Humanistic Treatment of Psychoses: In Honour of the History of the International Society for the Psychological Treatments of the Schizophrenias and Other Psychoses, 1956–2006* (pp. 11–16). Madrid: Fundación para la Investigación y Tratamiento de la Esquizofrenia y otras Psicosis.

Alanen, Y. O., González de Chávez, M., Silver, A.-L. S., & Martindale, B. (Eds.) (2009). *Psychotherapeutic Approaches to Schizophrenic Psychoses: Past, Present and Future.* Hove, East Sussex: Routledge.

Aldrich, C. K., & Coffin, M. (1948a). Clinical studies of psychoses in the navy: I. Prediction values of social histories and the Harrower–Erickson test. *Journal of Nervous and Mental Disease, 108*: 36–44.

Aldrich, C. K., & Coffin, M. (1948b). Clinical studies of psychoses in the navy: II. Prognosis. *Journal of Nervous and Mental Disease, 108*: 142–148.

Alexander, F. (1946). The principle of corrective emotional experience. In: F. Alexander, T. M. French, C. L. Bacon, T. Benedek, R. A. Fuerst, M. W. Gerard, R. R. Grinker, M. Grotjahn, A. M. Johnson, H. V. McLean, & E. Weiss (Eds.), *Psychoanalytic Therapy: Principles and Application* (pp. 66–70). New York: Ronald Press.

Allen, C. (1935). The diagnosis and treatment of the early psychotic and prepsychotic. *British Journal of Medical Psychology, 15*: 140–152.

Allen, H. A., Liddle, P. F., & Frith, C. D. (1993). Negative features, retrieval processes and verbal fluency in schizophrenia. *British Journal of Psychiatry, 163*: 769–775.

Altschule, M. D. (1970). Disease entity, syndrome, state of mind, or figment? In: R. Cancro (Ed.), *The Schizophrenic Reactions: A Critique of the Concept, Hospital Treatment, and Current Research. The Proceedings of The Menninger Foundation Conference on the Schizophrenic Syndrome* (pp. 13–24). New York: Brunner/Mazel.

American Psychiatric Association (1994). *Diagnostic and Statistical Manual of Mental Disorders, Fourth Edition.* Washington, DC: American Psychiatric Association.

An Ex-patient (1930). The asylum environment. *British Journal of Medical Psychology, 10*: 344–364.

Andre, L. (2009). *Doctors of Deception: What They Don't Want You to Know About Shock Treatment*. New Brunswick, NJ: Rutgers University Press.

Andreasen, N. C. (1984). *The Broken Brain: The Biological Revolution in Psychiatry*. New York: Harper and Row.

Andreasen, N. C. (1986). Cerebral localization: its revelance to psychiatry. In: N. C. Andreasen (Ed.), *Can Schizophrenia Be Localized in the Brain?* (pp. 3–16). Washington, DC: American Psychiatric Press.

Andreasen, N. C. (Ed.) (1994). *Schizophrenia: From Mind to Molecule*. Washington, DC: American Psychiatric Association Press.

Andrews, G., Hall, W., Goldstein, G., Lapsley, H., Bartels, R., & Silove, D. (1985). The economic costs of schizophrenia: implications for public policy. *Archives of General Psychiatry, 42*: 537–543.

Anonymous (1949). Problems of treatment in psychiatry. *Medical Echo, 25*: 40–44.

Antonova, E., Kumari, V., Morris, R., Halari, R., Anilkumar, A., Mehrotra, R., & Sharma, T. (2005). The relationship of structural alterations to cognitive deficits in schizophrenia: a voxel-based morphometry study. *Biological Psychiatry, 58*: 457–467.

Arieti, S. (1980). Psychotherapy of schizophrenia: new or revised procedures. *American Journal of Psychotherapy, 34*: 464–476.

Armstrong-Jones, R. (1918). The mind: its defects and disorders. an epitome of four lectures on physic delivered at the Gresham College. *St. Bartholomew's Hospital Journal, 26*: 28–29.

Armstrong-Perlman, E. A. (1995). Psychosis: the sacrifice that fails? In: J. Ellwood (Ed.), *Psychosis: Understanding and Treatment* (pp. 93–102). London: Jessica Kingsley.

Arnold, C. (2008). *Bedlam: London and its Mad*. London: Simon and Schuster.

Baird, H. (1941). Psychoses in officers in the 1914–1918 war. *Journal of Mental Science, 87*: 109–114.

Barnes, M., & Berke, J. (1971). *Mary Barnes: Two Accounts of a Journey Through Madness*. London: MacGibbon and Kee.

Barnes, M., & Scott, A. (1989). *Something Sacred: Conversations, Writings, Paintings*. London: Free Association Books.

Barnes, T. R. E., & Kerwin, R. (2003). Mortality and sudden death in schizophrenia. In: A. J. Camm (Ed.), *Cardiovascular Risk Associated with Schizophrenia and its Treatment* (pp. 7–23). London: Galliard Healthcare Communications.

Bartschinger, H., & Maier, H. W. (1920). The question of the causation of schizophrenia by head injuries, and some opinions on them. *Dementia Praecox Studies*, 3: 223–229.

Beaton, T. (1920). The psychoses and the psycho-neuroses. *Journal of the Royal Naval Medical Service*, 6: 132–155.

Bebbington, P., Wilkins, S., Jones, P., Foerster, A., Murray, R., Toone, B., & Lewis, S. (1993). Life events and psychosis: initial results from the Camberwell collaborative psychosis study. *British Journal of Psychiatry*, 162: 72–79.

Benedetti, G. (1973). Intrapsychic aspects of schizophrenic psychopathology. In: S. Arieti (Ed.), *The World Biennial of Psychiatry and Psychotherapy, Volume II* (pp. 219–231). New York: Basic Books.

Benedetti, G. (2006). The first three ISPS Symposia on the psychotherapy of schizophrenia in Cery (Lausanne) and Brestenberg (near Zurich), 1956, 1959 and 1964. In: Y. Alanen, A.-L. S. Silver, & M. González de Chávez (Eds.), *Fifty Years of Humanistic Treatment of Psychoses: In Honour of the History of the International Society for the Psychological Treatments of the Schizophrenias and Other Psychoses, 1956–2006* (pp. 31–45). Madrid: Fundación para la Investigación y Tratamiento de la Esquizofrenia y otras Psicosis.

Bentall, R. P. (Ed.) (1990). *Reconstructing Schizophrenia*. London: Routledge.

Bentall, R. P. (2003). *Madness Explained: Psychosis and Human Nature*. London: Allen Lane/Penguin Books.

Bentall, R. P. (2009). *Doctoring the Mind: Why Psychiatric Treatments Fail*. London: Allen Lane/Penguin Books.

Berlet, H. H., Bull, C., Himwich, H. E., Kohl, H., Matsumoto, K., Pscheidt, G. R., Spaide, J., Tourlentes, T. T., & Valverde, J. M. (1966). Effect of diet on schizophrenic behavior. In: P. H. Hoch & J. Zubin (Eds.), *Psychopathology of Schizophrenia* (pp. 425–452). New York: Grune and Stratton.

Berrios, G. E. (1991). Psychosurgery in Britain and elsewhere: a conceptual history. In: G. E. Berrios & H. Freeman (Eds.), *150 Years of British Psychiatry, 1841–1991* (pp. 180–196). London: Gaskell.

Berrios, G. E. (1996). Early electroconvulsive therapy in Britain, France and Germany: a conceptual history. In: H. Freeman & G. E. Berrios (Eds.), *150 Years of British Psychiatry: Volume II. The Aftermath*, (pp. 3–15). London: Athlone Press.

Berrios, G. E. (1997). The origins of psychosurgery: Shaw, Burckhardt and Moniz. *History of Psychiatry*, 8: 61–81.

Bettelheim, B. (1943). Individual and mass behavior in extreme situations. *Journal of Abnormal and Social Psychology*, 38: 417–452.

Bettelheim, B. (1956). Schizophrenia as a reaction to extreme situations. *American Journal of Orthopsychiatry*, 26: 507–518.

Bettelheim, B. (1967). *The Empty Fortress: Infantile Autism and the Birth of the Self*. New York: Free Press.

Bettelheim, B. (1979). Schizophrenia as a reaction to extreme situations. In: B. Bettelheim (Ed.), *Surviving and Other Essays* (pp. 112–124). New York: Alfred A. Knopf.

Billig, O., & Bradley, J. D. (1946). Combined shock and corpus luteum hormone therapy. *American Journal of Psychiatry*, 102: 783–787.

Birley, J. L. T., & Brown, G. W. (1970). Crises and life changes preceding the onset or relapse of acute schizophrenia: clinical aspects. *British Journal of Psychiatry*, 116: 327–333.

Bjerre, P. (1911). Zur Radikalbehandlung der chronischen Paranoia. *Jahrbuch für psychoanalytische und psychopathologische Forschungen*, 3: 795–847.

Blair, P. (1717). *A Letter from Dr. Patrick Blair (Fellow of the Royal Society) to Doctor Baynard: Concerning ſome Conſiderable Improvements Concerning the Uſe of Cold Bathing. To Which are Added ſeveral Very Remarkable Obſervations in the Practiſe of Physick, Anatomy, Surgery and Botany*. London: George Strahan/William Innys.

Blakemore, C. (1998). How the environment helps to build the brain. In: B. Cartledge (Ed.), *Mind, Brain, and the Environment: The Linacre Lectures 1995–1996* (pp. 28–56). Oxford: Oxford University Press.

Blandford, G. F. (1871). *Insanity and its Treatment: Lectures on the Treatment, Medical and Legal, of Insane Patients*. Edinburgh: Oliver and Boyd.

Bleckwenn, W. J. (1931). The use of sodium amytal in catatonia. In: G. H. Kirby, T. K. Davis, & H. A. Riley (Eds.), *Schizophrenia [Dementia Praecox]: An Investigation of the Most Recent Advances. The Proceedings of the Association. New York. December 27th and 28th, 1929* (pp. 224–229). Baltimore, MD: Williams and Wilkins.

Bleuler, E. (1911). Dementia Praecox oder Gruppe der Schizophrenien. In: G. Aschaffenburg (Ed.), *Handbuch der Psychiatrie: Spezieller Teil. 4. Abteilung, 1. Hälfte* (pp. vii–420). Vienna: Franz Deuticke.

Borges, E. (1995). A social critique of biological psychiatry. In: C. A. Ross & A. Pam (Eds.), *Pseudoscience in Biological Psychiatry: Blaming the Body* (pp. 211–240). New York: John Wiley.

Bourne, A. (1962). *A Doctor's Creed: The Memoirs of a Gynaecologist*. London: Victor Gollancz.

Bowlby, J. (1944a). Forty-four juvenile thieves: their characters and home-life. *International Journal of Psycho-Analysis*, 25: 19–53.

Bowlby, J. (1944b). Forty-four juvenile thieves: their characters and home-life (II). *International Journal of Psycho-Analysis, 25*: 107–128.

Bowlby, J. (1969). *Attachment and Loss: Volume I. Attachment*. London: Hogarth Press and the Institute of Psycho-Analysis.

Bowlby, J. (1973). *Attachment and Loss: Volume II. Separation. Anxiety and Anger*. London: Hogarth Press and the Institute of Psycho-Analysis.

Bowlby, J. (1980). *Attachment and Loss: Volume III. Loss. Sadness and Depression*. London: Hogarth Press and the Institute of Psycho-Analysis.

Bowlby, J. (1990). *Charles Darwin: A Biography*. London: Hutchinson.

Bowlby, J. (n.d.). Untitled Notebook. PP/BOW/A.1/20/14. (Edward) John (Mostyn) Bowlby (1907–1990) Collection, Contemporary Medical Archives Centre, Archives and Manuscripts, Rare Materials Room, The Wellcome Library for the History and Understanding of Medicine, Wellcome Collection, The Wellcome Building, London.

Boydell, J., Van Os, J., & Murray, R. M. (2004). Is there a role for social factors in a comprehensive developmental model for schizophrenia? In: M. S. Keshavan, J. L. Kennedy, & R. M. Murray (Eds.), *Neurodevelopment and Schizophrenia* (pp. 224–247). Cambridge: Cambridge University Press.

Boyer, L. B. (1967a). Historical development of psychoanalytic psychotherapy of the schizophrenias: Freud's contributions. Background information. In: L. B. Boyer & P. L. Giovacchini (Eds.), *Psychoanalytic Treatment of Schizophrenic and Characterological Disorders* (pp. 40–79). New York: Science House.

Boyer, L. B. (1967b). Historical development of psychoanalytic therapy of the schizophrenias: contributions of the followers of Freud. In: L. B. Boyer & P. L. Giovacchini (Eds.), *Psychoanalytic Treatment of Schizophrenic and Characterological Disorders* (pp. 80–142). New York: Science House.

Boyer, L. B., & Giovacchini, P. L. (1967). *Psychoanalytic Treatment of Schizophrenic and Characterological Disorders*. New York: Science House.

Boyle, M. (1990). *Schizophrenia: A Scientific Delusion?* London: Routledge.

Braslow, J. (1997). *Mental Ills and Bodily Cures: Psychiatric Treatment in the First Half of the Twentieth Century*. Berkeley, CA: University of California Press.

Breggin, P. R. (1983). *Psychiatric Drugs: Hazards to the Brain*. New York: Springer.

Breggin, P. R. (1991). *Toxic Psychiatry: Why Therapy, Empathy, and Love Must Replace the Drugs, Electroshock, and Biochemical Theories of the "New Psychiatry"*. New York: St Martin's Press.

Bremner, J. D. (2002). *Does Stress Damage the Brain? Understanding Trauma-Related Disorders from a Mind–Body Perspective.* New York: W. W. Norton.

Brenner, S., & Cohen, C. I. (2009). Medical health in aging persons with schizophrenia. In: J. M. Meyer & H. A. Nasrallah (Eds.), *Medical Illness and Schizophrenia: Second Edition* (pp. 377–413). Arlington, VA: American Psychiatric Association.

Brewer, W. J., Edwards, J., Anderson, V., Robinson, T., & Pantelis, C. (1996). Neuropsychological, olfactory, and hygiene deficits in men with negative symptom schizophrenia. *Biological Psychiatry, 40*: 1021–1031.

Brill, A. A. (1929). Schizophrenia and psychotherapy. *American Journal of Psychiatry, 9*: 519–537.

Brown, G. W., Birley, J. L. T., & Wing, J. K. (1972). Influence of family life on the course of schizophrenic disorders: a replication. *British Journal of Psychiatry, 121*: 241–258.

Brown, R. P., Gerbarg, P. L., & Muskin, P. R. (2009). *How to Use Herbs, Nutrients and Yoga in Mental Health Care.* New York: W. W. Norton.

Brown, S. (1997). Excess mortality of schizophrenia: a meta-analysis. *British Journal of Psychiatry, 171*: 502–508.

Brown, S., Kim, M., Mitchell, C., & Inskip, H. (2010). Twenty-five year mortality of a community cohort with schizophrenia. *British Journal of Psychiatry, 196*: 116–121.

Brown, W. (1920). Book review of Ernest Jones, *Treatment of the Neuroses. British Journal of Psychology: Medical Section, 1*: 84–86.

Bruch, H. (1978). A historical perspective of psychotherapy in schizophrenia. In: W. E. Fann, I. Karacan, A. D. Pokorny, & R. L. Williams (Eds.), *Phenomenology and Treatment of Schizophrenia* (pp. 311–324). Jamaica, New York: Spectrum Publications.

Bryer, J. B., Nelson, B. A., Miller, J. B., & Krol, P. A. (1987). Childhood sexual and physical abuse as factors in adult psychiatric illness. *American Journal of Psychiatry, 144*: 1426–1430.

Buckley, P. F., Hrouda, D. R., Friedman, L., Noffsinger, S. G., Resnick, P. J., & Camlin-Shingler, K. (2004). Insight and its relationship to violent behavior in patients with schizophrenia. *American Journal of Psychiatry, 161*: 1712–1714.

Buckley, P. F., Miller, B. J., Lehrer, D. S., & Castle, D. J. (2009). Psychiatric comorbidities and schizophrenia. *Schizophrenia Bulletin, 35*: 383–402.

Buckley, P. F., O'Callaghan, E., Larkin, C., & Waddington, J. L. (1992). Schizophrenia research: the problem of controls. *Biological Psychiatry, 32*: 215–217.

Bundy, H., Stahl, D., & MacCabe, J. H. (2011). A systematic review and meta-analysis of the fertility of patients with schizophrenia and their unaffected relatives. *Acta Psychiatrica Scandinavica, 123*: 98–106.

Burch, J. W. (1995). Typicality range deficit in schizophrenics' recognition of emotion in faces. *Journal of Clinical Psychology, 51*: 140–152.

Burckhardt, G. (1891). Ueber Rindenexcisionen, als Beitrag zur operativen Therapie der Psychosen. *Allgemeine Zeitschrift für Psychiatrie und psychisch-gerichtliche Medicin, 47*: 463–548.

Burke, R. D. (1995). *When the Music's Over: My Journey into Schizophrenia*, R. Gates & R. Hammond (Eds.), New York: Basic Books.

Bychowski, G. (1968a). Permanent character changes as an aftereffect of persecution. In: H. Krystal (Ed.), *Massive Psychic Trauma* (pp. 75–86). New York: International Universities Press.

Bychowski, G. (1968b). General discussion of the workshop themes. In: H. Krystal (Ed.), *Massive Psychic Trauma* (pp. 97–98). New York: International Universities Press.

Camm, A. J. (2003). Cardiovascular risk associated with schizophrenia and its treatment. In: A. J. Camm (Ed.), *Cardiovascular Risk Associated with Schizophrenia and its Treatment* (pp. 5–6). London: Galliard Healthcare Communications.

Carlier, M. (1980). La Méthode des adoptions dans l'analyse génétique des psychoses schizophréniques: Revue critique. *La Psychiatrie de l'enfant, 23*: 507–585.

Carvajal, A., Arias, L. H. M., & Jimeno, N. (2009). Antipsychotic drugs. In: J. K. Aronson (Ed.), *Side Effects of Drugs Annual 31: A Worldwide Yearly Survey of New Data and Trends in Adverse Drug Reactions and Interactions* (pp. 65–104). Amsterdam: Elsevier.

Casey, D. E., & Hansen, T. E. (2009). Excessive mortality and morbidity associated with schizophrenia. In: J. M. Meyer & H. A. Nasrallah (Eds.), *Medical Illness and Schizophrenia: Second Edition* (pp. 17–35). Arlington, VA: American Psychiatric Association.

Cassou, B., Schiff, M., & Stewart, J. (1980). Génétique et schizophrénie: Réévaluation d'un consensus. *La Psychiatrie de l'enfant, 23*: 87–201.

Chamberlin, J. (2004). User-run services. In: J. Read, L. R. Mosher, & R. P. Bentall (Eds.), *Models of Madness: Psychological, Social and Biological Approaches to Schizophrenia* (pp. 283–290). Hove: Brunner-Routledge.

Chapin, K. J., Rosenbaum, G., Fields, R. B., & Wightman, L. H. (1996). Multiple deficit theory of schizophrenia: incidence of markers vs. symptoms. *Journal of Clinical Psychology, 52*: 109–123.

Chapman, J., & McGhie, A. (1962). A comparative study of disordered attention in schizophrenia. *Journal of Mental Science, 108*: 487–500.

Chen, E. Y. H., & McKenna, P. J. (1996). Memory dysfunction in schizophrenia. In: C. Pantelis, H. E. Nelson & T. R. E. Barnes (Eds.), *Schizophrenia: A Neuropsychological Perspective* (pp. 107–124). Chichester, West Sussex: John Wiley and Sons.

Chen, L. P., Murad, M. H., Paras, M. L., Colbenson, K. M., Sattler, A. L., Goranson, E. N., Elamin, M. B., Seime, R. J., Shinozaki, G., Prokop, L. J., & Zirahzadeh, A. (2010). Sexual abuse and lifetime diagnosis of psychiatric disorders: systematic review and meta-analysis. *Mayo Clinic Proceedings, 85*: 618–629.

Chua, S. E., & McKenna, P. J. (2000). A sceptical view of the neuropathology of schizophrenia. In: P. J. Harrison & G. W. Roberts (Eds.), *The Neuropathology of Schizophrenia: Progress and Interpretation* (pp. 291–337). Oxford: Oxford University Press.

Clarke, B. (1975). *Mental Disorder in Earlier Britain: Exploratory Studies.* Cardiff: University of Wales Press.

Cohen, D. (1988). *Forgotten Millions.* London: Paladin/Grafton Books.

Cohen, P. (2011). Abuse in childhood and psychotic symptoms in later life. *American Journal of Psychiatry, 168*: 7–8.

Cohn, T. (2009). Obesity and schizophrenia. In: J. M. Meyer & H. A. Nasrallah (Eds.), *Medical Illness and Schizophrenia: Second Edition* (pp. 61–90). Arlington, VA: American Psychiatric Publishing.

Colbert, T. C. (1996). *Broken Brains or Wounded Hearts: What Causes Mental Illness.* Santa Ana, CA: Kevco.

Compton, M. T., & Walker, E. F. (2009). Physical manifestations of neurodevelopmental disruption: are minor physical anomalies part of the syndrome of schizophrenia? *Schizophrenia Bulletin, 35*: 425–436.

Cooper, D. (1978). *The Language of Madness.* London: Allen Lane.

Correia, M. (2006). *Egas Moniz e o Prémio Nobel: Enigmas, paradoxos e segredos.* Coimbra: Imprensa da Universidade de Coimbra.

Cott, A. (1973). The use of parenteral vitamins in the treatment of schizophrenia. In: D. Hawkins & L. Pauling (Eds.), *Orthomolecular Psychiatry: Treatment of Schizophrenia* (pp. 540–543). San Francisco, CA: W. H. Freeman.

Cox, J. M. (1804). *Practical Observations on Insanity. In Which Some Suggestions are Offered Towards an Improved Mode of Treating Diseases of the Mind, and Some Rules Proposed Which it is Hoped May Lead to a More Humane and Successful Method of Cure: To Which are Subjoined, Remarks on Medical Jurisprudence as Connected with Diseased Intellect.* London: C. & R. Baldwin/J. Murray.

Cox, M. (1997). The great feat of languages: passwords to the psychotic's inner world. In: C. Mace & F. Margison (Eds.), *Psychotherapy of Psychosis* (pp. 31–48). London: Gaskell.

Cozolino, L. (2006). *The Neuroscience of Human Relationships: Attachment and the Developing Social Brain*. New York: W. W. Norton.

Crider, A. (1979). *Schizophrenia: A Biopsychological Perspective*. Hillsdale, NJ: Lawrence Erlbaum Associates, Publishers.

Crossley, D. (1993). The introduction of leucotomy: a British case history. *History of Psychiatry*, 4: 553–564.

Crow, T. J. (1982). Positive and negative symptoms and the role of dopamine in schizophrenia. In: G. Hemmings (Ed.), *Biological Aspects of Schizophrenia and Addiction* (pp. 49–54). Chichester, West Sussex: John Wiley.

Crow, T. J. (1994). Prenatal exposure to influenza as a cause of schizophrenia: there are inconsistencies and contradictions in the evidence. *British Journal of Psychiatry*, 164: 588–592.

Crowe, R. R. (1994). Molecular genetic research in schizophrenia. In: N. C. Andreasen (Ed.), *Schizophrenia: From Mind to Molecule* (pp. 245–260). Washington, DC: American Psychiatric Press.

Cutting, J. (1985). *The Psychology of Schizophrenia*. Edinburgh: Churchill Livingstone.

Damasio, A. R. (2000). Egas Moniz, pioneer of angiography and leucotomy. In: A. L. Pereira & J. R. Pita (Eds.), *Egas Moniz: Em livre exame* (pp. 97–109). Coimbra: Edições MinervaCoimbra.

Davidson, M. (1937). A study of schizophrenic performance on the Stanford-Binet scale. *British Journal of Medical Psychology*, 17: 93–97.

Davis, J. E. (1957). *Recovery from Schizophrenia: The Roland Method*. Springfield, IL: Charles C. Thomas.

Dax, E. C. (1949). Physical methods of treatment. In: J. R. Rees (Ed.), *Modern Practice in Psychological Medicine 1949* (pp. 357–380). London: Butterworth.

Dearth, N., Labenski, B. J., Mott, M. E., & Pellegrini, L. M. (1986). *Families Helping Families: Living with Schizophrenia*. New York: W. W. Norton.

deMause, L. (Ed.) (1974). *The History of Childhood*. New York: Psychohistory Press.

Devine, H. (1914). The biological significance of delusions. *Proceedings of the Royal Society of Medicine, Section of Psychiatry*, 7: 89–103.

Devine, H. (1920). Observations on the psychogenetic psychoses. *Proceedings of the Royal Society of Medicine, Section of Psychiatry*, 13: 1–17.

Devine, H. (1929). *Recent Advances in Psychiatry*. London: J. & A. Churchill.

Devine, H. (1933). *Recent Advances in Psychiatry* (2nd edn). London: J. & A. Churchill.

Diamond, M. C. (1988). *Enriching Heredity: The Impact of the Environment on the Anatomy of the Brain*. New York: Free Press/Macmillan; London: Collier Macmillan.

Diethelm, O. (1939). An historical review of somatic therapy in psychiatry. *American Journal of Psychiatry*, 95: 1165–1178.

Dohrenwend, B. P., Shrout, P. E., Link, B. G., Skodol, A. E., & Stueve, A. (1995). Life events and other possible psychosocial risk factors for episodes of schizophrenia and major depression: a case-control study. In: C. M. Mazure (Ed.), *Does Stress Cause Psychiatric Illness?* (pp. 43–65). Washington, DC: American Psychiatric Press.

Dorman, D. (2003). *Dante's Cure: A Journey Out of Madness*. New York: Other Press.

Double, D. B. (Ed.) (2006). *Critical Psychiatry: The Limits of Madness*. Houndmills, Hampshire: Palgrave Macmillan.

Duval, A. M. (1944). Psychoses in officers in World War II. *War Medicine*, 5: 1–5.

Duval, A. M., & Hoffman, J. L. (1941). Dementia praecox in military life as compared with dementia praecox in civil life. *War Medicine*, 1: 854–862.

Dynes, J. B. (1939). Affective sequelae of convulsant drug therapy. *Journal of Mental Science*, 85: 489–492.

Eagles, J. M., Hunter, D., & Geddes, J. R. (1995). Gender-specific changes since 1900 in the season-of-birth effect in schizophrenia. *British Journal of Psychiatry*, 167: 469–472.

Eccleston, D. (1986). Organic aspects of schizophrenia: overview. In: A. Kerr, P. Snaith, S. Thorley, & A. Campbell (Eds.), *Contemporary Issues in Schizophrenia* (pp. 199–206). London: Gaskell.

Eissler, K. R. (1951). Remarks on the psycho-analysis of schizophrenia. *International Journal of Psycho-Analysis*, 32: 139–156.

Eitinger, L. (1961). Pathology of the concentration camp syndrome: preliminary report. *Archives of General Psychiatry*, 5: 371–379.

Eitinger, L. (1964). *Concentration Camp Survivors in Norway and Israel*. Oslo: Universitetsforlaget/Norwegian Research Council for Science and the Humanities.

El-Hai, J. (2005). *The Lobotomist: A Maverick Medical Genius and His Tragic Quest to Rid the World of Mental Illness*. Hoboken, NJ: John Wiley.

Ellery, R. S. (1941). *Schizophrenia: The Cinderella of Psychiatry*. Sydney: Australasian Medical.

English, W. M. (1929). Report of the treatment with manganese chloride of 181 cases of schizophrenia, 33 of manic depression, and 16 of other defects or psychoses at the Ontario Hospital, Brockville, Ontario. *American Journal of Psychiatry*, 9: 569–579.

Esquirol, É. (1838a). *Des Maladies mentales considérées sous les rapports médical, hygiénique et médico-légal*. Tome Premier. Paris: J.-B. Baillière/ Librairie de l'Académie Royale de Médicine.

Esquirol, É. (1838b). *Des Maladies mentales considérées sous les rapports médical, hygiénique et médico-légal*. Tome Second. Paris: J.-B. Baillière/ Librairie de l'Académie Royale de Médicine.

Esterson, A. (1970). *The Leaves of Spring: A Study in the Dialectics of Madness*. London: Tavistock.

Everett, B., & Gallop, R. (2001). *The Link Between Childhood Trauma and Mental Illness: Effective Interventions for Mental Health Professionals*. Thousand Oaks, CA: Sage.

Farber, S. L. (1981). *Identical Twins Reared Apart: A Reanalysis*. New York: Basic Books.

Fay, D. W. (1922). *A Psychoanalytic Study of Psychoses with Endocrinoses*. Washington, DC: Nervous and Mental Disease.

Fear, N. T., Jones, M., Murphy, D., Hull, L., Iversen, A. C., Coker, B., Machell, L., Sundin, J., Woodhead, C., Jones, N., Greenberg, N., Landau, S., Dandeker, C., Rona, R. J., Hotopf, M., & Wessely, S. (2010). What are the consequences of deployment to Iraq and Afghanistan on the mental health of the UK armed forces? A cohort study. *Lancet*, 22–28 May: 1783–1797.

Federn, P. (1952). *Ego Psychology and the Psychoses*. E. Weiss (Ed.). New York: Basic Books.

Feinsilver, D. B. (Ed.) (1986). *Towards a Comprehensive Model for Schizophrenic Disorders: Psychoanalytic Essays in Memory of Ping-Nie Pao, M.D.* Hillsdale, NJ: Analytic Press.

Fennell, P. (1996). *Treatment without Consent: Law, Psychiatry and the Treatment of Mentally Disordered People Since 1845*. London: Routledge.

Ferenczi, S. (1929). The unwelcome child and his death-instinct. *International Journal of Psycho-Analysis*, 10: 125–129.

Filik, R., Sipos, A., Kehoe, P. G., Burns, T., Cooper, S. J., Stevens, H., Laugharne, R., Young, G., Perrington, S., McKendrick, J., Stephenson, D., & Harrison, G. (2006). The cardiovascular and respiratory health of people with schizophrenia. *Acta Psychiatrica Scandinavica*, 113: 298–305.

Fink, M. (1999). *Electroshock: Restoring the Mind*. New York: Oxford University Press.

Fisher, S., & Greenberg, R. P. (1997). What are we to conclude about psychoactive drugs? Scanning the major findings. In: S. Fisher & R. P. Greenberg (Eds.), *From Placebo to Panacea: Putting Psychiatric Drugs to the Test* (pp. 359–384). New York: John Wiley.

Fliess, R. (1973). *Symbol, Dream, and Psychosis: Volume III. Psychoanalytic Series*. New York: International Universities Press.

Forsyth, D. (1920). Psycho-analysis of a case of early paranoid dementia. *Proceedings of the Royal Society of Medicine, Section of Psychiatry, 13*: 65–81.

Foster, H. D. (2003). *What Really Causes Schizophrenia*. Victoria, British Columbia: Trafford.

Fox, H. M. (1944). A variety of furlough psychosis. *Psychiatry, 7*: 207–213.

Freeman, H. (1994). Schizophrenia and city residence. In: Y. O. Alanen, V. Lehtinen, V. Räkköläinen, R. K. R. Salokangas, & E. K. G. Syvälahti (Eds.), *Integrated Approach to Schizophrenia: Symposium Held in Turku, Finland, 3–5 June 1992. British Journal of Psychiatry, 164*(Suppl.): 39–50.

Freeman, H. (1998). Mental health and urban environment. In: B. Cartledge (Ed.), *Mind, Brain, and the Environment: The Linacre Lectures 1995–1996* (pp. 124–143). Oxford: Oxford University Press.

Freeman, T. (1962). A psycho-analytic approach to the diagnosis of schizophrenic reactions. *Journal of Mental Science, 108*: 286–299.

Freeman, T. (1975). Schizophrenia from the psychoanalytical standpoint. In: A. Forrest & J. Affleck (Eds.), *New Perspectives in Schizophrenia* (pp. 117–137). Edinburgh: Churchill Livingstone.

Freeman, W. (1931). Deficiency of catalytic iron in the brain in schizophrenia. In: G. H. Kirby, T. K. Davis, & H. A. Riley (Eds.), *Schizophrenia [Dementia Praecox]: An Investigation of the Most Recent Advances. The Proceedings of the Association, New York, 27 & 28 December 1929* (pp. 16–32). Baltimore, MD: Williams and Wilkins.

Freeman, W., & Watts, J. W. (1942). *Psychosurgery: Intelligence, Emotion and Social Behavior Following Prefontal Lobotomy for Mental Disorders*. Springfield, IL: Charles C. Thomas.

Freud, S. (1895). Draft H: Paranoia (Extracts from the Fliess papers). *S.E., 1*: 206–212. London: Hogarth Press and the Institute of Psycho-Analysis.

Freud, S. (1909b). *Analysis of a Phobia in a Five-Year-Old Boy. S.E., 10*: 5–147. London: Hogarth Press and the Institute of Psycho-Analysis.

Freud, S. (1911). Psychoanalytische Bemerkungen über einen autobiographisch beschriebenen Fall von Paranoia (Dementia Paranoides). *Jahrbuch für psychoanalytische und psychopathologische Forschungen, 3*, 9–68.

Freud, S. (1911c). Psycho-analytic notes on an autobiographical account of a case of paranoia (dementia paranoides). *S.E.*, *12*: 9–79. London: Hogarth Press and the Institute of Psycho-Analysis.

Freud, S. (1937d). Constructions in analysis. *S.E.*, *23*: 257–269. London: Hogarth Press and the Institute of Psycho-Analysis.

Freudenberg, R. (1941). On the curability of mental diseases by "shock" treatment: (an analysis of cases treated). *Journal of Mental Science*, *87*: 529–544.

Frith, C., & Johnstone, E. (2003). *Schizophrenia: A Very Short Introduction*. Oxford: Oxford University Press.

Geddes, J. R., & Lawrie, S. M. (1995). Obstetric complications and schizo-phrenia: a meta-analysis. *British Journal of Psychiatry*, *167*: 786–793.

Gibson, R. W. (1966). The ego defect in schizophrenia. In: G. L. Usdin (Ed.), *Psychoneurosis and Schizophrenia* (pp. 88–97). Philadelphia, PA: J. B. Lippincott.

Gilbert, M. (2006). *Kristallnacht: Prelude to Destruction*. London: HarperCollins.

Gilman, S. L. (1982). *Seeing the Insane: A Cultural History of Madness and Art in the Western World, Showing How the Portrayal of Stereotypes Has Both Reflected and Shaped the Perception and Treatment of the Mentally Disturbed as Depicted in Manuscripts, Woodcuts, Engravings, Drawings, Paintings, Sculptures, Lithographs and Photographs, from the Middle Ages to the End of the Nineteenth Century*. New York: John Wiley, in associa-tion with Brunner/Mazel.

Gilman, S. L. (2008a). Constructing schizophrenia as a category of mental illness. In: E. R. Wallace IV & J. Gach (Eds.), *History of Psychiatry and Medical Psychology: With an Epilogue on Psychiatry and the Mind–Body Relation* (pp. 461–483). New York: Springer Science and Business Media.

Gilman, S. L. (2008b). Electrotherapy and mental illness: then and now. *History of Psychiatry*, *19*: 339–357.

Glover, E. (1968). *The Birth of the Ego: A Nuclear Hypothesis*. London: George Allen and Unwin.

Goodwin, J. M. (1990). Applying to adult incest victims what we have learned from victimized children. In: R. P. Kluft (Ed.), *Incest-Related Syndromes of Adult Psychopathology* (pp. 55–74). Washington, DC: American Psychiatric Publishing.

Gottdiener, W. H. (2004). Psychodynamic psychotherapy for schizophre-nia: empirical support. In: J. Read, L. R. Mosher, & R. P. Bentall (Eds.), *Models of Madness: Psychological, Social and Biological Approaches to Schizophrenia* (pp. 307–318). Hove: Brunner-Routledge.

Gould, S. J. (1981). *The Mismeasure of Man*. New York: W. W. Norton.

Grace, A. A. (2004). Developmental dysregulation of the dopamine system and the pathophysiology of schizophrenia. In: M. S. Keshavan, J. L. Kennedy, & R. M. Murray (Eds.), *Neurodevelopment and Schizophrenia* (pp. 273–294). Cambridge: Cambridge University Press.

Grebelskaja, S. (1912). Psychologische Analyse einer Paranoiden. *Jahrbuch für psychoanalytische und psychopathologische Forschungen*, 4: 116–140.

Greden, J. F., & Tandon, R. (Eds.) (1991). *Negative Schizophrenic Symptoms: Pathophysiology and Clinical Implications*. Washington, DC: American Psychiatric Press.

Green, M. F., Nuechterlein, K. H., & Satz, P. (1987). Electrodermal activity and symptomatology in schizophrenia. In: P. D. Harvey & E. F. Walker (Eds.), *Positive and Negative Symptoms in Psychosis: Description, Research, and Future Directions* (pp. 243–257). Hillsdale, NJ: Lawrence Erlbaum.

Greenfield, D. (1985). *The Psychotic Patient: Medication and Psychotherapy*. New York: Free Press.

Greenfield, S. F., Strakowski, S. M., Tohen, M., Batson, S. C., & Kolbrener, M. L. (1994). Childhood abuse in first-episode psychosis. *British Journal of Psychiatry*, 164: 831–834.

Grinspoon, L., Ewalt, J. R., & Shader, R. I. (1972). *Schizophrenia: Pharmacotherapy and Psychotherapy*. Baltimore, MD: Williams and Wilkins.

Gross, D. (1998). Der Beitrag Gottlieb Burckhardts (1836–1907) zur Psychochirurgie in medizinhistorischer und ethischer Sicht. *Gesnerus*, 55: 221–248.

Guislan, J. (1826a). *Traité sur l'aliénation mentale et sur les hospices des aliénés*. Tome I. Amsterdam: J. van der Hey et Fils, et Les Héritiers H. Gartman.

Guislan, J. (1826b). *Traité sur l'aliénation mentale et sur les hospices des aliénés*. Tome II. Amsterdam: J. van der Hey et Fils, et Les Héritiers H. Gartman.

Gunderson, J. G., & Mosher, L. R. (Eds.) (1975). *Psychotherapy of Schizophrenia*. New York: Jason Aronson.

Günther-Genta, F., Bovet, P., & Hohlfeld, P. (1994). Obstetric complications and schizophrenia: a case-controlled study. *British Journal of Psychiatry*, 164: 165–170.

Hare, E. H. (1962). Masturbatory insanity: the history of an idea. *Journal of Mental Science*, 108: 1–25.

Harms, M. P., Wang, L., Campanella, C., Aldridge, K., Moffitt, A. J., Kuelper, J., Ratnanather, J. T., Miller, M. I., Barch, D. M., & Csernansky, J. G. (2010). Structural abnormalities in the gyri of the prefrontal cortex in individuals with schizophrenia and their unaffected siblings. *British Journal of Psychiatry*, 196: 150–157.

Harrow, M., & Quinlan, D. M. (1985). *Disordered Thinking and Schizophrenic Psychopathology*. New York: Gardner Press.

Harvey, P. D., & Walker, E. F. (Eds.) (1987). *Positive and Negative Symptoms in Psychosis: Description, Research, and Future Directions*. Hillsdale, NJ: Lawrence Erlbaum.

Hawkins, D., & Pauling, L. (1973). *Orthomolecular Psychiatry: Treatment of Schizophrenia*. San Francisco, CA: W. H. Freeman.

Henn, F. A., & Nasrallah, H. A. (Eds.) (1982). *Schizophrenia as a Brain Disease*. New York: Oxford University Press.

Herman, J. L., & Hirschman, L. (1981). *Father–Daughter Incest*. Cambridge, MA: Harvard University Press.

Herman, J. L., Russell, D., & Trocki, K. (1986). Long-term effects of incestuous abuse in childhood. *American Journal of Psychiatry, 143*: 1293–1296.

Hill, H. (1938). Histamine and insulin in the treatment of schizophrenia and other mental diseases. *Journal of Mental Science, 84*: 581–588.

Hill, H. (1940). *The Histamine and Insulin Treatment of Schizophrenia and Other Mental Diseases*. London: Baillière, Tindall and Cox.

Hippisley-Cox, J., Vinogradova, Y., Coupland, C., & Parker, C. (2007). Risk of malignancy in patients with schizophrenia or bipolar disorder: nested case-control study. *Archives of General Psychiatry, 64*: 1368–1376.

Hirsch, S. R., & Leff, J. P. (1975). *Abnormalities in Parents of Schizophrenics: A Review of the Literature and an Investigation of Communication Defects and Deviances*. London: Oxford University Press.

Hirsch, S. R., Bowen, J., Emami, J., Cramer, P., Jolley, A., Haw, C., & Dickinson, M. (1996). A one year prospective study of the effect of life events and medication in the aetiology of schizophrenic relapse. *British Journal of Psychiatry, 168*: 49–56.

Hitschman, M., & Yarrell, Z. (1943). Psychoses occurring in soldiers during the training period. *American Journal of Psychiatry, 100*: 301–305.

Holmes, B. (1918). A personal view of the victim of dementia praecox. *Dementia Praecox Studies, 1*: 35–48.

Honig, A. M. (1972). *The Awakening Nightmare: A Breakthrough in Treating the Mentally Ill*. Rockaway, NJ: American Faculty Press.

Hoppe, K. D. (1971). The aftermath of Nazi persecution reflected in recent psychiatric literature. In: H. Krystal & W. G. Niederland (Eds.), *Psychic Traumatization: Aftereffects in Individuals and Communities* (pp. 169–204). Boston, MA: Little, Brown.

Horsley, J. S. (1943). *Narco-Analysis: A New Technique in Short-Cut Psychotherapy. A Comparison with Other Methods. And Notes on the Barbiturates*. London: Oxford University Press/Humphrey Milford.

Hoskins, R. G. (1943). Psychosexuality in schizophrenia: some endocrine considerations. *Psychosomatic Medicine, 5:* 3–9.

Hoskins, R. G. (1946). *The Biology of Schizophrenia.* New York: W. W. Norton.

Hovens, J. G. F. M., Wiersma, J. E., Gittay, E. J., Van Oppen, P., Spinhoven, P., Penninx, B. W. J. H., & Zitman, F. G. (2010). Childhood life events and childhood trauma in adult patients with depressive, anxiety and comorbid disorders vs. controls. *Acta Psychiatrica Scandinavica, 122:* 66–74.

Hultman, C. M., Öhman, A., Cnattingius, S., Wieselgren, I.-M., & Lindström, L. H. (1997). Prenatal and neonatal risk factors for schizophrenia. *British Journal of Psychiatry, 170:* 128–133.

Humphreys, M. S., Johnstone, E. C., Macmillan, J. F., & Taylor, P. J. (1992). Dangerous behaviour preceding first admissions for schizophrenia. *British Journal of Psychiatry, 161:* 501–505.

Hunter, R., & Macalpine, I. (1963). *Three Hundred Years of Psychiatry: 1535–1860. A History Presented in Selected English Texts.* London: Oxford University Press.

Hussar, A. E. (1966). Leading causes of death in institutionalized schizophrenic patients: a study of 1,275 autopsy protocols. *Journal of Nervous and Mental Disease, 142:* 45–57.

Itkin, O., Nemets, B., & Einat, H. (2001). Smoking habits in bipolar and schizophrenic outpatients in southern Israel. *Journal of Clinical Psychiatry, 62:* 269–272.

Jackson, D. D. (1957). A note on the importance of trauma in the genesis of schizophrenia. *Psychiatry, 20:* 181–184.

Jackson, H. F. (1990). Are there biological markers of schizophrenia? In: R. P. Bentall (Ed.), *Reconstructing Schizophrenia* (pp. 118–156). London: Routledge.

Jacobsen, L. K., D'Souza, D. C., Mencl, W. E., Pugh, K. H., Skudlarski, P., & Krystal, J. H. (2004). Nicotine effects on brain function and functional connectivity in schizophrenia. *Biological Psychiatry, 55:* 850–858.

Jernigan, T. L., Zatz, L. M., Moses, J. A. Jr, & Berger, P. A. (1982). Computed tomography in schizophrenics and normal volunteers: I. Fluid volume. *Archives of General Psychiatry, 39:* 765–770.

Jernigan, T. L., Zatz, L. M., Moses, J. A. Jr, & Cardellino, J. P. (1982). Computed tomography in schizophrenics and normal volunteers: II. Cranial asymmetry. *Archives of General Psychiatry, 39:* 771–773.

Johnstone, L. (2006). The limits of the biomedical model of distress. In: D. B. Double (Ed.), *Critical Psychiatry: The Limits of Madness* (pp. 81–98). Houndmills, Hampshire: Palgrave Macmillan.

Jones, M. (1940). Intravenous insulin in the treatment of schizophrenia. *Lancet*, 21 April: 361.

Jones, P. B., & Buckley, P. F. (2003). *Schizophrenia Schizophrenia*. London: Mosby.

Jones, P. B., & Buckley, P. F. (2006). *Schizophrenia*. Edinburgh: Churchill Livingstone/Elsevier.

Jones, P. B., & Marder, S. R. (2008). Psychosocial and pharmacological treatments for schizophrenia. In: P. Tyrer & K. R. Silk (Eds.), *Cambridge Textbook of Effective Treatments in Psychiatry* (pp. 469–479). Cambridge: Cambridge University Press.

Jones, P. B., Bebbington, P., Foerster, A., Lewis, S. W., Murray, R. M., Russell, A., Sham, P. C., Toone, B. K., & Wilkins, S. (1993). Premorbid social underachievement in schizophrenia: results from the Camberwell collaborative psychosis study. *British Journal of Psychiatry, 162*: 65–71.

Jones, P. B., Rantakallio, P., Hartikainen, A.-L., Isohanni, M., & Sipila, P. (1998). Schizophrenia as a long-term outcome of pregnancy, delivery, and perinatal complications: a 28-year follow-up of the 1966 North Finland general population birth cohort. *American Journal of Psychiatry, 155*: 355–364.

Jones, W. L. (1983). *Ministering to Minds Diseased: A History of Psychiatric Treatment*. London: William Heinemann Medical Books.

Joseph, J. (2003). *The Gene Illusion: Genetic Research in Psychiatry and Psychology Under the Microscope*. Ross-on-Wye: PCCS Books.

Joseph, J. (2004). Schizophrenia and heredity: why the Emperor has no genes. In: J. Read, L. R. Mosher, & R. P. Bentall (Eds.), *Models of Madness: Psychological, Social and Biological Approaches to Schizophrenia* (pp. 67–83). Hove: Brunner-Routledge.

Joseph, J. (2006). *The Missing Gene: Psychiatry, Heredity, and the Fruitless Search for Genes*. New York: Algora.

Justo, D. (2006). Smoldering systemic inflammation: a link between schizophrenia, smoking and obesity. *Acta Psychiatrica Scandinavica, 113*: 245–246.

Juvonen, H., Reunanen, A., Haukka, J., Muhonen, M., Suvisaari, J., Arajärvi, R., Partonen, T., & Lönnqvist, J. (2007). Incidence of schizophrenia in a nationwide cohort of patients with Type 1 Diabetes Mellitus. *Archives of General Psychiatry, 64*: 894–899.

Kahlbaum, K. (1874). *Die Katatonie oder das Spannungsirresein: Eine klinische Form psychischer Krankheit*. Berlin: Verlag von August Hirschwald.

Kahr, B. (1984). Interview with John Bowlby, 20 February.

Kahr, B. (1993). Ancient infanticide and modern schizophrenia: the clinical uses of psychohistorical research. *Journal of Psychohistory, 20*: 267–273.

Kahr, B. (1994). The historical foundations of ritual abuse: an excavation of ancient infanticide. In: V. Sinason (Ed.), *Treating Survivors of Satanist Abuse* (pp. 45–56). London: Routledge.

Kahr, B. (1997). Teaching the psychotherapy of schizophrenia. Collection of lectures and abstracts presented at ISPS 97, 12–16 October, 1997. London, United Kingdom. Conference on "Building Bridges: The Psychotherapies and Psychosis", Twelfth International Symposium for the Psychotherapy of Schizophrenia, The International Society for the Psychological Treatments of the Schizophrenias and Other Psychoses, The Queen Elizabeth II Conference Centre, Westminster, London, p. 54.

Kahr, B. (2001). The legacy of infanticide. *Journal of Psychohistory, 29*: 40–44.

Kahr, B. (2002). Multiple personality disorder and schizophrenia: an interview with Professor Flora Rheta Schreiber. In: V. Sinason (Ed.), *Attachment, Trauma and Multiplicity: Working with Dissociative Identity Disorder* (pp. 240–264). London: Brunner-Routledge.

Kahr, B. (2007a). *Sex and the Psyche*. London: Allen Lane/Penguin Books.

Kahr, B. (2007b). The infanticidal attachment. *Attachment: New Directions in Psychotherapy and Relational Psychoanalysis, 1*: 117–132.

Kahr, B. (2007c). The infanticidal attachment in schizophrenia and dissociative identity disorder. *Attachment: New Directions in Psychotherapy and Relational Psychoanalysis, 1*: 305–309.

Kahr, B. (2011). Multiple personality disorder and schizophrenia: an interview with Professor Flora Rheta Schreiber [revised version]. In: V. Sinason (Ed.), *Attachment, Trauma and Multiplicity: Working with Dissociative Identity Disorder, Second Edition* (pp. 204–214). Hove: Routledge.

Kalinowsky, L. B. (1939). Electric-convulsion therapy in schizophrenia. *Lancet*, 9 December: 1232–1233.

Kalinowsky, L. B., & Hoch, P. H. (1946). *Shock Treatments and Other Somatic Procedures in Psychiatry*. New York: Grune and Stratton.

Kallmann, F. J. (1946). The genetic theory of schizophrenia: an analysis of 691 schizophrenic twin index families. *American Journal of Psychiatry, 103*: 309–322.

Kallmann, F. J., & Rypins, S. J. (1938). *Schizophrenia: A Study of Heredity and Reproduction in the Families of 1,087 Schizophrenics*. New York: J. J. Augustin.

Kamin, L. J. (1984). Schizophrenia: the clash of determinisms. In: R. C. Lewontin, S. Rose, & L. J. Kamin (Eds.), *Not in Our Genes: Biology, Ideology, and Human Nature* (pp. 197–231). New York: Pantheon Books.

Kane, J., & Di Scipio, W. J. (1979). Acupuncture treatment of schizophrenia: report on three cases. *American Journal of Psychiatry, 136:* 297–302.

Karon, B. P. (1996). Foreword: in search of truth. In: J. Modrow (Ed.), *How to Become a Schizophrenic: The Case Against Biological Psychiatry* (2nd edn) (pp. xi–xiv). Seattle, Washington: Apollyon Press.

Karon, B. P., & VandenBos, G. R. (1981). *Psychotherapy of Schizophrenia: The Treatment of Choice*. New York: Jason Aronson.

Karpas, M. J. (1908). Contribution to our knowledge of the aetiology of dementia praecox: (preliminary communication), Part I. *New York Medical Journal,* 5 December: 1061–1068.

Kasanin, J. S. (Ed.) (1944). *Language and Thought in Schizophrenia: Collected Papers. Presented at the Meeting of the American Psychiatric Association, May 12, 1939, Chicago, Illinois and Brought Up to Date*. Berkeley, CA: University of California Press.

Kaufmant, Y. (1989). Crucial moments in the cure of psychotics. *Le Bulletin du GRAPP (Groupe de Recherche et d'Application des Concepts Psychanalytiques à la Psychose), April:* 3.

Kendler, K. S., & Prescott, C. A. (2006). *Genes, Environment, and Psychopathology: Understanding the Causes of Psychiatric and Substance Use Disorders*. New York: Guilford Press.

Killick, K. (1995). Working with psychotic processes in art therapy. In: J. Ellwood (Ed.), *Psychosis: Understanding and Treatment* (pp. 105–119). London: Jessica Kingsley.

Kingdon, D. G., Ashcroft, K., Bhandari, B., Gleeson, S., Warikoo, N., Symons, M., Taylor, L., Lucas, E., Mahendra, R., Ghosh, S., Mason, A., Badrakalimuthu, R., Hepworth, C., Read, J., & Mehta, R. (2010). Schizophrenia and borderline personality disorder: similarities and differences in the experience of auditory hallucinations, paranoia, and childhood trauma. *Journal of Nervous and Mental Disease, 198:* 399–403.

Klempan, T. A., Muglia, P., & Kennedy, J. L. (2004). Genes and brain development. In: M. S. Keshavan, J. L. Kennedy, & R. M. Murray (Eds.), *Neurodevelopment and Schizophrenia* (pp. 3–34). Cambridge: Cambridge University Press.

Klinge, V. (1979). Facilitating oral hygiene in patients with chronic schizophrenia. *Journal of the American Dental Association, 99:* 644–645.

Klingmann, T. (1946). Physical signs in schizophrenia. *American Journal of Psychiatry, 103:* 69–71.

Klow, S. D. (1943). Acute psychosis in selectees. *Illinois Medical Journal, 83*: 125–128.

Kluft, R. P. (Ed.) (1990). *Incest-Related Syndromes of Adult Psychopathology*. Washington, DC: American Psychiatric Publishing.

Knapp, M. (1997). Costs of schizophrenia. *British Journal of Psychiatry, 171*: 509–518.

Kneeland, T. W., & Warren, C. A. B. (2002). *Pushbutton Psychiatry: A History of Electroshock in America*. Westport, CT: Praeger.

Krabbendam, L., & Van Os, J. (2004). Can the social environment cause schizophrenia? In: C. McDonald, K. Schulze, R. M. Murray, & P. Wright (Eds.), *Schizophrenia: Challenging the Orthodox* (pp. 47–55). London: Taylor and Francis.

Kraepelin, E. (1913a). *Psychiatrie: Ein Lehrbuch für Studierende und Ärzte. Achte, vollständig umgearbeitete Auflage. III. Band. Klinische Psychiatrie. II. Teil*. Leipzig: Verlag von Johann Ambrosius Barth.

Kraepelin, E. (1913b). *Dementia Praecox and Paraphrenia*, G. M. Robertson (Ed.), R. M. Barclay (Trans.). Edinburgh: E. & S. Livingstone, 1919.

Kral, V. A. (1951). Psychiatric observations under severe chronic stress. *American Journal of Psychiatry, 108*: 185–192.

Krystal, H. (Ed.) (1968a). *Massive Psychic Trauma*. New York: International Universities Press.

Krystal, H. (1968b). General discussion of the workshop themes. In: H. Krystal (Ed.), *Massive Psychic Trauma* (p. 98). New York: International Universities Press.

Krystal, H. (1968c). Introduction: the massively traumatized individuals as a challenge to humane medicine. In: H. Krystal (Ed.), *Massive Psychic Trauma* (pp. 109–110). New York: International Universities Press.

Krystal, H., & Niederland, W. G. (Eds.) (1971). *Psychic Traumatization: Aftereffects in Individuals and Communities*. Boston, MA: Little, Brown.

Kuipers, L., Leff, J., & Lam, D. (1992). *Family Work for Schizophrenia: A Practical Guide*. London: Gaskell/Royal College of Psychiatrists.

Kurth, A. (2007). Personal communication to the author, 4 January.

Kvarnes, R. G., & Parloff, G. H. (Eds.) (1976). *A Harry Stack Sullivan Case Seminar: Treatment of a Young Male Schizophrenic*. New York: W. W. Norton.

Laan, W., Grobbee, D. E., Selten, J.-P., Heijnen, C. J., Kahn, R. S., & Burger, H. (2010). Adjuvant aspirin therapy reduces symptoms of schizophrenia spectrum disorders: results from a randomized, double-blind, placebo-controlled trial. *Journal of Clinical Psychiatry, 71*: 520–527.

Lacan, J. (1981). *Le Séminaire de Jacques Lacan: Livre III. Les Psychoses, 1955–1956*. J.-A. Miller (Ed.). Paris: Éditions du Seuil.

Laing, R. D. (1960). *The Divided Self: A Study of Sanity and Madness*. London: Tavistock.

Laing, R. D. (1964). Is schizophrenia a disease? *International Journal of Social Psychiatry, 10*: 184–193.

Laing, R. D. (1976). A critique of Kallmann's and Slater's genetic theory of schizophrenia. In: R. I. Evans (Ed.), *Dialogue with R.D. Laing: The Man and His Ideas* (pp. 97–156). New York: E. P. Dutton.

Laing, R. D. (1981). A critique of Kallmann's and Slater's genetic theory of schizophrenia. In: R. I. Evans (Ed.), *Dialogue with R.D. Laing* (revised edn) (pp. 97–156). New York: Praeger.

Landau, R., Harth, P., Othnay, N., & Sharfhertz, C. (1972). The influence of psychotic parents on their children's development. *American Journal of Psychiatry, 129*: 38–43.

Langfeldt, G. (1939). *The Schizophreniform States: A Katamnestic Study Based on Individual Re-Examinations. With Special Reference to Diagnostic and Prognostic Clues, and with a View to Presenting a Standard Material for Comparison with the Remissions Effected by Shock Treatment*. Copenhagen: Ejnar Munksgaard International.

Lardinois, M., Lataster, T., Mengelers, R., Van Os, J., & Myin-Germeys, I. (2011). Childhood trauma and increased stress sensitivity in psychosis. *Acta Psychiatrica Scandinavica, 123*: 28–35.

Lawrie, S. M. (1999). Social and psychological treatments. In: E. C. Johnstone, M. S. Humphreys, F. H. Lang, S. M. Lawrie, & R. Sandler (Eds.), *Schizophrenia: Concepts and Clinical Management* (pp. 222–237). Cambridge: Cambridge University Press.

Lawrie, S. M. (2004). Premorbid structural abnormalities in schizophrenia. In: M. S. Keshavan, J. L. Kennedy, & R. M. Murray (Eds.), *Neurodevelopment and Schizophrenia* (pp. 347–372). Cambridge: Cambridge University Press.

Lawrie, S. M., & Abukmeil, S. S. (1998). Brain abnormality in schizophrenia: a systematic and quantitative review of volumetric magnetic resonance imaging studies. *British Journal of Psychiatry, 172*: 110–120.

Lawrie, S. M., Weinberger, D. R., & Johnstone, E. C. (Eds.) (2004). *Schizophrenia: From Neuroimaging to Neuroscience*. Oxford: Oxford University Press.

Lebensohn, Z. M. (1945). Psychoses in naval officers: a plea for psychiatric selection. *American Journal of Psychiatry, 101*: 511–516.

Leclaire, S. (1999). *Principes d'une psychothérapie des psychoses*. Paris: Librairie Arthème Fayard.

Leff, J. (2001). *The Unbalanced Mind*. London: Weidenfeld and Nicolson.

Leff, J. (2002). Keynote lecture: relatives' expressed emotion. From measurement technique to practical help for families. In: K. Haruo, I. R. H. Falloon, M. Masafumi, & A. Masahiro (Eds.), *Comprehensive Treatment of Schizophrenia: Linking Neurobehavioral Findings to Psychosocial Approaches* (pp. 83–93). Tokyo: Springer-Verlag.

Leff, J. (2005). *Advanced Family Work for Schizophrenia: An Evidence-Based Approach.* London: Gaskell.

Leigh, D. (1961). *The Historical Development of British Psychiatry: Volume 1. 18th and 19th Century.* New York: Pergamon Press.

Lenzenweger, M. F., & Dworkin, R. H. (Eds.) (1998). *Origins and Development of Schizophrenia: Advances in Experimental Psychopathology.* Washington, DC: American Psychological Association.

Levin, M. (1946). Transitory schizophrenias produced by bromide intoxication. *American Journal of Psychiatry, 103:* 229–237.

Lewis, D. A., Mimics, K., & Levitt, P. (2004). Transcriptomes in schizophrenia: assessing altered gene expression with microarrays. In: M. S. Keshavan, J. L. Kennedy, & R. M. Murray (Eds.), *Neurodevelopment and Schizophrenia* (pp. 210–223). Cambridge: Cambridge University Press.

Lewis, G., David, A., Andréasson, S., & Allebeck, P. (1992). Schizophrenia and city life. *Lancet,* 18 July: 137–140.

Lewis, M., McCrone, P., & Frangou, S. (2001). Service use and costs of treating schizophrenia with atypical antipsychotics. *Journal of Clinical Psychiatry, 62:* 749–756.

Lewis, N. D. C., & Engle, B. (Eds.) (1954). *Wartime Psychiatry: A Compendium of the International Literature.* New York: Oxford University Press.

Liddle, P. F. (2001). *Disordered Mind and Brain: The Neural Basis of Mental Symptoms.* London: Gaskell.

Lidz, T. (1973). *The Origin and Treatment of Schizophrenic Disorders.* New York: Basic Books.

Lidz, T. (1983). Danish data show weak genetic factor. *American Journal of Psychiatry, 141:* 1308.

Lidz, T., & Blatt, S. (1983). Critique of the Danish-American studies of the biological and adoptive relatives of adoptees who became schizophrenic. *American Journal of Psychiatry, 140:* 426–435.

Lidz, T., Blatt, S., & Cook, B. (1981). Critique of the Danish-American studies of the adopted-away offspring of schizophrenic parents. *American Journal of Psychiatry, 138:* 1063–1068.

Lidz, T., Fleck, S., & Cornelison, A. (1965). *Schizophrenia and the Family.* New York: International Universities Press.

Lifton, R. J. (1967). *Death in Life: Survivors of Hiroshima.* New York: Random House.

Lifton, R. J. (1968). Observations on Hiroshima survivors. In: H. Krystal (Ed.), *Massive Psychic Trauma* (pp. 168–189). New York: International Universities Press.

Liotti, G., & Gumley, A. (2008). An attachment perspective on schizophrenia: the role of disorganized attachment, dissociation and mentalization. In: A. Moskowitz, I. Schäfer, & M. J. Dorahy (Eds.), *Psychosis, Trauma and Dissociation: Emerging Perspectives on Severe Psychopathology* (pp. 117–133). Chichester: Wiley-Blackwell.

Littlewood, R., & Lipsedge, M. (1982). *Aliens and Alienists: Ethnic Minorities and Psychiatry*. Harmondsworth: Penguin.

Littlewood, R., & Lipsedge, M. (1988). Psychiatric illness among British Afro-Caribbeans. *British Medical Journal*, 2 April: 950–951.

Lux, K. E. (1976). A mystical–occult approach to psychosis. In: P. A. Magaro (Ed.), *The Construction of Madness: Emerging Conceptions and Interventions into the Psychotic Process* (pp. 93–132). Oxford: Pergamon Press.

MacCarthy, B. (1988). Are incest victims hated? *Psychoanalytic Psychotherapy*, 3: 113–120.

MacCarthy, B. (2005). Counterpoints. In: G. Ambrosio (Ed.), *On Incest: Psychoanalytic Perspectives* (pp. 115–120). London: Karnac.

Maeder, A. (1910). Psychologische Untersuchungen an Dementia Praecox-Kranken. *Jahrbuch für psychoanalytische und psychopathologische Forschungen*, 2: 185–245.

Magaro, P. A. (Ed.) (1976). *The Construction of Madness: Emerging Conceptions and Interventions into the Psychotic Process*. Oxford: Pergamon Press.

Magid, B. (1984). Some contributions of self psychology to the treatment of borderline and schizophrenic patients. *Dynamic Psychotherapy*, 2: 101–111.

Mahadik, S. P. (2004). Nutritional factors and schizophrenia. In: M. S. Keshavan, J. L. Kennedy, & R. M. Murray (Eds.), *Neurodevelopment and Schizophrenia* (pp. 156–173). Cambridge: Cambridge University Press.

Main, D. C. (1923). Catatonic dementia praecox, physiotherapeutics, and results obtained in a series of twenty cases. *American Journal of Psychiatry*, 2: 473–483.

Malamud, W., & Malamud, I. (1943). A socio-psychiatric investigation of schizophrenia occurring in the armed forces. *Psychosomatic Medicine*, 5: 364–375.

Malla, A. K., Norman, R. M. G., Aguilar, O., Carnahan, H., & Cortese, L. (1995). Relationship between movement planning and psychopathology profiles in schizophrenia. *British Journal of Psychiatry*, 167: 211–215.

Malzberg, B. (1934). *Mortality Among Patients with Mental Disease*. Utica, NY: State Hospitals Press.

Malzberg, B., & Lee, E. S. (1956). *Migration and Mental Disease: A Study of First Admissions to Hospitals for Mental Disease, New York, 1939–1941*. New York: Social Science Research Council.

Marshall, J. R. (1984). The genetics of schizophrenia revisited. *Bulletin of the British Psychological Society, 37*: 177–181.

Marshall, J. R. (1990). The genetics of schizophrenia: axiom or hypothesis? In: R. P. Bentall (Ed.), *Reconstructing Schizophrenia* (pp. 89–117). London: Routledge.

Marshall, J. R. (1995). Schizophrenia: a constructive analogy or a convenient construct? In: J. Ellwood (Ed.), *Psychosis: Understanding and Treatment* (pp. 54–69). London: Jessica Kingsley.

Marwaha, S., Johnson, S., Bebbington, P., Stafford, M., Angermeyer, M. C., Brugha, T., Azorin, J.-M., Kilian, R., Hansen, K., & Tuomi, M. (2007). Rates and correlates of employment in people with schizophrenia in the UK, France and Germany. *British Journal of Psychiatry, 191*: 30–37.

Matthysse, S. W., & Kety, S. S. (Eds.) (1975). *Catecholamines and Schizophrenia*. Oxford: Pergamon Press.

Maudsley, H. (1868). Illustrations of a variety of insanity. *Journal of Mental Science, 14*: 149–162.

Mayer-Gross, W., Slater, E., & Roth, M. (1954). *Clinical Psychiatry*. London: Cassell.

Maynard, A. (1996). Financing and paying for care in schizophrenia. In: M. Moscarelli, A. Rupp, & N. Sartorius (Eds.), *Handbook of Mental Health Economics and Health Policy: Volume I. Schizophrenia* (pp. 423–431). Chichester: John Wiley.

Mazure, C. M., & Druss, B. G. (1995). A historical perspective on stress and psychiatric illness. In: C. M. Mazure (Ed.), *Does Stress Cause Psychiatric Illness?* (pp. 1–41). Washington, DC: American Psychiatric Association Press.

McConnell, J. (1945). Two years' experience of female schizophrenics treated by insulin coma therapy. *Journal of Mental Science, 91*: 506–510.

McCrae, N. (2006). 'A violent thunderstorm': cardiazol treatment in British mental hospitals. *History of Psychiatry, 17*: 67–90.

McCreadie, R. G., Main, C. J., & Dunlop, R. A. (1978). Token economy, pimozide and chronic schizophrenia. *British Journal of Psychiatry, 133*: 179–181.

McDonald, C., & Murray, R. M. (2004). Can structural magnetic resonance imaging provide an alternative phenotype for genetic studies of schizophrenia? In: M. S. Keshavan, J. L. Kennedy, & R. M. Murray (Eds.), *Neurodevelopment and Schizophrenia* (pp. 138–155). Cambridge: Cambridge University Press.

McGrath, J., Saha, S., Chant, D., & Welham, J. (2008). Schizophrenia: a concise overview of incidence, prevalence, and mortality. *Epidemiologic Reviews, 30*: 67–76.

McGrath, J., Welham, J., & Pemberton, M. (1995). Month of birth, hemisphere of birth and schizophrenia. *British Journal of Psychiatry, 167*: 783–785.

McGregor, J. S., & Crumbie, J. R. (1941). Surgical treatment of mental diseases. *Lancet,* 5 July: 7–8.

McKenzie, K., Fearon, P., & Hutchinson, G. (2008). Migration, ethnicity and psychosis. In: C. Morgan, K. McKenzie, & P. Fearon (Eds.), *Society and Psychosis* (pp. 143–160). Cambridge: Cambridge University Press.

McNeil, T. F., & Kaij, L. (1978). Obstetric factors in the development of schizophrenia: complications in the births of preschizophrenics and in reproduction by schizophrenic parents. In: L. C. Wynne, R. L. Cromwell, S. Matthysse, M. L. Toohey, B. J. Spring, & J. Sugarman (Eds.), *The Nature of Schizophrenia: New Approaches to Research and Treatment* (pp. 401–429). New York: John Wiley.

Mednick, S. A., Cannon, T. D., & Barr, C. E. (1991). Obstetrical events and adult schizophrenia. In: S. A. Mednick, T. D. Cannon, C. E. Barr, & M. Lyon (Eds.), *Fetal Neural Development and Adult Schizophrenia* (pp. 115–149). Cambridge: Cambridge University Press.

Mednick, S. A., Cannon, T. D., Barr, C. E., & Lyon, M. (Eds.) (1991). *Fetal Neural Development and Adult Schizophrenia*. Cambridge: Cambridge University Press.

Meerloo, J. A. M. (1968). Delayed mourning in victims of extermination camps. In: H. Krystal (Ed.), *Massive Psychic Trauma* (pp. 72–75). New York: International Universities Press.

Menninger, K. A. (1922). Reversible schizophrenia: a study of the implications of delirium schizophrenoides and other post-influenzal syndromes. *American Journal of Psychiatry, 1*: 573–587.

Mercier, C. (1916). Diet as a factor in the causation of mental disease. *Journal of Mental Science, 62*: 505–529.

Metzl, J. M. (2009). *The Protest Psychosis: How Schizophrenia Became a Black Disease*. Boston, MA: Beacon Press.

Miller, A. (1986). Personal communication to the author. Date unknown.

Milne, S., Curson, D., Wilkie, A., & Pantelis, C. (1993). Social morbidity of a long-stay mental hospital population with chronic schizophrenia. *Psychiatric Bulletin, 17*: 647–649.

Mishler, E. G., & Waxler, N. E. (Eds.) (1968). *Family Processes and Schizophrenia*. New York: Science House.

Mispelbaum, F. (1891). Ueber Psychosen nach Influenza. *Allgemeine Zeitschrift für Psychiatrie und psychisch-gerichtliche Medicin, 47*: 127–153.

Moncrieff, J. (2008). *The Myth of the Chemical Cure: A Critique of Psychiatric Drug Treatment*. Basingstoke: Palgrave Macmillan.

Moncrieff, J. (2011). Questioning the 'neuroprotective' hypothesis: does drug treatment prevent brain damage in early psychosis or schizophrenia? *British Journal of Psychiatry, 198*: 85–87.

Moniz, E. (1936). *Tentatives opératoires dans le traitement de certaines psychoses*. Paris: Masson et Compagnie, Éditeurs.

Morgan, C., & Fisher, H. (2007). Environmental factors in schizophrenia: childhood trauma—a critical review. *Schizophrenia Bulletin, 33*: 3–10.

Morrens, M., Hulstijn, W., & Sabbe, B. (2007). Psychomotor slowing in schizophrenia. *Schizophrenia Bulletin, 33*: 1038–1053.

Mortensen, P. B., & Juel, K. (1993). Mortality and causes of death in first admitted schizophrenic patients. *British Journal of Psychiatry, 163*: 183–189.

Mortensen, P. B., Norgaard-Pedersen, B., Waltoft, B. L., Sørensen, T. L., Hougaard, D., & Yolken, R. H. (2007). Early infections of *Toxoplasma gondii* and the later development of schizophrenia. *Schizophrenia Bulletin, 33*: 741–744.

Moscarelli, M., Rupp, A., & Sartorius, N. (Eds.) (1996). *Handbook of Mental Health Economics and Health Policy: Volume I. Schizophrenia*. Chichester: John Wiley.

Mott, F. W. (1920). Studies in the pathology of dementia praecox. *Proceedings of the Royal Society of Medicine, Section of Psychiatry, 13*: 25–63.

Mueser, K. T., & Berenbaum, H. (1990). Psychodynamic treatment of schizophrenia: is there a future? *Psychological Medicine, 20*: 253–262.

Müller, C. (2006). Beginnings of the International Symposia for the psychotherapy of schizophrenia. In: Y. Alanen, A.-L. S. Silver, & M. González de Chávez (Eds.), *Fifty Years of Humanistic Treatment of Psychoses: In Honour of the History of the International Society for the Psychological Treatments of the Schizophrenias and Other Psychoses, 1956–2006* (pp. 23–29). Madrid: Fundación para la Investigación y Tratamiento de la Esquizofrenia y otras Psicosis.

Murphy, K. C., & Owen, M. J. (1996). Minor physical anomalies and their relationship to the aetiology of schizophrenia. *British Journal of Psychiatry, 168*: 139–142.

Murray, R. M., Chen, C.-K., Grech, A., Arseneault, L., Cannon, M., & Zanelli, J. (2004). What is the relationship between methamphetamine abuse and schizophrenia? In: C. McDonald, K. Schulze, R. M. Murray, & P. Wright (Eds.), *Schizophrenia: Challenging the Orthodox* (pp. 75–80). London: Taylor and Francis.

Myrhman, A., Rantakallio, P., Isohanni, M., Jones, P., & Partanen, U. (1996). Unwantedness of a pregnancy and schizophrenia in the child. *British Journal of Psychiatry, 169*: 637–640.

Nagel, D. B. (1991). Psychotherapy of schizophrenia: 1900–1920. In: J. G. Howells (Ed.), *The Concept of Schizophrenia: Historical Perspectives* (pp. 191–201). Washington, DC: American Psychiatric Publishing.

Nasrallah, H. A., Schwarzkopf, S. B., Coffman, J. A., & Olson, S. C. (1991). Developmental brain abnormalities on MRI in schizophrenia: the role of genetic and perinatal factors. In: S. A. Mednick, T. D. Cannon, C. E. Barr, & M. Lyon (Eds.), *Fetal Neural Development and Adult Schizophrenia* (pp. 216–223). Cambridge: Cambridge University Press.

Nemeth, M. C. (1971). Psychosis in a concentration camp survivor: a case presentation. In: H. Krystal & W. G. Niederland (Eds.), *Psychic Traumatization: Aftereffects in Individuals and Communities* (pp. 135–146). Boston, MA: Little, Brown.

Niederland, W. G. (1959a). The "miracled-up" world of Schreber's childhood. *Psychoanalytic Study of the Child, 14*: 383–413.

Niederland, W. G. (1959b). Schreber: father and son. *Psychoanalytic Quarterly, 28*: 151–169.

Niederland, W. G. (1961). The problem of the survivor. *Journal of the Hillside Hospital, 10*: 233–247.

Niederland, W. G. (1963). Further data and memorabilia pertaining to the Schreber case. *International Journal of Psycho-Analysis, 44*: 201–207.

Niederland, W. G. (1968a). Clinical observations on the "survivor syndrome". *International Journal of Psycho-Analysis, 49*: 313–315.

Niederland, W. G. (1968b). An interpretation of the psychological stresses and defenses in concentration-camp life and late aftereffects. In: H. Krystal (Ed.), *Massive Psychic Trauma* (pp. 60–70). New York: International Universities Press.

Niederland, W. G. (1974). *The Schreber Case: Psychoanalytic Profile of a Paranoid Personality*. New York: Quadrangle/The New York Times Book Company.

Niederland, W. G. (1980). *Folgen der Verfolgung: Das Überlebenden-Syndrom Seelenmord*. Frankfurt am Main: Suhrkamp Verlag.

Niederland, W. G. (1984). *The Schreber Case: Psychoanalytic Profile of a Paranoid Personality* (2nd edn). Hillsdale, NJ: Analytic Press.

Nielsen, J., & Toft, E. (2009). The spectrum of cardiovascular disease in patients with schizophrenia. In: J. M. Meyer & H. A. Nasrallah (Eds.), *Medical Illness and Schizophrenia: Second Edition* (pp. 169–202). Arlington, VA: American Psychiatric Publishing.

Noll, R. (2006a). Infectious insanities, surgical solutions: Bayard Taylor Holmes, dementia praecox and laboratory science in early 20th-century America. Part 1. *History of Psychiatry*, 17: 183–204.

Noll, R. (2006b). Infectious insanities, surgical solutions: Bayard Taylor Holmes, dementia praecox and laboratory science in early 20th-century America. Part 2. *History of Psychiatry*, 17: 299–311.

Noll, R. (2006c). The blood of the insane. *History of Psychiatry*, 17: 395–418.

Noll, R. (2007). Kraepelin's 'lost biological psychiatry'?: autointoxication, organotherapy and surgery for dementia praecox. *History of Psychiatry*, 18: 301–320.

North, C. S. (1987). *Welcome, Silence: My Triumph Over Schizophrenia*. New York: Simon and Schuster.

Norton, N., & Owen, M. J. (2004). Can we find the genes that predispose to schizophrenia? In: C. McDonald, K. Schulze, R. M. Murray, & P. Wright (Eds.), *Schizophrenia: Challenging the Orthodox* (pp. 17–22). London: Taylor and Francis.

Obregia, A., Tomesco, P., & Dimolesco, A. (1936). Les Psychoses émotionelles: Le Rôle psychogène des traumatismes affectifs. *Bulletin de la Société de Psychiatrie de Bucarest*, 1: 157–170.

Oldham, J. M., & Bone, S. (Eds.) (1994). *Paranoia: New Psychoanalytic Perspectives*. Madison, CT: International Universities Press.

Osnato, M. (1930). The rôle of trauma in various neuro-psychiatric conditions. *American Journal of Psychiatry*, 9: 643–659.

Owens, D. G. C., & Johnstone, E. C. (1980). The disabilities of chronic schizophrenia: their nature and the factors contributing to their development. *British Journal of Psychiatry*, 136: 384–395.

Pajonk, F.-G., Wobrock, T., Gruber, O., Scherk, H., Berner, D., Kaizl, I., Kierer, A., Müller, S., Oest, M., Meyer, T., Backens, M., Schneider-Axmann, T., Thornton, A. E., Honer, W. G., & Falkai, P. (2010). Hippocampal plasticity in response to exercise in schizophrenia. *Archives of General Psychiatry*, 67: 133–143.

Pam, A. (1995). Biological psychiatry: science or pseudoscience? In: C. A. Ross & A. Pam (Eds.), *Pseudoscience in Biological Psychiatry: Blaming the Body* (pp. 7–84). New York: John Wiley.

Pankow, G. (2006). *Les Dangers du "on-dit" et autres réflexions: Abord analytique de la parole de l'autre*. Paris: Éditions CampagnePremière.

Pao, P.-N. (1979). *Schizophrenic Disorders: Theory and Treatment from a Psychodynamic Point of View*. New York: International Universities Press.

Partridge, M. (1950). *Pre-Frontal Leucotomy: A Survey of 300 Cases Followed Over $1^1/_2$–3 Years*. Oxford: Blackwell Scientific.

Paskind, H. A., & Brown, M. (1940). Psychoses resembling schizophrenia occurring with emotional stress and ending in recovery. *American Journal of Psychiatry, 96*: 1379–1388.

Passione, R. (2004). Italian psychiatry in an international context: Ugo Cerletti and the case of electroshock. *History of Psychiatry, 15*: 83–104.

Passione, R. (2006). Introduzione. In: R. Passione (Ed.), *Ugo Cerletti: Scritti sull' elettroshock* (pp. 9–47). Milano: FrancoAngeli.

Paster, S. (1948). Psychotic reactions among soldiers of World War II. *Journal of Nervous and Mental Disease, 108*: 54–66.

Patterson, T., Spohn, H. E., Bogia, D. P., & Hayes, K. (1986). Thought disorder in schizophrenia: cognitive and neuroscience approaches. *Schizophrenia Bulletin, 12*: 460–472.

Peralta, V., & Cuesta, M. J. (1996). Symptoms of the schizophrenic negative syndrome. *British Journal of Psychiatry, 169*: 209–212.

Perry, H. S. (1982). *Psychiatrist of America: The Life of Harry Stack Sullivan*. Cambridge, MA: Belknap Press of Harvard University Press.

Pettegrew, J. W., & Minshew, N. J. (1994). Molecular insights into schizophrenia. In: N. C. Andreasen (Ed.), *Schizophrenia: From Mind to Molecule* (pp. 221–243). Washington, DC: American Psychiatric Press.

Phillips, M. R., West, C. L., & Wang, R. (1996). Erotomanic symptoms in 42 Chinese schizophrenic patients. *British Journal of Psychiatry, 169*: 501–508.

Power, T. D. (1942). *The Mechanism of Convulsion Therapy*. Dorking: Adlard and Son/Bartholomew Press.

Pressman, J. D. (1998). *Last Resort: Psychosurgery and the Limits of Medicine*. Cambridge: Cambridge University Press.

Prout, C. T. (1946). Psychiatric reactions to war-time stress as seen in members of the armed services, referred to a private mental hospital. *Psychiatric Quarterly, 20*: 434–446.

Racamier, P.-C. (1980). *Les Schizophrènes*. Paris: Petite Bibliothèque Payot.

Raphael, T., & Gregg, S. (1921). Reaction in dementia praecox to the intravenous administration of non-specific protein. *American Journal of Psychiatry*, 1: 31–39.

Ray, W. A., Chung, C. P., Murray, K. T., Hall, K., & Stein, C. M. (2009). Atypical antipsychotic drugs and the risk of sudden cardiac death. *New England Journal of Medicine*, 15 January: 225–235.

Raz, M. (2010). Psychosurgery, industry and personal responsibility, 1940–1965. *Social History of Medicine*, 23: 116–133.

Read, J., & Hammersley, P. (2005). Child sexual abuse and schizophrenia. *British Journal of Psychiatry*, 186: 76.

Read, J., & Hammersley, P. (2006). Can very bad childhoods drive us crazy? Science, ideology and taboo. In: J. O. Johannessen, B. V. Martindale, & J. Cullberg (Eds.), *Evolving Psychosis: Different Stages, Different Treatments* (pp. 270–292). Hove: Routledge.

Read, J., Goodman, L., Morrison, A. P., Ross, C. A., & Aderhold, V. (2004). Childhood trauma, loss and stress. In: J. Read, L. R. Mosher, & R. P. Bentall (Eds.), *Models of Madness: Psychological, Social and Biological Approaches to Schizophrenia* (pp. 223–252). Hove, East Sussex: Brunner-Routledge.

Read, J., Rudegeair, T., & Farrelly, S. (2006). The relationship between child abuse and psychosis: public opinion, evidence, pathways and implications. In: W. Larkin & A. P. Morrison (Eds.), *Trauma and Psychosis: New Directions for Theory and Therapy* (pp. 23–57). Hove: Routledge.

Rees, W. L. (1957). Physical characteristics of the schizophrenic patient. In: D. Richter (Ed.), *Schizophrenia: Somatic Aspects* (pp. 1–14). London: Pergamon Press.

Reich, A. (1936). Klinischer Beitrag zum Verständnis der paranoiden Persönlichkeit. *Internationale Zeitschrift für Psychoanalyse*, 22: 315–337.

Reid, R. (1990). Dr Russell Reid: transexual specialist. In: D. Danziger (Ed.), *The Noble Tradition: Interviews with the Medical Profession* (pp. 155–159). London: Viking.

Reil, J. C. (1803). *Rhapsodien über die Anwendung der psychischen Curmethode auf Geisteszerrüttungen*. Halle: Curtschen Buchhandlung.

Reilly, S. P. (1997). Psychoanalytic and psychodynamic approaches to psychosis: an overview. In: C. Mace & F. Margison (Eds.), *Psychotherapy of Psychosis* (pp. 13–30). London: Gaskell.

Rhinewine, J. P., Lencz, T., Thaden, E. P., Cervellione, K. L., Burdick, K. E., Henderson, I., Bhaskar, S., Keehlisen, L., Kane, J., Kohn, N., Fisch,

G. S., Bilder, R. M., & Kumra, S. (2005). Neurocognitive profile in adolescents with early-onset schizophrenia: clinical correlates. *Biological Psychiatry, 58*: 705–712.

Rickers-Ovsiankina, M. (1938). The Rorschach Test as applied to normal and schizophrenic subjects. *British Journal of Medical Psychology, 17*: 227–257.

Rizzo, L., Danion, J.-M., Van der Linden, M., & Grangé, D. (1996). Patients with schizophrenia remember that an event has occurred, but not when. *British Journal of Psychiatry, 168*: 427–431.

Roberts, G. W. (1991). Temporal lobe pathology and schizophrenia. In: R. Kerwin (Ed.), *Cambridge Medical Reviews: Neurobiology and Psychiatry. Volume 1* (pp. 15–38). Cambridge: Cambridge University Press.

Roberts, N. (1967). *Mental Health and Mental Illness*. London: Routledge and Kegan Paul.

Rochester, S., & Martin, J. R. (1979). *Crazy Talk: A Study of the Discourse of Schizophrenic Speakers*. New York: Plenum Press.

Rockland, L. H. (2010). Psychotherapeutic and psychosocial interventions in schizophrenia: clinical outcomes and cost-effectiveness. In: S. G. Lazar (Ed.), *Psychotherapy is Worth It: A Comprehensive Review of Cost-Effectiveness* (pp. 31–60). Arlington, VA: American Psychiatric Publishing.

Rogues de Fursac, J. (1918). Traumatic and emotional psychoses: so-called shell shock, A. J. Rosanoff (Trans.). *American Journal of Insanity, 75*: 19–51.

Rosen, H., & Kiene, H. E. (1947). The paranoiac officer and the officer paranee. *American Journal of Psychiatry, 103*: 614–621.

Rosen, J. N. (1953). *Direct Analysis: Selected Papers*. New York: Grune and Stratton.

Rosenberg, S. D., Goodman, L. A., Osher, F. C., Swartz, M. S., Essock, S. M., Butterfield, M. I., Constantine, N. T., Wolford, G. L., & Salyers, M. P. (2001). Prevalence of HIV, Hepatitis B, and Hepatitis C in people with severe mental illness. *American Journal of Public Health, 91*: 31–37.

Rosenfeld, D. (1992). *The Psychotic: Aspects of the Personality*. London: Karnac.

Rosenfeld, H. (1947). Analysis of a schizophrenic state with depersonalization. *International Journal of Psycho-Analysis, 28*: 130–139.

Rosenfeld, H. (1949). Remarks on the relation of male homosexuality to paranoia, paranoid anxiety and narcissism. *International Journal of Psycho-Analysis, 30*: 36–47.

Rosenfeld, H. (1950). Note on the psychopathology of confusional states in chronic schizophrenias. *International Journal of Psycho-Analysis, 31*: 132–137.

Rosenfeld, H. (1952). Notes on the psycho-analysis of the super-ego conflict of an acute schizophrenic patient. *International Journal of Psycho-Analysis, 33*: 111–131.

Rosenthal, D. (1970). *Genetic Theory and Abnormal Behavior.* New York: McGraw-Hill.

Rosenzweig, S. (1943). Sibling death as a psychological experience with special reference to schizophrenia. *Psychoanalytic Review, 30*: 177–186.

Rosenzweig, S., & Bray, D. (1943). Sibling deaths in the anamneses of schizophrenic patients. *Archives of Neurology and Psychiatry, 49*: 71–92.

Ross, C. A. (1995). Errors of logic in biological psychiatry. In: C. A. Ross & A. Pam (Eds.), *Pseudoscience in Biological Psychiatry: Blaming the Body* (pp. 85–128). New York: John Wiley.

Ross, C. A. (2000). *The Trauma Model: A Solution to the Problem of Comorbidity in Psychiatry.* Richardson, TX: Manitou Communications.

Ross, C. A. (2008). Dissociative schizophrenia. In: A. Moskowitz, I. Schäfer, & M. J. Dorahy (Eds.), *Psychosis, Trauma and Dissociation: Emerging Perspectives on Severe Psychopathology* (pp. 281–294). Chichester: Wiley-Blackwell.

Sacco, K. A., Termine, A., Seyal, A., Dudas, M. M., Vessicchio, J. C., Krishnan-Sarin, S., Jatlow, P. I., Wexler, B. E., & George, T. P. (2005). Effects of cigarette smoking on spatial working memory and attentional deficits in schizophrenia: involvement of nicotinic receptor mechanisms. *Archives of General Psychiatry, 62*: 649–659.

Saccuzzo, D. P., & Braff, D. L. (1986). Information-processing abnormalities: trait- and state-dependent components. *Schizophrenia Bulletin, 12*: 447–559.

Salzinger, K., Portnoy, S., & Feldman, R. S. (1978). Communicability deficit in schizophrenics resulting from a more general deficit. In: S. Schwartz (Ed.), *Language and Cognition in Schizophrenia* (pp. 35–53). Hillsdale, NJ: Lawrence Erlbaum.

Sampson, H., Messinger, S. L., Towne, R. D., Ross, D., Livson, F., Bowers, M., Cohen, L., & Dorst, K. (1964). *Schizophrenic Women: Studies in Marital Crisis.* New York: Atherton Press.

Sarbin, T. R., & Mancuso, J. C. (1980). *Schizophrenia: Medical Diagnosis or Moral Verdict?* New York: Pergamon Press.

Sargant, W. (1967). *The Unquiet Mind: The Autobiography of a Physician in Psychological Medicine.* London: William Heinemann.

Sashidharan, S. P. (1993). Afro-Caribbeans and schizophrenia: the ethnic vulnerability hypothesis re-examined. *International Review of Psychiatry, 5*: 129–143.

Scazfuca, M., & Kuipers, E. (1996). Links between expressed emotion and burden of care in relatives of patients with schizophrenia. *British Journal of Psychiatry, 168*: 580–587.

Schäfer, I., Ross, C. A., & Read, J. (2008). Childhood trauma in psychotic and dissociative disorders. In: A. Moskowitz, I. Schäfer, & M. J. Dorahy (Eds.), *Psychosis, Trauma and Dissociation: Emerging Perspectives on Severe Psychopathology* (pp. 137–150). Chichester: Wiley-Blackwell.

Schetky, D. H. (1990). A review of the literature on the long-term effects of childhood sexual abuse. In: R. P. Kluft (Ed.), *Incest-Related Syndromes of Adult Psychopathology* (pp. 35–54). Washington, DC: American Psychiatric Press.

Schork, N. J., Greenwood, T. A., & Braff, D. L. (2007). Statistical genetics concepts and approaches in schizophrenia and related neuropsychiatric research. *Schizophrenia Bulletin, 33*: 95–104.

Schreiber, F. R. (1983). *The Shoemaker: The Anatomy of a Psychotic*. New York: Simon and Schuster.

Schultz-Hencke, H. (1952). *Das Problem der Schizophrenie: Analytische Psychotherapie und Psychose*. Stuttgart: Georg Thieme Verlag.

Schwartz, S. (Ed.) (1978). *Language and Cognition in Schizophrenia*. Hillsdale, NJ: Lawrence Erlbaum

Schwing, G. (1940). *Ein Weg zur Seele des Geisteskranken*. Zurich: Rascher Verlag.

Scott, R. D., & Ashworth, P. L. (1965). The 'axis value' and the transfer of psychosis: a scored analysis of the interaction in the families of schizophrenic patients. *British Journal of Medical Psychology, 38*: 97–116.

Scott, R. D., & Ashworth, P. L. (1967). 'Closure' at first schizophrenic break-down: a family study. *British Journal of Medical Psychology, 40*: 109–149.

Scott, R. D., & Ashworth, P. L. (1969). The shadow of the ancestor: a historical factor in the transmission of schizophrenia. *British Journal of Medical Psychology, 42*: 13–32.

Scull, A. (1993). *The Most Solitary of Afflictions: Madness and Society in Britain 1700–1900*. New Haven, CT: Yale University Press.

Scull, A. (2005). *Madhouse: A Tragic Tale of Megalomania and Modern Medicine*. New Haven, CT: Yale University Press.

Searles, H. F. (1963). The place of neutral therapist-responses in psychotherapy with the schizophrenic patient. *International Journal of Psycho-
Analysis*, 44: 42–56.

Sechehaye, M. (1956). *A New Psychotherapy in Schizophrenia: Relief of
Frustrations by Symbolic Realization*, G. Rubin-Rabson (Trans.). New
York: Grune and Stratton.

Seeman, M. V., Lang, M., & Rector, N. (1990). Chronic schizophrenia: a
risk factor for HIV? *Canadian Journal of Psychiatry*, 35: 765–768.

Segal, H. (1950). Some aspects of the analysis of a schizophrenic.
International Journal of Psycho-Analysis, 31: 268–278.

Segal, H. (1956). Depression in the schizophrenic. *International Journal of
Psycho-Analysis*, 37: 339–343.

Segal, H. (1975). Psycho-analytical approach to the treatment of schizophrenia. In: M. H. Lader (Ed.), *Studies of Schizophrenia: Papers Read at
the World Psychiatric Association Symposium, "Current Concepts of
Schizophrenia", London, November, 1972* (pp. 94–97). Ashford: Headley
Brothers.

Segal, H. (1994). Paranoid anxiety and paranoia. In: J. M. Oldham & S.
Bone (Eds.), *Paranoia: New Psychoanalytic Perspectives* (pp. 17–26).
Madison, CT: International Universities Press.

Semrad, E. V. (1966). Long-term therapy of schizophrenia: formulation
of the clinical approach. In: G. L. Usdin (Ed.), *Psychoneurosis
and Schizophrenia* (pp. 155–173). Philadelphia, Pennsylvania: J. B.
Lippincott.

Shakespeare, W. (ca. 1601). *The Riverside Shakespeare*. G. Blakemore Evans
(Ed.). Boston, MA: Houghton Mifflin Company, 1974.

Sharma, T., & Chitnis, X. (2000). *Brain Imaging in Schizophrenia: Insights and
Applications*. London: ReMedica.

Sharpley, M., Hutchinson, G., McKenzie, K., & Murray, R. M. (2001).
Understanding the excess of psychosis among the African-Caribbean
population in England: review of current hypotheses. *British Journal of
Psychiatry*, 178(Suppl. t40): s60–s68.

Shaw, T. C. (1889). The surgical treatment of general paralysis. *British
Medical Journal*, 16 November: 1090–1091.

Shengold, L. (1989). *Soul Murder: The Effects of Childhood Abuse and
Deprivation*. New Haven, CT: Yale University Press.

Shields, J., Heston, L. L., & Gottesman, I. I. (1975). Schizophrenia and the
schizoid: the problem for genetic analysis. In: R. R. Fieve, D. Rosenthal,
& H. Brill (Eds.), *Genetic Research in Psychiatry* (pp. 167–197). Baltimore,
MD: Johns Hopkins University Press.

Shin, L. M., McNally, R. J., Kosslyn, S. M., Thompson, W. L., Rauch, S. L., Alpert, N. M., Metzger, L. J., Lasko, N. B., Orr, S. P., & Pitman, R. K. (1999). Regional cerebral blow flow during script-driven imagery in childhood sexual abuse-related PTSD: a PET investigation. *American Journal of Psychiatry, 156*: 575–584.

Shin, L. M., Rauch, S. L., & Pitman, R. K. (2005). Structural and functional anatomy of PTSD: findings from neuroimaging research. In: J. J. Vasterling & C. R. Brewin (Eds.), *Neuropsychology of PTSD: Biological, Cognitive, and Clinical Perspectives* (pp. 59–82). New York: Guilford Press.

Shin, L. M., Wright, C. I., Cannistrato, P. A., Wedig, M. M., McMullin, K., Martis, B., Macklin, M. L., Lasko, N. B., Cavanagh, S. R., Krangel, T. S., Orr, S. P., Pitman, R. K., Whalen, P. J., & Rauch, S. L. (2005). A functional magnetic resonance imaging study of amygdala and medial prefrontal cortex responses to overtly presented fearful faces in posttraumatic stress disorder. *Archives of General Psychiatry, 62*: 273–281.

Shorter, E. (1997). *A History of Psychiatry: From the Era of the Asylum to the Age of Prozac*. New York: John Wiley.

Shorter, E., & Healy, D. (2007). *Shock Therapy: A History of Electroconvulsive Treatment in Mental Illness*. New Brunswick, NJ: Rutgers University Press.

Shuttleworth, G. E. (1904). Juvenile psychoses originating in whooping-cough. *British Journal of Children's Diseases, 1*: 143.

Shutts, D. (1982). *Lobotomy: Resort to the Knife*. New York: Van Nostrand Reinhold.

Silver, A.-L. S. (Ed.) (1989). *Psychoanalysis and Psychosis*. Madison, CT: International Universities Press.

Silverman, I. (1983). *Pure Types are Rare: Myths and Meanings of Madness*. New York: Praeger.

Sinason, V. (2001). Children who kill their teddy bears. In: B. Kahr (Ed.), *Forensic Psychotherapy and Psychopathology: Winnicottian Perspectives* (pp. 43–49). London: Karnac.

Slater, E. (1971). *Man, Mind, and Heredity: Selected Papers of Eliot Slater on Psychiatry and Genetics*, J. Shields & I. I. Gottesman (Eds.). Baltimore, MD: Johns Hopkins University Press.

Slater, E., & Cowie, V. (1971). *The Genetics of Mental Disorders*. London: Oxford University Press.

Smith, J., & Hucker, S. (1994). Schizophrenia and substance abuse. *British Journal of Psychiatry, 165*: 13–21.

Speers, R. W., & Lansing, C. (1965). *Group Therapy in Childhood Psychosis.* Chapel Hill, NC: University of North Carolina Press.

Spielrein, S. (1911). Über den psychologischen Inhalt eines Falles von Schizophrenie (Dementia Praecox). *Jahrbuch für psychoanalytische und psychopathologische Forschungen,* 3: 329–400.

Stefan, M. D., & Catalán, J. (1995). Psychiatric patients and HIV infection: a new population at risk? *British Journal of Psychiatry,* 167: 721–727.

Stern, E., & Silbersweig, D. A. (1998). Neural mechanisms underlying hallucinations in schizophrenia: the role of abnormal fronto-temporal interactions. In: M. F. Lenzenweger & R. H. Dworkin (Eds.), *Origins and Development of Schizophrenia: Advances in Experimental Psychopathology* (pp. 235–246). Washington, DC: American Psychological Association.

Stevens, J. R. (1982). Neurology and neuropathology of schizophrenia. In: F. A. Henn & H. A. Nasrallah (Eds.), *Schizophrenia as a Brain Disease* (pp. 112–147). New York: Oxford University Press.

Stockings, G. T. (1945). Schizophrenia in military psychiatric practice. *Journal of Mental Science,* 91: 110–112.

Stone, J. L. (2001). Dr. Gottlieb Burckhardt: the pioneer of psychosurgery. *Journal of the History of the Neurosciences,* 10: 79–92.

Stone, M. H. (1983). The history of the psychoanalytic treatment of schizophrenia: the early period. In: M. H. Stone, H. D. Albert, D. V. Forrest, & S. Arieti (Eds.), *Treating Schizophrenic Patients: A Clinico-Analytical Approach* (pp. 65–92). New York: McGraw-Hill.

Stone, M. H. (1991a). The psychodynamics of schizophrenia I: introduction and psychoanalysis. In: J. G. Howells (Ed.), *The Concept of Schizophrenia: Historical Perspectives* (pp. 125–151). Washington, DC: American Psychiatric Press.

Stone, M. H. (1991b). The psychodynamics of schizophrenia II: other contributors and discussion. In: J. G. Howells (Ed.), *The Concept of Schizophrenia: Historical Perspectives* (pp. 153–172). Washington, DC: American Psychiatric Press.

Stotsky, B. A., & Zolik, E. S. (1965). Group psychotherapy with psychotics: 1921–1963. A review. *International Journal of Group Psychotherapy,* 15: 321–344.

Strachey, G. L. (1956). Letter to Virginia Stephen, 3 January. In: L. Woolf & J. Strachey (Eds.) V. Woolf & L. Strachey. *Letters* (pp. 24–26). London: Hogarth Press/Chatto and Windus.

Strauss, J. S., & Carpenter, W. T. Jr (1981). *Schizophrenia.* New York: Plenum Medical Books.

Strean, H. (1976). A note on the treatment of schizophrenia. In: H. S. Strean (Ed.), *Crucial Issues in Psychotherapy* (pp. 280–288). Metuchen, NJ: Scarecrow Press.

Strean, H., & Freeman, L. (1990). *The Severed Soul: A Psychoanalyst's Heroic Battle to Heal the Mind of a Schizophrenic.* New York: St Martin's Press.

Sueuer, L. (1996). French psychiatrists on the causes of madness, 1800–1870: an ambiguous attitude before an epistemological obstacle. *History of Psychiatry, 8*: 267–275.

Sugarman, P. A., & Craufurd, D. (1994). Schizophrenia in the Afro-Caribbean community. *British Journal of Psychiatry, 164*: 474–480.

Sullivan, H. S. (1944). The language of schizophrenia. In: J. S. Kasanin (Ed.), *Language and Thought in Schizophrenia: Collected Papers. Presented at the Meeting of the American Psychiatric Association, May 12, 1939, Chicago, Illinois and Brought Up to Date* (pp. 4–16). Berkeley, CA: University of California Press.

Sullivan, H. S. (1953). *The Interpersonal Theory of Psychiatry,* H. S. Perry & M. L. Gawel (Eds.). New York: W. W. Norton.

Sullivan, P. F., Owen, M. J., O'Donovan, M. C., & Freedman, R. (2006). Genetics. In: J. A. Lieberman, T. S. Stroup, & D. O. Perkins (Eds.), *The American Psychiatric Publishing Textbook of Schizophrenia* (pp. 39–53). Washington, DC: American Psychiatric Publishing.

Sutherland, G. F., & Barnes, M. E. (1946). "Furlough" psychosis. *American Journal of Psychiatry, 102*: 670–673.

Sutton, D. G. (1940). Naval psychiatric problems. *American Journal of Psychiatry, 97*: 255–275.

Szasz, T. S. (1961). *The Myth of Mental Illness: Foundations of a Theory of Personal Conduct.* New York: Paul B. Hoeber / Medical Division, Harper Brothers.

Szasz, T. S. (1976). *Schizophrenia: The Sacred Symbol of Psychiatry.* New York: Basic Books.

Szasz, T. S. (2006). *"My Madness Saved Me": The Madness and Marriage of Virginia Woolf.* New Brunswick, NJ: Transaction.

Tandon, R., & Greden, J. F. (1991). Cholinergic excess and negative schizophrenic symptoms. In: J. F. Greden & R. Tandon (Eds.), *Negative Schizophrenic Symptoms: Pathophysiology and Clinical Implications* (pp. 99–111). Washington, DC: American Psychiatric Publishing.

Taylor, D. M. (2006). *Schizophrenia in Focus.* London: Pharmaceutical Press.

Thakore, J. H. (2005). Metabolic syndrome and schizophrenia. *British Journal of Psychiatry, 186*: 455–456.

Theodoropoulou-Vaidaki, S., Alexopoulos, C., & Stefanis, C. N. (1988). A study of the immunological state of schizophrenic patients. In: C. N. Stefanis & A. D. Rabavilas (Eds.), *Schizophrenia: Recent Biosocial Developments* (pp. 69–85). New York: Human Sciences Press.

Thiels, C. (2005). Obesity and schizophrenia. *British Journal of Psychiatry*, 187: 489.

Tierney, A. J. (2000). Egas Moniz and the origins of psychosurgery: a review commemorating the 50th anniversary of Moniz's Nobel Prize. *Journal of the History of the Neurosciences*, 9: 22–36.

Tiihonen, J., Lönnqvist, J., Wahlbeck, K., Klaukka, T., Niskanen, L., Tanskanen, A., & Haukka, J. (2009). 11-year follow-up of mortality in patients with schizophrenia: a population-based cohort study (FIN11 Study). *Lancet*, 22–28 August: 620–627.

Tomes, N. (1984). *A Generous Confidence: Thomas Story Kirkbride and the Art of Asylum-Keeping, 1840–1883*. Cambridge: Cambridge University Press.

Torrey, E. F. (1983). *Surviving Schizophrenia: A Family Manual*. New York: Harper and Row.

Trautman, E. C. (1971). Violence and victims in Nazi concentration camps and the psychopathology of the survivors. In: H. Krystal & W. G. Niederland (Eds.), *Psychic Traumatization: Aftereffects in Individuals and Communities* (pp. 115–133). Boston, MA: Little, Brown.

Tsuang, M. T. (1993). Genotypes, phenotypes, and the brain: a search for connections in schizophrenia. *British Journal of Psychiatry*, 163: 299–307.

Tsuang, M. T., Woolson, R. F., & Fleming, J. A. (1980). Causes of death in schizophrenia and manic-depression. *British Journal of Psychiatry*, 136: 239–242.

Valenstein, E. S. (1986). *Great and Desperate Cures: The Rise and Decline of Psychosurgery and Other Radical Treatments for Mental Illness*. New York: Basic Books.

Valenstein, E. S. (1998). *Blaming the Brain: The Truth About Drugs and Mental Health*. New York: Free Press.

Van Os, J., & Kapur, S. (2009). Schizophrenia. *Lancet*, 22–28 August: 635–645.

Van Os, J., & Selten, J.-P. (1998). Prenatal exposure to maternal stress and subsequent schizophrenia: the May 1940 invasion of The Netherlands. *British Journal of Psychiatry*, 172: 324–326.

Vaughn, C. E., & Leff, J. P. (1976). The influence of family and social factors on the course of psychiatric illness: a comparison of schizophrenic and depressed neurotic patients. *British Journal of Psychiatry*, 129: 125–137.

Vaughn, C. E., & Leff, J. P. (1981). Patterns of emotional response in rela-tives of schizophrenic patients. *Schizophrenia Bulletin, 7*: 43–44.

Venzlaff, U. (1964). Mental disorders resulting from racial persecution outside of concentration camps. *International Journal of Social Psychiatry, 10*: 177–183.

Venzlaff, U. (1968). Forensic psychiatry of schizophrenia in survivors. In: H. Krystal (Ed.), *Massive Psychic Trauma* (pp. 110–125). New York: International Universities Press.

Ver Eecke, W. (2006). A post-Lacanian view of psychosis. In: J. O. Johannessen, B. V. Martindale, & J. Cullberg (Eds.), *Evolving Psychosis: Different Stages, Different Treatments* (pp. 49–63). Hove: Routledge.

Vermetten, E., Lanius, R., & Bremner, J. D. (2008). Contributions of trau-matic stress studies to the neurobiology of dissociation and dissocia-tive disorders: implications for schizophrenia. In: A. Moskowitz, I. Schäfer, & M. J. Dorahy (Eds.), *Psychosis, Trauma and Dissociation: Emerging Perspectives on Severe Psychopathology* (pp. 221–238). Chichester: Wiley-Blackwell.

Vonnegut, M. (1975). *The Eden Express*. New York: Praeger.

Vyas, N. S., Patel, N. H., & Puri, B. K. (2011). Neurobiology and pheno-typic expression in early onset schizophrenia. *Early Intervention in Psychiatry, 5*: 3–14.

Waddington, J. L., O'Callaghan, E., Buckley, P., Madigan, C., Redmond, O., Stack, J. P., Kinsella, A., Larkin, C., & Ennis, J. T. (1995). Tardive dyskinesia in schizophrenia: relationship to minor physical anomalies, frontal lobe dysfunction and cerebral structure on magnetic resonance imaging. *British Journal of Psychiatry, 167*: 41–44.

Wahl, C. W. (1956). Some antecedent factors in the family histories of 568 male schizophrenics of the United States navy. *American Journal of Psychiatry, 113*: 201–210.

Wake, N. (2006). "The full story by no means all told": Harry Stack Sullivan at Sheppard-Pratt, 1922–1930. *History of Psychology, 9*: 325–358.

Walsh, E., Buchanan, A., & Fahy, T. (2002). Violence and schizophrenia: examining the evidence. *British Journal of Psychiatry, 180*: 490–495.

Walsh, M. (1985). *Schizophrenia: Straight Talk for Families and Friends*. New York: William Morrow.

Wehring, H. J., & Kelly, D. L. (2009). Sexual dysfunction and schizophre-nia. In: J. M. Meyer & H. A. Nasrallah (Eds.), *Medical Illness and Schizophrenia: Second Edition* (pp. 303–342). Arlington, VA: American Psychiatric Publishing.

Weinberger, D. R. (1995). Schizophrenia as a neurodevelopmental disorder. In: S. R. Hirsch & D. R. Weinberger (Eds.), *Schizophrenia* (pp. 293–323). Oxford: Blackwell Science.

Weiss, A. A., Winnik, H. Z., & Assael, M. (1961). One-year psychodiagnostic follow-up and clinical study of six cases of psychiatric complications after Asian influenza. *Psychiatria et Neurologia, 141*: 319–346.

Weiss, I. I. (1947a). Psychoses in military prisoners: Part I. *Journal of Clinical Psychopathology, 8*: 689–705.

Weiss, I. I. (1947b). Psychoses in military prisoners: Part II. *Journal of Clinical Psychopathology, 8*: 801–815.

Weisskopf-Joelson, E. (1988). *Father, Have I Kept My Promise? Madness as Seen from Within*. West Lafayette, IN: Purdue University Press.

Welldon, E. V. (2006). Personal communication to the author, 8 March.

Welldon, R. M. C. (1971). The "shadow-of-death" and its implications in four families, each with a hospitalized schizophrenic member. *Family Process, 10*: 281–300.

Wexler, M. (1951). The structural problem in schizophrenia: therapeutic implications. *International Journal of Psycho-Analysis, 32*: 157–166.

Whitehorn, J. C., & Betz, B. (1975). *Effective Psychotherapy with the Schizophrenic Patient*. New York: Jason Aronson.

Wiener, H. (1995). The genetics of preposterous conditions. In: C. A. Ross & A. Pam (Eds.), *Pseudoscience in Biological Psychiatry: Blaming the Body* (pp. 193–210). New York: John Wiley.

Wilkinson, M. (2010). *Changing Minds in Therapy: Emotion, Attachment, Trauma, and Neurobiology*. New York: W. W. Norton.

Will, O. A. Jr (1944). Psychoses in naval inductees with less than fifteen days' active duty. *United States Naval Medical Bulletin, 43*: 909–921.

Williamson, P. (2006). *Mind, Brain, and Schizophrenia*. New York: Oxford University Press.

Winkelman, J. W. (2001). Schizophrenia, obesity, and obstructive sleep apnea. *Journal of Clinical Psychiatry, 62*: 8–11.

Winnicott, D. W. (1943a). Prefontal leucotomy. *Lancet*, 10 April: 475.

Winnicott, D. W. (1943b). Shock treatment of mental disorder. *British Medical Journal*, 25 December: 829–830.

Winnicott, D. W. (1943c). Treatment of mental disease by induction of fits. In: C. Winnicott, R. Shepherd, & M. Davis (Eds.), *Psycho-Analytic Explorations* (pp. 516–521). London: Karnac, 1989.

Winnicott, D. W. (1944a). Shock therapy. *British Medical Journal*, 12 February: 234–235.

Winnicott, D. W. (1944b). Introduction to a symposium on the psycho-analytic contribution to the theory of shock therapy. In: C. Winnicott, R. Shepherd, & M. Davis (Eds.), *Psycho-Analytic Explorations* (pp. 525–528). London: Karnac, 1989.

Winnicott, D. W. (1944c). Kinds of psychological effect of shock therapy. In: C. Winnicott, R. Shepherd, & M. Davis (Eds.), *Psycho-Analytic Explorations* (pp. 529–533). London: Karnac, 1989.

Winnicott, D. W. (1945). Physical therapy in mental disorder. *British Medical Journal*, 22 December: 901–902.

Winnicott, D. W. (1947a). Physical therapy of mental disorder. *British Medical Journal*, 17 May: 688–689.

Winnicott, D. W. (1947b). Battle neurosis treated with leucotomy. *British Medical Journal*, 13 December: 974.

Winnicott, D. W. (1949a). Hate in the counter-transference. *International Journal of Psycho-Analysis*, 30: 69–74.

Winnicott, D. W. (1949b). Leucotomy. *British Medical Students' Journal*, 3(2): 35–38.

Winnicott, D. W. (1951a). Leucotomy in psychosomatic disorders. *Lancet*, 18 August: 314–315.

Winnicott, D. W. (1951b). Ethics of prefrontal leucotomy. *British Medical Journal*, 25 August: 496–497.

Winnicott, D. W. (1951c). Notes on the general implications of leucotomy. In: C. Winnicott, R. Shepherd, & M. Davis (Eds.), *Psycho-Analytic Explorations* (pp. 548–552). London: Karnac, 1989.

Winnicott, D. W. (1953). Symptom tolerance in paediatrics. *Proceedings of the Royal Society of Medicine*, 46: 675–684.

Winnicott, D. W. (1956). Prefrontal leucotomy. *British Medical Journal*, 28 January: 229–230.

Winnicott, D. W. (1963). Dependence in infant care, in child care, and in the psycho-analytic setting. *International Journal of Psycho-Analysis*, 44: 339–344.

Wolman, B. B. (1973). *Call No Man Normal*. New York: International Universities Press.

Wu, E. Q., Birnbaum, H. G., Shi, L., Ball, D. E., Kessler, R. C., Moulis, M., & Aggarwal, J. (2005). The economic burden of schizophrenia in the United States. *Journal of Clinical Psychiatry*, 66: 1122–1129.

Wyden, P. (1998). *Conquering Schizophrenia: A Father, His Son, and a Medical Breakthrough*. New York: Alfred A. Knopf.

Youssef, H. A., & Youssef, F. A. (1996). Evidence for the existence of schiz-ophrenia in medieval Islamic society. *History of Psychiatry*, 7: 55–62.

Zilboorg, G., & Henry, G. W. (1941). *A History of Medical Psychology*. New York: W. W. Norton.

Zwelling, S. S. (1985). *Quest for a Cure: The Public Hospital in Williamsburg, Virginia. 1773–1885*. Williamsburg, VA: Colonial Williamsburg Foundation.

CHAPTER THREE

Disorganized attachment and the therapeutic relationship with people in shattered states

Giovanni Liotti

D uring the clinical dialogue with some of the most severely troubled psychiatric patients, in those moments when the patient's state of mind is deeply shattered, it is vital to preserve the intersubjectivity of the experience from sinking into reciprocal withdrawal of attention and understanding. Empirical evidence and clinical reflections stemming from attachment theory might be of great assistance to psychotherapists engaged in the difficult task of maintaining an empathic understanding of their patients' states of mind when, during the clinical dialogue, they become fragmented and imbued with contradictory, dramatic emotions such as those indicated by quick shifts between expressions of hope and expressions of rage, sorrow, and fright.

The empirical inquiry into the intersubjective roots of severe psychiatric disorders, offering a well-researched theory contributing to the understanding of the therapeutic relationship with deeply traumatized patients, is among the most valuable legacies from John Bowlby's work. This chapter aims to introduce the reader to this aspect of attachment theory and research. It begins with a summary of the empirical evidence concerning the genesis of early attachment disorganization, proceeds to reviewing the evidence linking early disorganized attachment to adult psychopathology characterized by fragmentation of the self, and ends with a reflection on some of the implications of these empirical studies for psychotherapy.

Research into early disorganized attachment

Research into early attachment supports the statement that in the case of disorganization of attachment behaviour, attention and conscious experience might be a purely intersubjective event. Disorganization of infant attachment behaviour is statistically linked to unresolved traumas or losses in the caregiver (Main & Hesse, 1990; Van IJzendoorn, Schuengel, & Bakermans-Kranenburg, 1999), or to a caregiver's state of mind characterized by non-integrated hostile and helpless representations of the self and the attachment figures (Lyons-Ruth, Yellin, Melnick, & Atwood, 2003, 2005). The caregiver's states of mind that are related to infant attachment are assessed through the Adult Attachment Interview (AAI: Hesse, 1999). The caregivers' attitudes and behaviours that mediate between their unresolved/disaggregated states of mind and disorganization of infant attachment have been hypothesized to be frightening to the infant, either because these attitudes involve abrupt emotional and physical aggression, or because they express carers' fear, helplessness, and dissociative absorption in painful memories (Main & Hesse, 1990). Empirical evidence that not only aggressive attitudes, but also frightened and dissociative behaviour of the caregiver toward the infant can cause disorganization in the infant's attachment behaviour has been collected by Schuengel, Van IJzendoorn and Bakermans-Kranenburg (1999). The hypothesis that genetic factors might play a significant role in early attachment disorganization (Lakatos et al., 2000) has been refuted by more recent studies (Bakermans-Kranenburg & Van IJzendoorn, 2004; Bokhorst et al., 2003). Genetic factors could modulate the environmental influences that are responsible for infant attachment disorganization, but not be its direct cause.

Summarizing the evidence coming from empirical studies, we can assume that infant attachment disorganization is, at least in a substantial proportion of infants showing it, the outcome of purely intersubjective experiences linked to deficits in the regulation of emotion within the infant–parent dyad, and not to genetic risk factors or to overtly traumatic experiences (DeOliveira, Neufeld-Bailey, Moran, & Pederson, 2004; Hesse, Main, Abrams, & Rifkin, 2003; Lyons-Ruth, 2003). In other words, at least some instances of attachment disorganization are the outcome of subtle relational trauma (Schore, 2003), not adverse influences such as overt abuse or primary neurobiological anomalies.

Theories about the genesis of attachment disorganization

Attachment theory explains the origins of disorganized attachment behaviour in terms of conflict between two different inborn control systems, the attachment system and the fight/flight (i.e., defence) system. The attachment and the defence systems normally operate in harmony as exemplified in flight from the source of fear to find refuge in proximity to the attachment figure. However, where the caregiver is at the same time the source and the solution of the infant's fear, there is a clash (Liotti, 2004a,b). Being exposed to frequent interactions with a helplessly frightened, hostile, frightening, or confused caregiver, infants are caught in a relational trap: their defence system motivates them to flee from the frightened and/or frightening caregivers, while at the same time their attachment system motivates them, under the commanding influence of separation fear, to strive to achieve comforting proximity to them. Thus, the disorganized infant is bound to the experience of "fright without solution" (Cassidy & Mohr, 2001; Main & Hesse, 1990, p. 163).

This experience may be holistically understood as a type of early relational trauma that exerts an adverse influence on the development of the system in the infant's brain that copes with stress (Schore, 2003). A reductionist view of the genesis of attachment disorganization traces it back to the activity of an innate contingency detection module, whose function is to explore the environment in search of mirroring experiences (Koos & Gergely, 2001). In a deviant contingency environment such as the one created by a frightened and frightening caregiver, this module operates in a seriously dysfunctional manner. The unpredictable states of mind of the unresolved caregiver—whose moods and attitudes oscillate between availability, unwitting absorption in painful unresolved memories, fear and sometimes frightening aggression—may induce a rigidly operating flickering switch mechanism in the infant's contingency detection module. This switch oscillates between two dominant and competing targets for the infant's attention, one self-oriented and the other oriented toward the attachment figure (Koos & Gergely, 2001). The flickering switch mechanism causes a dissociative style of attention and information processing that researchers and theoreticians regard as typical of attachment disorganization (Liotti, 1992, 1999; Lyons-Ruth, 2003; Main & Morgan, 1996).

Early attachment disorganization and adult psychopathology

The empirical study of the sequelae of infant attachment disorganization, from early childhood to adolescence, has provided evidence that one consequence is the proneness toward dissociative experiences throughout development (Carlson, 1998; Hesse & Van IJzendoorn, 1999; Ogawa, Sroufe, Weinfield, Carlson, & Egeland, 1997). Other likely consequences of early attachment disorganization are deficits in emotional regulation (Conklin, Bradley, & Westen, 2006; DeOliveira, Neufeld-Bailey, Moran, & Pederson, 2004; Hesse, Main, Abrams, & Rifkin, 2003), in stress coping capacity (Schore, 2003; Spangler & Grossmann, 1999), in the control of aggressive impulses (Lyons-Ruth, 1996) and in the development of mentalization (Bateman & Fonagy, 2004; Fonagy, Target, Gergely, Allen, & Bateman, 2003). These findings support the hypothesis that attachment disorganization is a risk factor in the development of a wide range of psychiatric disorders, a hypothesis that is supported by an increasing number of clinical and empirical studies (for reviews, see Dozier, Stovall, & Albus, 1999; Levy, 2005).

Although early attachment disorganization is linked to the development of a wide range of *DSM* psychiatric diagnoses, it is essentially a dissociative process. Therefore, we could expect that it is statistically more strongly linked to disorders characterized by severe dissociation, splitting among ego states, and fragmentation of the self than to other psychiatric disorders (Howell, 2005; Liotti, 1992, 1995, 1999, 2004a). In support of this expectation, a recent controlled study found that the hostile–helpless, non-integrated states of mind that are typical of the caregivers of infants disorganized in their attachments are also significantly more frequent in the AAI of patients labelled as "borderline" than in the AAI of patients labelled as "dysthymic" (Lyons-Ruth, Melnick, Patrick, & Hobson, 2007).

Evidence compatible with the hypothesis of a particularly strong link between early attachment disorganization and disorders characterized by fragmentation of self-experience also comes from two other controlled studies. The first study (Liotti, Pasquini, & The Italian Group for the Study of Dissociation, 2000) explores the relationship between borderline personality disorder and severe traumas or losses suffered by mothers of adult patients two years before or after the patients' birth (a variable indicative of disorganized attachment). The second study explores the link between this variable and adult dissociative disorders (Pasquini et al., 2002; see also West, Adam, Spreng, & Rose, 2001). In the first study, a group of sixty-six borderline patients was matched with a control group composed of 146 psychiatric patients whose disturbances were not characterized by splitting or fragmentation of the self (anxiety disorders, affective disorders, and cluster C personality disorders). In the second study, the same control group was matched with a group of fifty-two patients suffering from dissociative disorders. Both the dissociative and the borderline group showed a higher frequency of major losses and severe traumas in the life of the patients' mothers in the two years preceding and following the patients' birth. The difference between the research group and the control group was statistically highly significant. In the light of the robust statistical evidence linking unresolved traumas and losses in the mother to attachment disorganization in the offspring (Van IJzendoorn, Schuengel, & Bakermans-Kranenburg, 1999), we could hypothesize that the specific pathogenic effect of traumas and losses in the life of the patients' mothers, fostering fragmentation and splitting of the self in the patients, is mediated by early disorganized attachment.

The two studies (Liotti, Pasquini, & The Italian Group for the Study of Dissociation, 2000; Pasquini et al., 2002) also examined the role of direct traumatic experiences during patients' childhoods in determining the dissociative or split features of patients' sense of self in comparison to the controls. In accordance with the extensive literature on this topic, childhood traumas proved to be a significant risk factor for adults labelled as having borderline and dissociative disorders. Statistically, losses and traumas in the lives of the mothers and childhood traumas in the borderline and dissociative patients' lives were independent risk factors in the genesis of their disorders. That is, in adult patients, the risk of developing a dissociative or a borderline personality disorder, rather than another type of mental disorder less bound to fragmentation of self experience is increased by two potentially independent past conditions:

1. the patient's mother was mourning a loss (or was dealing with a serious trauma) during the patient's infancy;
2. the patient's childhood had been plagued by severe traumatic experiences (e.g. sexual, emotional, or physical abuse).

The control group in the two case-control studies mentioned above excluded schizophrenic patients, because the authors wished to avoid the confounding effect of patients who, although diagnosed in different categories, borderline personality disorder and the dissociative disorders, were afflicted by at least equally shattered mental states. However, another study (Miti & Chiaia, 2003), compared a group of forty-one in-patients diagnosed as suffering from dissociative or borderline personality disorders and a group of sixty-two controls widely composed of schizophrenic in-patients (Miti & Chiaia, 2003, p. 30). Interestingly, the study by Miti and Chiaia found a high frequency of losses and traumas reported by the controls' mothers in the two years preceding and following the patient's birth. The hypothesis that early disorganized attachment plays a role in the development not only of adult borderline and dissociative disorders, but also of schizophrenic disorders seems a not unreasonable one. In support of this hypothesis, Tyrrell and Dozier (1997, quoted by Dozier, Stovall, & Albus, 1999, p. 510) found a high rate of unresolved AAI classifications in samples of schizophrenic patients (unresolved and hostile–helpless states of mind characterize, statistically, the attachment relationship between the caregivers and their disorganized infants). This finding might be interpreted as a consequence of the schizophrenic thought disorder influencing the patient's response to the AAI. However, it is also compatible with the hypothesis that disorganized attachment intervenes in the developmental pathways, leading to schizophrenic disorders.

It is important to emphasize that research on attachment and psychopathology supports the hypothesis that disorganized attachment is a general vulnerability factor rather than a specific risk factor for any single diagnostic category among the disorders listed by the *DSM* (for a review of studies hinting at this conclusion, see

Levy, 2005). One reason for this widespread influence of attachment disorganization in the genesis of psychiatric disorders could be that dissociative processes not only lie at the heart of *DSM* dissociative disorders, but might also be of significance in disorders that, according to the *DSM*, should be labelled psychotic and borderline. In addition, albeit at a latent level, dissociation might also be at the core of many other psychopathological developments, a point of view originally held by Pierre Janet that is now explored anew by psychoanalytic theorists such as Bromberg (2003) and Howell (2005). At any rate, disorders implying an immediately evident fragmentation of the self are a likely outcome, but not the only possible final step of psychopathological developments stemming from early attachment disorganization. However, I would argue that other risk factors must intervene during later development in determining the final, specific psychopathological outcome.

Pathways leading from early attachment disorganization to adult psychopathology

Bowlby (1973) suggested that the metaphor of branching railway lines could aptly represent his idea that multiple possible pathways can lead from any type of early attachment pattern either to mental health or to different types of psychopathology. Secure patterns of early attachment are more likely than other patterns to lead to mental health throughout development and during adulthood, while insecure patterns open up developmental pathways that tend to deviate from healthy outcomes in the direction of specific types of mental suffering. Any untoward pathway, however, can be gradually reversed towards mental health, and any favourable pathway can be left behind as a result of later negative influences, to follow the railroads leading to the development of psychopathology.

The psychiatric literature provides abundant evidence that childhood psychological traumas play a major role in paving the way toward adult disorders characterized by fragmentation of the self (for some recent reviews and critical comments on the role of traumas in dissociative, borderline, and schizophrenic disorders, see: Bradley, Jeney, & Westen, 2005; Briere, 2006). We might, therefore, assume that the pathways to these disorders, stemming from infant disorganized attachment, are characterized by traumatic experiences intervening after infancy. The central concept that allows for an understanding of such psychopathological developments is related to the reciprocal influence between pre-existing attachment patterns and later traumatic experiences, and to the fact that all types of mental pain, and intense prolonged mental pain in particular, activate the attachment system "from the cradle to the grave" (Bowlby, 1979, p. 129).

As a general rule, the quality of attachment is an important factor in children's capacity to resolve traumatic experiences, while at the same time traumas suffered at the hands of attachment figures throughout childhood and adolescence have a damaging effect on the quality of existing attachments (Lieberman, 2004). In terms of the organizational theories stemming from Piaget's work (Flavell, 1963), development is seen as a series of qualitative reorganizations: earlier patterns of adaptation provide the framework for later ones, and at the same time are transformed by them. Development is a cumulative process whereby early experiences are strongly influential on later ones, but do not determine them according to linear causality and might also be changed by them.

A pre-existing disorganized attachment is particularly likely to instigate dissociative reactions to new traumatic experiences (Cassidy & Mohr, 2001; Liotti, 2004a). Reciprocally, traumas inflicted on children by family members are likely to cause fright without solution throughout childhood and adolescence, and, therefore, to reinforce disorganization of earlier attachments, or to induce further attachment disorganization, both towards the abuser and towards other members of the family who fail to protect the victim.

The concept of internal working models (IWMs) is of crucial importance in understanding how early attachment experiences might influence responses to life events later in development. The IWM of early attachment is a structure of implicit memory (Amini et al., 1996): that is, it is hardly accessible to consciousness. It determines expectations about what is likely to happen in later attachment interactions. Life events that activate the attachment system also activate the IWM of attachment.

The reason why the activation of a disorganized IWM in response to mental pain is likely to yield dissociative responses is that this mental structure is intrinsically dissociated and yields catastrophic expectations linked to the experience of fright without solution. When traumas activate a disorganized IWM, both peritraumatic and post-traumatic dissociative experiences become extremely likely. Peri-traumatic dissociation predicts chronic post-traumatic stress disorder (Marmar et al., 1994). In contrast, the IWM of early secure attachment, providing an expectation of being soothed and helped by competent caregivers, reduces the likelihood of peritraumatic dissociation, and therefore acts as a protective factor against the development of chronic and complex types of trauma-related disorders (Liotti, 1999, 2004a).

A deeper understanding of the dynamic interactions between traumas and attachments in determining fragmentation of the self requires an enquiry into the early antecedents of the internal working model (IWM) of disorganized attachment, and detailed reflections on the controlling strategies developed by disorganized children before they reach school age.

The disorganized IWM and the development of controlling strategies

The disorganized IWM represents caregivers' responses to the child's need for help and comfort that are unpredictable, uncontrollable, and frightening without solution. It also represents switches in the child's state of mind that are equally uncontrollable and oscillate between the multiple polarities of desperate craving for protective closeness, fear, attachment anger, defensive rage, helplessness, and a tendency to invert the direction of the attachment relationship. George and Solomon (1999) convincingly argue for the inborn nature of the behavioural system that motivates primates, from an early age, to respond with concern and caregiving behaviours to cues of vulnerability and pain coming from members of the same species. When the caregivers' non-verbal attitudes hardly conceal, and might reveal in an all too obvious way, their painful reactions to unresolved memories of traumas and losses, their children are likely to experience in themselves the activation of the caregiving system, with its emotions of protectiveness and concern. Therefore, a disorganized child is likely to have an experience of the self during attachment interactions of at least three types of contradictory and reciprocally incompatible ways of responding: care-seeking, caregiving, and defensive fight/flight. With repeated experiences, these contradictory self–other interactions are then encoded in procedural memory and become the IWMs.

The IWM of disorganized attachment, therefore, contains a pattern of incompatible expectations of how others will respond to needs for help and comfort that are structurally multiple, non-integrated, and dramatic (Hesse, Main, Abrams, & Rifkin, 2003; Liotti, 1995, 1999, 2004a,b; Main, 1991; Main & Hesse, 1990). This conceptualization of the IWM of disorganized attachment is in keeping with observations of the states of mind of school age children and adults who are likely to have been disorganized infants (see Hesse, Main, Abrams, & Rifkin, 2003 for a review). Adults who report histories of traumatic attachments, and whose children have developed disorganized attachments towards them, typically show multiple, non-integrated dramatic representations of self and attachment figures, shifting between hostility, helplessness, and compulsive caregiving (Lyons-Ruth, Yellin, Melnick, & Atwood, 2003, 2005). Liotti (1995, 1999, 2004a,b) has suggested that this multiple, dramatic, and dissociated representation of self and attachment figures is captured, in a clinically useful way, by the metaphor of the "drama triangle", in which both self and significant others are represented, simultaneously or in quick sequence, according to three reciprocally incompatible roles: the helpless victim, the powerful–benevolent rescuer, and the equally powerful but malevolent persecutor (for the original description of the drama triangle, see Karpman, 1968).

The disorganized IWM, thus, is likely to yield multiple, dramatic, fragmented representations of self and others whenever it becomes active; that is, whenever the attachment behavioural system is triggered by loneliness, fear, or pain. This assumption, we should notice, does not imply that children who have been disorganized infants constantly show, during their development, dissociated, utterly incoherent and dysregulated mental states and behaviour in their interactions with other people. On the contrary, before they reach school age, the great majority of children who have been disorganized in their infant attachments develop an organized behavioural and attentional strategy towards their caregivers. They achieve such an organization by exerting active control over the parents' attention and behaviour, either through caregiving or through domineering–punitive strategies (Hesse, Main, Abrams, & Rifkin, 2003; Lyons-Ruth & Jacobvitz, 1999). These observations may be explained as follows (cf. Liotti, 2004a).

When a disorganized IWM dominates someone from infancy, the activities of the attachment system tend to be defensively inhibited throughout development, in order to protect both the child and his/her relationship with parents from the unbearably chaotic experience of disorganization. The relative inhibition of the attachment motivational system is achieved through co-opting another, equally inborn, interpersonal motivational system during the daily interactions with the caregiver: that is, another system tends to intervene instead of the attachment system to regulate the interactions between child and parent, so that behaviour and intersubjective experience can achieve at least a degree of organization. The activation of the caregiving system (George & Solomon, 1999) in the service of a defensive inhibition of the attachment system yields controlling–caregiving strategies in the child. The activation of dominance/submission strategies (ranking system: Gilbert, 1989; Sloman, Atkinson, Milligan, & Liotti, 2002) is at the base of controlling–punitive strategies.

While controlling–punitive and controlling–care–giving strategies have been well documented in the developmental studies of the sequelae of early attachment disorganization, there could be other strategies devised by some children in order to cope with the shattered states brought on by the activation of the disorganized IWM. For instance, one could hypothesize that some disorganized children resort to a general inhibition of relational needs and tend to withdraw from all types of close affective interaction, a response that might pave the way to schizoid personality disorder and to disorders in the schizophrenic spectrum. One could also hypothesize that some disorganized children resort, at times, to activation of the sexual system in order to deal defensively with attachment motivations and the activation of a disorganized IWM. Indeed, abnormal sexualization of parent–child interactions has been convincingly attributed, through evolutionary and anthropological analyses, to dysfunction of the attachment motivational system (Erickson, 2000).

The defensive activation of another motivational system in response to a disorganized IWM of attachment should not be construed as a purely intrapsychic process, or be related to the child's temperamental variables. Rather, the choice of the motivational system that defensively substitutes for the attachment system, or the inhibition of relational needs, is likely to be influenced by the caregivers' attitudes. Evidence supporting this hypothesis is beginning to emerge in the literature. For instance, parents who show frightened/ frightening behaviours towards their children are also more likely than other parents to display unusual arrays of submissive, care-seeking, violently domineering, and sometimes sexualized behaviours together with caregiving (Hesse, Main, Abrams, & Rifkin, 2003).

Shattered states and the collapse of controlling strategies

The competitively aggressive, caregiving, or sexualized interactions, substituting for the activation of the attachment system, limit the dissociating influence of the disorganized IWM on the child's current thought, emotion, and behaviour. However, they neither correct nor cancel the IWM of disorganized attachment in the child's mind, as becomes obvious when the child's attachment system is activated by conditions that are able to overcome its relative inhibition. For instance, six-year-old controlling children appear well orientated and organized in their thinking, behavioural, and attentional strategies until they are shown the pictures of a version of the Separation Anxiety Test (Main, Kaplan, & Cassidy, 1985). These pictures portray situations that are able powerfully to activate a child's attachment system (e.g., parents leaving a child alone). Once the system is thus activated, the formerly organized strategies of thought and behaviour collapse in the controlling children: the underlying disorganization of their mental operations is suddenly revealed by the unrealistic, catastrophic, and utterly incoherent narratives produced in response to the pictures (an illustration of these narratives may be found in Hesse, Main, Abrams, & Rifkin, 2003).

The collapse of the seemingly coherence-yielding strategy of controlling–disorganized children in the face of a powerful activation of the attachment system illustrates an important process in the pathogenesis of trauma-related disorders based on a disorganized IWM. The relative inhibition of the attachment system through the defensive activation of other equally inborn motivational systems (the caregiving or the social ranking system) allows for coherent styles of relating in people otherwise prone to shattered states. These relational styles can meet social approval and be appraised as pleasant and healthy (as often happens with controlling–caregiving children and adults), or, on the contrary, they can be regarded as problematic but not necessarily indicative of a disorder (as with controlling–punitive people). Adult survivors of childhood abuse and early attachment disorganization might, therefore, run lives that are not considered abnormal, either subjectively or by standard diagnostic psychiatric criteria, until the controlling strategy is forcefully suspended under the influence of a powerful stressor. This stressor need not necessarily be an obviously traumatic event. For example, changes in the balance of affectional bonds because of separations or the making of new bonds can activate the attachment system beyond the limit imposed on it by the controlling strategy. It is on these occasions that unmistakable psychopathological symptoms make their appearance. These symptoms imply the emotional dysregulation (Schore, 2003), the reduced mentalizing capacity (Bateman & Fonagy, 2004), the dissociative experiences (e.g., depersonalization) and the dramatic, non-integrated self-representations (Liotti, 1999, 2004a) that characterize the shattered states of mind typical of dissociative, borderline, and psychotic disorders.

A particularly clear non-clinical example of how dissociated self-representations (previously unnoticed both by the person and by his/her relatives and doctors) can appear in the context of an intense and durable activation of the attachment system is provided by the AAI transcripts coded "Cannot Classify" (CC: Hesse, 1996, 1999). Sometimes, the response of the person who is coded CC is formally indistinguishable, albeit clinically less intense, from the response of a patient diagnosed as suffering from a dissociative identity disorder (Steele & Steele, 2003). Research findings in keeping with the hypothesis that dissociative symptoms emerge from a strong activation of the attachment system are reported by a recent neuro-imaging study (Buchheim & George, 2011; Buchheim, George, Kächele, Erk, & Walter, 2006). Only subjects with unresolved disorganized attachment showed increasing activation of medial temporal regions, including the amygdala and the hippocampus, in the course of attachment activation caused by the pictures from the Adult Attachment Projective (AAP: George & West, 2001). This pattern was demonstrated especially at the end of the AAP task, where the pictures are drawn to portray traumatic situations. The abnormal pattern of brain activity during the AAP task might be explained by dissociative processes and emotional dysregulation produced as a consequence of the activation of a disorganized IWM.

An illustration of the collapse of a controlling strategy causing a seemingly delayed dissociative response to an early traumatic experience is provided by the following clinical example.

Clinical vignette: Diana

Diana, a thirty-two-year-old physician, had remembered throughout her life that her father had sexually abused her when she was a school age child. Her mother failed to protect her because she had suffered from recurrent major depression since well before Diana was born. (Maternal depression is a frequent antecedent of attachment disorganization in the infant: DeMulder & Radke-Yarrow, 1991; Teti, Gelfand, Messinger, & Isabella, 1995.) Memories of Diana's childhood suggest that it was very likely that, having been a baby disorganized in her attachment to her mother, she developed a controlling–caregiving strategy in the relationship with her. This strategy might have motivated an important aspect of Diana's reaction to the incest: she strove to safeguard her younger sister from her father's incestuous sexuality. For almost twenty years, she was convinced that she had been totally successful in this task. The controlling–caregiving strategy might also have motivated Diana's professional vocation. By devoting herself to preventing and alleviating other people's illnesses, she had been able to attribute meaning to her own sufferings.

As an adult, Diana never manifested either subjectively experienced or externally observable dissociative symptoms until she was thirty-two years old. She did suffer from recurrent depressive episodes from the time she was a medical student, which she treated through self-prescriptions of antidepressant drugs. The tendency to avoid asking for other people's help when she felt depressed is a sign of deactivation of the attachment system. Such deactivation is quite frequent in adults who have been disorganized in their childhood attachments (Main, Hesse, & Kaplan, 2005). When Diana was thirty-two years old, her sister, then twenty-six, told her that she, too, had been sexually abused by their father. Immediately thereafter, Diana started having problems with memory, concentration, and sleep (she had terrifying nightmares). She also experienced episodes of derealization and depersonalization: she had the uncanny feeling of impending grotesque transformations both of outside reality and of her own body.

The therapeutic relationship with people in shattered states

The role of disorganized attachment in the genesis of dissociative, borderline, and psychotic disorders invites us to trace the interpersonal difficulties of these patients back to the activation of the attachment system. At the root of these difficulties, according to attachment theory, there is a repetition of the situation which has led to the disorganized attachment: to relinquish the only relationship that appears capable of affording comfort from unbearable emotional pain is frightening, but to approach the same attachment figure is equally frightening. Each pole of this approach–avoidance dilemma increases the intensity of the painful emotions implied by the other, leading to repetition of the experience of unresolvable fear.

The reactivation of a disorganized (dissociated) IWM might also lead to disruption of the integrative functions of memory and consciousness, manifested by disorientation, depersonalization, or other feelings of unreality, and dramatic shifts between the representation of self and the attachment figure as an almost omnipotent rescuer, a persecutor/abuser, and a helpless victim. When these intolerable states of mind, related to the dramatic and multiple IWM, are experienced in the psychotherapy setting, they can make the therapeutic relationship unbearable to both partners, and force one or the other to interrupt the treatment prematurely.

Strains and ruptures in the therapeutic alliance can also be provoked by the attempts of patients to avoid the unpleasant experiences that accompany activation of the attachment system. Such an avoidance of attachment emotions might be obtained by rehearsing in the therapeutic dialogue familiar controlling strategies. The patients' mental state then shifts from attachment to another inborn motivational system, whose operations manifest themselves with partially similar emotions. For instance, patients might quickly shift from attachment anger (the type of anger characterizing the secure child's protest during separation from the mother) to competitive anger (ritualized aggression aimed at defining the social rank), thereby inhibiting the co-operative and the caregiving systems in the therapists (Liotti, 2004a,b). It is well known that the most complicated challenge arising in the treatment of these patients concerns how to deal with their tendency to externalize unbearable self-states, and the strong countertransference responses which this can produce (Bateman & Fonagy,

2004). That countertransferential fear and feelings of being over-whelmed are by no means unlikely events is evidenced by recent research data collected by Bradley and Westen (2005). Although the overt expression of these emotions can be controlled by the therapist, their presence can be apprehended by the patient at a non-verbal, implicit level. They act as reminders of the formerly frightened, and, therefore, frightening primary attachment figure. In turn, such an apprehension can retraumatize the patient by re-creating the relational atmosphere of attachment disorganization.

A further comment on the possible role played by attachment disorganization and its developmental sequelae in the relational diffi-culties of dissociative, borderline, and psychotic patients is crucial here. The shattered states that appear in the psychotherapy of these patients are closely related to impaired mentalization (Bateman & Fonagy, 2004), and such an impairment is contingent upon the activa-tion of the attachment system. This means that interventions requir-ing self-reflective abilities (such as psychodynamic interpretations) might not be understood properly by the patient, at least in the begin-ning phases of the treatment. On the other hand, therapists' empathic (or compassionate and solicitous) responses could open the road to intense activation of the patients' attachment system within the ther-apeutic relationship, and, therefore, to worsening of symptoms, further hindrance to the use of metacognitive abilities, and increasing relational difficulties in the clinical dialogue. This is illustrated by the following clinical example.

Clinical vignette: Ugo

Ugo asked for psychotherapy shortly after having been diagnosed, when he was twenty-seven years old, as suffering from primary pulmonary hypertension. PPH is a fatal disease that usually leads to death within five years of diagnosis. Its only treatment is a heart and lungs transplant which, although it is very often unsuccessful, is indi-cated when heart failure, usually about three years from the diagno-sis, becomes impending. Ugo had suffered from borderline person-ality disorder (BPD) since his late teens, when he began to consider suicide as a solution to his deep emotional suffering. A previous psychotherapy he had begun when he was twenty-three years old did not help him significantly. His reason for a new psychotherapy was to reconstruct his life experiences, in order to achieve a less vague and less unpleasant sense of self. "Before dying," he said, "I wish to know who I really am."

During the intake interview, Ugo stated quite clearly that he was planning to refuse the transplant. He had wished for years to put an end to his life, and now the prospect of dying came as a relief. His therapist usually followed the prescription of the dialectic–behavioural model of psychotherapy with suicidal BPD patients (Linehan, 1993), beginning psychotherapy only after the patients have signed a contract stating that they renounce committing suicide during the planned two years of treatment. However, to ask for such an explicit contract seemed insensible of Ugo's idea not to commit suicide, but simply to let his illness run its unavoidable course.

During the first months of psychotherapy Ugo idealized his therapist, who regarded this as the outward sign of a progressive activation of his patient's attachment system within the therapeutic relationship. Having reasons for expecting that the early IWM was disorganized (Ugo reported that his mother had suffered from recurrent major depression following her marriage), the therapist was looking for any sign in the clinical dialogue that could foretell a state of latent fear (the "fright without solution" of attachment disorganization). The therapist was able to detect only one such sign: the moist, cold hand he met while shaking hands at the end of each session. (In Italy, this is a customary equivalent of saying "goodbye" after each meeting with a person.) This could have been an indication of latent anxiety during the session, but it could also have been understood as a symptom of Ugo's poor circulatory and respiratory balance: therefore, the therapist decided not to comment on it.

During the fourth month of psychotherapy, explicit signs of discomfort suddenly appeared within the clinical dialogue. Ugo began to hint at the emerging idea that it was pointless to wait until the illness ran its fatal course. He repeatedly expressed self-attacking thoughts that grew in intensity session after session, until he finally stated, with convincing determination, that he had decided to kill himself soon. Every attempt the therapist made to express disagreement with Ugo's violent self-attacks, and to convince him to give up his suicidal intentions, was sternly rejected. However, notwithstanding his dismissal of the therapist's arguments, Ugo also said that his psychotherapeutic experience had been a very positive one, and that he wished to continue the dialogue until the very last days of his life: "I will come here till the very end, till I eventually kill myself."

The therapist thought that by assuming this suicidal attitude within the clinical dialogue, Ugo might unconsciously be testing a pathogenic belief (Weiss, 1993). He might believe himself to be such a bad person (the "persecutor" of the drama triangle characterizing the IWM of disorganized attachment) as to be an unbearable burden to any attachment figure, who would, therefore, feel relieved by his death. Ugo might have constructed this belief as a child, thinking that his mother's depression was caused by his misbehaviour. On the basis of such a hypothesis, the therapist decided to offer a strong refutation of this pathogenic belief. The therapist stated that he had tacitly accepted, at the beginning of the treatment, Ugo's expressed intention to refuse the transplant. Now, however, the therapist thought that such a tacit acceptance had been a mistake, and he wanted to correct it: the therapist asked explicitly for Ugo's commitment not only to renouncing suicide, but also to disposing himself to accept the prospect of the transplant. The reason the therapist offered for wanting to discuss this request was that life was more important than any relationship, however good the relationship might be, since there could be no possible relationship when there was no life any more. If, therefore, Ugo thought (as he seemed to do) that the relationship with the therapist was more important than his own life, their dialogue would be based on such a logical and affective paradox that it could not possibly be productive. In order to go on with their dialogue, this paradox would have to be dismissed by Ugo first accepting to live as long as possible.

Ugo reacted to the challenge with sheer rage, shouting that the therapist had betrayed him, and that he would quit the treatment. The therapist disagreed: since Ugo had not been able to refute the idea that to regard a relationship as more important than life is an unmanageable paradox, he would have to wait for Ugo's next scheduled appointment, and would remain committed to their joint enterprise. During the next session, Ugo restated vehemently his disappointment at having lost forever the possibility of a dialogue that had been so free and accepting as to have constituted the best experience in his life. The therapist replied that he was convinced that their dialogue would be better if it went on, at least until Ugo could prove that a dialogue could be more important than life. When Ugo and his therapist shook hands at the end of their meeting Ugo was still saying, "I'll not come to the next session". And then the therapist noticed that, for the first time since he had met Ugo, his patient's hand was warm and dry. Ugo's hand communicated that he had been, but was now no longer, afraid of meeting his therapist.

When Ugo idealized the therapist and seemed relatively serene in the clinical dialogue, he was harbouring a pathogenic belief linked to the activation of attachment dynamics. The therapist's empathic listening to Ugo's suffering had fostered the activation of the patient's attachment system within the therapeutic relationship, and the rehearsal, at an implicit or unconscious level of mental processing, of an IWM conveying the experience of fright without solution. Not having explicitly challenged Ugo's intention to avoid the transplant at the beginning of the treatment, the therapist had not provided any hint that could refute the pathogenic belief that attachment figures would have somehow welcomed Ugo's disappearance from their world. Now the belief had been efficiently refuted and Ugo, while feeling disappointed at the conscious level of mental activity, was experiencing, at the unconscious level, a secure attachment to his therapist.

Ugo's treatment proceeded without interruptions and without further idealization or devaluation of the therapist for the following four years, until the time when Ugo, who, in the meantime, had asked to be placed on a national waiting list for heart–lung transplants, died of heart failure before a suitable donor could be found.

Relational dilemmas and parallel interventions

On the basis of the above considerations, the role of attachment disorganization in the structure of mental disorders might be regarded as the source of relational dilemmas which are very difficult to resolve. One way of conceptualizing the relational dilemma brought to the psychotherapist by patients with histories of disorganized attachment and later traumas is to state that the patient oscillates between a "phobia of attachment" and an abnormally clinging dependency on the therapist (Steele, Van der Hart, & Nijenhuis, 2001). In these circumstances, the therapist feels that every clinical choice leads to a blind alley. Searching for meaning in the clinical dialogue might be the only way of increasing the clinging patients' sense of security and autonomy, but, at the same time, the very words used in such a quest for meaning might arouse terrifying memories of attachment trauma and lead to withdrawal (Blizard, 2001; Holmes, 2004).

Another conceptualization might be summarized as follows: while the patients' traumatic memories and disorganized IWM distort the construing of the therapeutic dialogue, the metacognitive deficit hampers the usefulness of psychodynamic interpretations (Bateman & Fonagy, 2004). A third conceptualization focuses on the predictable failure both of an empathic approach and of a more detached interpretative approach: the therapist's empathic attitude could foster the activation of the disorganized IWM, while more emotionally detached interpretations of the meaning of transferential–countertransferential responses could be perceived as repetition of the indifference, or even neglect, of former attachment figures.

Since these dilemmas are linked to the dynamics between disorganized attachment and defensive, controlling strategies involving the caregiving, the ranking, and the sexual systems, therapists might try to solve them by resorting to relational approaches that foster co-operative exchanges (for a discussion of the basic motivational systems that regulate human interactions, see Gilbert, 2000). The co-operative motivational system is the only one with an evolved base that is not negatively influenced by early attachment disorganization and its developmental sequelae (Farina & Liotti, 2005; Liotti, Cortina, & Farina, 2008). Therefore, therapists should strive for a dialectical balance between sympathetic emotional closeness and a more egalitarian co-operative attitude of exploration and co-construction of new meanings. The knowledge of attachment disorganization is instrumental in achieving this balance, both in individual psychotherapy and in parallel integrated interventions, where the treatment is conducted by different clinicians operating in separate settings (e.g., individual and group settings, as in dialectical behaviour therapy and in mentalization-based psychotherapy of BPD: Bateman & Fonagy, 2004; Linehan, 1993). When the exercise of co-operative interactions has yielded sufficient corrective relational experiences and related insights, the IWM of disorganized attachment can be consciously revised within the therapeutic dialogue.

Parallel integrated treatments, such as dialectical–behavioural and mentalization-based therapies for borderline patients (Bateman & Fonagy, 2004; Linehan, 1993), offer interesting opportunities for co-operative patient–therapist interactions, as I will discuss later on. It is noteworthy that having two therapists operating in two parallel settings is held as useful by the guidelines of the American Psychiatric Association (2001) for the treatment of borderline personality disorder. Whatever types of treatment are simultaneously provided (individual psychotherapy and pharmachotherapy, individual psychotherapy and family therapy, individual and group psychotherapy) the co-ordination of two (or more) therapists operating in parallel settings might prove superior to any single setting in coping successfully with the relational strains characterizing the therapeutic relationship with these severely traumatized patients (Corcos, 2005; Farina & Liotti, 2005; Liotti, Cortina, & Farina, 2008; Vaslamatzis, Coccossis, Zervis, Panagiotopoulou & Chatziandreu, 2004).

The usefulness of the two-therapist model can be explained if we consider the basic dynamics of the attachment system. Where two therapists are involved in a patient's treatment, it might be less likely that the patient's disorganized IWM, and the relational dilemmas linked to it, will be activated. For instance, as the primary therapist's holidays are foreseen, the contingent security offered by the presence of a second source of potential help could reduce the emotional strain that would otherwise impinge on the first therapeutic relationship as a result of separation anxiety and the subsequent activation of the disorganized IWM.

The two-therapist model, however, has its difficulties, since it may easily become "a recipe for dangerous splitting with one professional being idealised and the other denigrated" (Bateman & Fonagy, 2004, p. 146). If parallel integrated treatments are to achieve corrective relational experiences rather than instigate dangerous splitting, the two (or more) therapists operating in the parallel settings must share theoretical agreement, must be able to co-operate on an equal basis, and must regularly exchange information about the outcomes of their interventions (Bateman & Fonagy, 2004; Farina & Liotti, 2005; Linehan, 1993; Liotti, Cortina, & Farina, 2008).

Parallel interventions, provided that they are thus organized as "one-team interventions" (Bateman & Fonagy, 2004), offer precious opportunities for corrective relational experiences that do not require in advance the use of mentalization capacities, but can foster their development. Fonagy and his collaborators have repeatedly and convincingly argued that attachment-related traumatic experiences and their rehearsal within the therapeutic relationship seriously impede the capacity to reflect on one's own and the other's state of mind (Bateman & Fonagy, 2004; Fonagy, Target, Gergely, Allen, & Bateman, 2003). This happens because the patient automatically construes the mind of the other as containing destructive intentions against their own mind, a deeply negative interpersonal schema that is rather easily activated by a disorganized IWM. While the relational strain within the primary therapeutic relationship hinders the patient's mentalization, the second therapist can assist the patient in construing alternative hypotheses about the primary therapist's beliefs and intentions. Perceiving the same interpersonal episode simultaneously from different perspectives improves both the complexity of internal representations of self and others and the capacity to reflect upon them. The less threatening interpersonal context the patient might perceive within the second therapeutic setting could facilitate a better understanding of mental states. In turn, this could have a positive feedback effect on the capacity to tolerate and modulate unpleasant emotions. This widened capacity for considering alternative hypotheses about the first therapist's mental state, and for modulating and tolerating unpleasant emotions, might protect the primary therapeutic relationship from premature interruption and therapeutic stalemates.

Another therapeutic effect of parallel integrated treatments on the patient's mentalizing capacity is linked to the possibility of presenting to the patient, within different relationships, coherent representations of self and others. Psychoanalytic orientated therapists suggest that the possibility of two therapists offering the patient a coherent perception of "self-with-other" might have a corrective effect on the splitting defence mechanism, quite typical of BPD. The partial, split representation that could appear in each of the two settings might become more easily integrated when the comments or interpretations of the two therapists converge towards the same view of what is happening (Bateman & Fonagy, 2004; Gunderson, 2001; Vaslamatzis, Coccossis, Zervis, Panagiotopoulou & Chatziandreu, 2004).

The knowledge of attachment dynamics suggests a further, particularly promising, way of dealing with situations where the patient idealizes one therapist—construed as the "rescuer" according to one aspect of a disorganized IWM—and devalues or fears the other, construed as helplessly vulnerable ("victim") or as threatening ("persecutor"), according to the other basic aspects of the same IWM. The idealized therapist, rather than commenting on the patient's de-valuation of the other therapist, strives to co-operate on equal grounds with the patient toward the very same goal that is now hindered in the relationship with the second therapist. In order to pursue this goal, it is mandatory that the idealized therapist not only avoids taking sides, however subtly, with the patient against the second therapist, but also limits classic psychoanalytic interpretations on the reported problems in the other therapeutic relationship. The reason for this is that interpretations might be understood by the patient as evidence that the idealized therapist knows better than the other one, which would disrupt the goal of preserving co-operation on equal terms as a main objective of all the people involved in these parallel settings. The activation of co-operative social states of mind (Gilbert, 2000), rather than attachment, caregiving, or competitive/ranking states of mind, preserves the therapeutic relationship both from the enactment of the disorganized IWM and from the defensive controlling strategies by which it is usually dealt with.

Finally, another important positive effect of multiple settings inte-grated treatments is the therapist's increased sense of security. BDP patients, especially those with aggressive, impulsive behaviours, quite often evoke very difficult feelings in their therapists. Fear, anger, a sense of deep impotence, and a wish to discontinue the therapy are therapists' responses not uncommonly experienced during the treat-ment of severe BDP (Bradley & Westen, 2005). If these countertrans-ferential reactions are expressed (however subtly), they retraumatize the patient by reproducing at least one aspect of the interpersonal situ-ation that originally yielded disorganization of attachment: a fragile, fragmented self meeting a vulnerable, frightened attachment figure (Liotti, Cortina, & Farina, 2008). The involvement of a second, co-oper-ating clinician in the therapy of these severely traumatized patients can reduce the emotional strain on the first therapist, in so far as it allows for the sharing of difficulties, worries, and responsibilities (Gunderson, 2001; Liotti, Cortina, & Farina, 2008; Vaslamatzis, Coccossis, Zervis, Panagiotopoulou & Chatziandreu, 2004).

Conclusion

Attachment theory provides us with a conceptual framework that allows for a developmental understanding of the dynamic and intersubjective processes capable of causing shattered self-states from the early attachment relationship to later traumatic interactions and to the relationships that should repair the experience of the self. In these repairing relationships, the presence of two (or more) therapists in parallel but integrated settings might provide important opportunities for three major goals: (1) modulating and diluting the activation of the attachment system (and, thereby, allowing for better coping with the approach–avoidance dilemma typical of attachment disorganization); (2) improving mentalization (by mirroring the representations of "self-with-others" in more than one relationship); (3) increasing the sense of security of the therapist while dealing with patients who might become completely dysregulated and then might lash out in fear.

Thus, instead of repeating the tragic interpersonal cycle of the original attachment trauma, risking the provocation of defensive controlling behaviour and producing shattered states due to the retraumatizing collapse of controlling strategies, new roads of intersubjective experience can be opened up more easily in the context of a new attachment relationship.

References

American Psychiatric Association (2001). Practice guideline for the treatment of patients with borderline personality disorder. *American Journal of Psychiatry, 158*(Oct. Suppl.): 1–52.

Amini, F., Lewis, T., Lannon, R., Louie, A., Baumbacher, G., McGuinnes, T., & Zirker, E. (1996). Affect, attachment, memory: contributions toward psychobiologic integration. *Psychiatry, 59*: 213–239.

Bakermans-Kranenburg, M. J., & Van IJzendoorn, M. H. (2004). No association of the dopamine D4 receptor (DRD4) and -521 C/T promotor polymorphism with infant attachment disorganization. *Attachment and Human Development, 6*: 211–219.

Bateman, A. W., & Fonagy, P. (2004). *Psychotherapy for Borderline Personality Disorder: Mentalization-Based Treatment*. New York: Oxford University Press.

Blizard, R. A. (2001). Masochistic and sadistic ego states: dissociative solutions to the dilemma of attachment to an abusive caregiver. *Journal of Trauma & Dissociation, 2*: 37–58.

Bokhorst, C. L., Bakermans-Kranenburg, M. J., Fearon, P., Van IJzendoorn, M. H., Fonagy, P., & Schuengel, C. (2003). The importance of shared environment in mother-infant attachment security: a behavioural-genetic study. *Child Development, 74*: 1769–1782.

Bowlby, J. (1973). *Attachment and loss: Vol. 2, Separation*. London: Hogarth Press.

Bowlby, J. (1979). *The Making and Breaking of Affectional Bonds*. London: Tavistock.

Bradley, R., & Westen, D. (2005). The psychodynamics of borderline personality disorder: a view from developmental psychopathology. *Development and Psychopathology, 17*: 927–957.

Bradley, R., Jeney, J., & Westen, D. (2005). Etiology of borderline personality disorder: disentangling the contributions of intercorrelated antecedents. *Journal of Nervous and Mental Disease, 193*: 24–31.

Briere, J. (2006). Dissociative symptoms and trauma exposure: specificity, affect disregulation and post-traumatic stress. *Journal of Nervous and Mental Disease, 194*: 78–82.

Bromberg, P. (2003). Something wicked this way comes. Trauma, dissociation and conflict: the space where psychoanalysis, cognitive science and neuroscience overlap. *Psychoanalytic Psychology, 20*: 558–574.

Buchheim, A., & George, C. (2011). The representational and neurobiological foundations of attachment in borderline personality disorder. In: J. Solomon & C. George (Eds.), *Disorganized Attachment and Caregiving* (pp. 343–382). New York: Guilford Press.

Buchheim, A., George, C., Kächele, H., Erk, S., & Walter, H. (2006). Measuring attachment representation in an fMRI environment: concepts and assessment. *Psychopathology, 39*: 136–143.

Carlson, E. A. (1998). A prospective longitudinal study of disorganized/disoriented attachment. *Child Development, 69*: 1970–1979.

Cassidy, J., & Mohr, J. J. (2001). Unsolvable fear, trauma and psychopathology: theory, research and clinical considerations related to disorganized attachment across the life cycle. *Clinical Psychology: Science and Practice, 8*: 275–298.

Conklin, C. Z., Bradley, R., & Westen, D. (2006). Affect regulation in borderline personality disorder. *Journal of Nervous and Mental Disease, 194*: 69–77.

Corcos, M. (2005). Bifocal therapy for borderline personality disorders in adolescence: a psychodynamic perspective. *Clinical Neuropsychiatry, 2*: 270–276.

DeMulder, E. K., & Radke-Yarrow, M. (1991). Attachment with affectively ill and well mothers: concurrent behavioral correlates. *Development and Psychopathology, 3*: 227–242.

DeOliveira, C. A., Neufeld-Bailey, H., Moran, G., & Pederson, D. R. (2004). Emotion socialization as a framework for understanding the development of attachment disorganization. *Social Development, 13*: 437–467.

Dozier, M., Stovall, K. C., & Albus, K. E. (1999). Attachment and psychopathology in adulthood. In: J. Cassidy & P. R. Shaver (Eds.), *Handbook of Attachment*. (pp. 497–519). New York: Guilford.

Erickson, M. T. (2000). The evolution of incest avoidance: Oedipus and the psychopathology of kinship. In: P. Gilbert & K. G. Bailey (Eds.), *Genes on The Couch* (pp. 211–231). Hove: Brunner-Routledge.

Farina, B., & Liotti, G. (2005). Two therapists for one patient: attachment theory as a framework for co-therapies in the treatment of borderline patients. *Clinical Neuropsychiatry, 2*: 260–269.

Flavell, J. (1963). *The Developmental Psychology of Jean Piaget*. New York: Nostrand.

Fonagy, P., Target, M., Gergely, G., Allen, J. G., & Bateman, A. W. (2003). The developmental roots of borderline personality disorder in early attachment relationships: a theory and some evidence. *Psychoanalytic Inquiry, 23*: 412–459.

George, C., & Solomon, J. (1999). Attachment and caregiving: the caregiving behavioral system. In: J. Cassidy & P. R. Shaver (Eds.), *Handbook of Attachment* (pp. 649–671). New York: Guilford.

George, C., & West, M. (2001). The development and preliminary validation of a new measure of adult attachment: the Adult Attachment Projective. *Attachment and Human Development, 3*: 55–86.

Gilbert, P. (1989). *Human Nature and Suffering*. London: LEA.

Gilbert, P. (2000). Social mentalities: internal 'social' conflict and the role of inner warmth and compassion in cognitive therapy. In: P. Gilbert & K. G. Bailey (Eds.), *Genes on The Couch* (pp. 118–150). Hove: Brunner-Routledge.

Gunderson, J. G. (2001). *Borderline Personality Disorder: A Clinical Guide*. Washington, DC: American Psychiatric Association.

Hesse, E. (1996). Discourse, memory and the Adult Attachment Interview: a note with emphasis on the emerging cannot classify category. *Infant Mental Health Journal, 17*: 4–11.

Hesse, E. (1999). The Adult Attachment Interview: historical and current perspectives. In: J. Cassidy & P. R. Shaver (Eds.), *Handbook of Attachment* (pp. 395–433). New York: Guilford Press.

Hesse, E., & Van IJzendoorn, M. H. (1999). Propensities toward absorption are related to lapses in the monitoring of reasoning or discourse during the Adult Attachment Interview: a preliminary investigation. *Attachment and Human Development, 1*: 67–91.

Hesse, E., Main, M., Abrams, K. Y., & Rifkin, A. (2003). Unresolved states regarding loss or abuse can have "second-generation" effects: disorganized, role-inversion and frightening ideation in the offspring of traumatized non-maltreating parents. In: D. J. Siegel & M. F. Solomon (Eds.), *Healing Trauma: Attachment, Mind, Bbody and Brain* (pp. 57–106). New York: Norton.

Holmes, J. (2004). Disorganised attachment and borderline personality disorder: a clinical perspective. *Attachment & Human Development, 6*: 181–190.

Howell, E. F. (2005). *The Dissociative Mind.* London: Analytic Press.

Karpman, S. (1968). Fairy tales and script drama analysis. *Transactional Analysis Bulletin, 7*: 39–43.

Koos, O., & Gergely, G. (2001). A contingency-based approach to the etiology of "disorganized" attachment: the "flickering switch" hypothesis. *Bulletin of the Menninger Clinic, 65*: 397–410.

Lakatos, K., Toth, I., Nemoda, Z., Ney, K., Sasvari, M., & Gervai, J. (2000). Dopamine D4 receptor gene polymorphism is associated with attachment disorganization in infants. *Molecular Psychiatry, 5*: 633–637.

Levy, K. N. (2005). The implications of attachment theory and research for understanding borderline personality disorder. *Development and Psychopathology, 17*: 959–986.

Lieberman, A. F. (2004). Traumatic stress and attachment: reality and internalization in disorders of infant mental health. *Infant Mental Health Journal, 25*: 336–351.

Linehan, M. M. (1993). *Cognitive-behavioral Treatment of Borderline Personality Disorder.* New York: Guilford Press.

Liotti, G. (1992). Disorganized/ disoriented attachment in the etiology of the dissociative disorders. *Dissociation, 5*: 196–204.

Liotti, G. (1995). Disorganized/disoriented attachment in the psychotherapy of the dissociative disorders. In: S. Goldberg, R. Muir & J. Kerr (Eds.), *Attachment Theory: Social, Developmental and Clinical Perspectives* (pp.343–363). Hillsdale, NJ: Analytic Press.

Liotti, G. (1999). Understanding the dissociative processes: the contribution of attachment theory. *Psychoanalytic Inquiry, 19*: 757–783.

Liotti, G. (2004a). Trauma, dissociation and disorganized attachment: three strands of a single braid. *Psychotherapy: Theory, Research, Practice, Training, 41*: 472–486.

Liotti, G. (2004b). The inner schema of borderline states and its correction during psychotherapy: a cognitive–evolutionary approach. In: P. Gilbert (Ed.), *Evolutionary Theory and Cognitive Psychotherapy* (pp. 137–160). New York: Springer.

Liotti, G., Cortina, M., & Farina, B. (2008). Attachment theory and the multiple integrated treatments of borderline patients. *Journal of the American Academy of Psychoanalysis and Dynamic Psychiatry*, 36: 293–312.

Liotti, G., Pasquini, P., & The Italian Group for the Study of Dissociation (2000). Predictive factors for borderline personality disorder: patients' early traumatic experiences and losses suffered by the attachment figure. *Acta Psychiatrica Scandinavica*, 102: 282–289.

Lyons-Ruth, K. (1996). Attachment relationships among children with aggressive behaviour problems: the role of disorganized early attachment patterns. *Journal of Consulting and Clinical Psychology*, 64: 64–73.

Lyons-Ruth, K. (2003). Dissociation and the parent–infant dialogue: a longitudinal perspective from attachment research. *Journal of the American Psychoanalytic Association*, 51: 883–911.

Lyons-Ruth, K., & Jacobvitz, D. (1999). Attachment disorganization: unresolved loss, relational violence and lapses in behavioral and attentional strategies. In: J. Cassidy & P. R. Shaver (Eds.), *Handbook of Attachment* (pp. 520–554). New York: Guilford Press.

Lyons-Ruth, K., Melnick, S., Patrick, M., & Hobson, P. R. (2007). A controlled study of hostile-helpless states of mind among borderline and dysthimic women. *Attachment and Human Development*, 9: 1–16.

Lyons-Ruth, K., Yellin, C., Melnick, S., & Atwood, G. (2003). Childhood experiences of trauma and loss have different relations to maternal unresolved and hostile-helpless states of mind on the AAI. *Attachment and Human Development*, 5: 330–352.

Lyons-Ruth, K., Yellin, C., Melnick, S., & Atwood, G. (2005). Expanding the concept of unresolved mental states: hostile/helpless states of mind on the Adult Attachment Interview are associated with disrupted mother–infant communication and infant disorganization. *Development and Psychopathology*, 17: 1–23.

Main, M. (1991). Metacognitive knowledge, metacognitive monitoring, and singular (coherent) versus multiple (incoherent) models of attachment. In: C. M. Parkes, J. Stevenson-Hinde, & P. Marris (Eds.), *Attachment Across the Life Cycle* (pp. 127–160). London: Routledge.

Main, M., & Hesse, E. (1990). Parents' unresolved traumatic experiences are related to infant disorganized attachment status: is frightened and/or frightening parental behavior the linking mechanism? In: M. T. Greenberg, D. Cicchetti, & E. M. Cummings (Eds.), *Attachment in the Preschool Years* (pp. 161–182). Chicago, IL: Chicago University Press.

Main, M., & Morgan, H. (1996). Disorganization and disorientation in infant strange situation behavior: phenotypic resemblance to dissociative states? In: L. Michelson & W. Ray (Eds.), *Handbook of Dissociation* (pp. 107–137). New York: Plenum Press.

Main, M., Hesse, E., & Kaplan, N. (2005). Predictability of attachment behaviour and representation processes at 1, 6 and 19 years of age. In: K. E. Grossman & K. Grossman (Eds.), *Attachment From Infancy to Adulthood: The Major Longitudinal Studies* (pp. 245–304). New York: Guilford.

Main, M., Kaplan, K., & Cassidy, J. (1985). Security in infancy, childhood and adulthood: a move to the level of representation. *Monographs of the Society for Research in Child Development, 50*: 66–104.

Marmar, C. R., Weiss, D. S., Schlenger, W. E., Fairbank, J. A., Jordan, B. K., Kulka, R. A., & Hough, R. L. (1994). Peritraumatic dissociation and posttraumatic stress in male Vietnam theater veterans. *American Journal of Psychiatry, 151*: 902–907.

Miti, G., & Chiaia, E. (2003). Patterns of attachment and the etiology of dissociative disorders and borderline personality disorder. *Journal of Trauma Practice, 2*(2): 19–35.

Ogawa, J. R., Sroufe, L. A., Weinfield, N. S., Carlson, E. A., & Egeland, B. (1997). Development and the fragmented self: longitudinal study of dissociative symptomatology in a nonclinical sample. *Development and Psychopathology, 9*: 855–879.

Pasquini, P., Liotti, G., Mazzotti, E., Fassone, G., Picardi, A., & The Italian Group for the Study of Dissociation (2002). Risk factors in the early family life of patients suffering from dissociative disorders. *Acta Psychiatrica Scandinavica, 105*: 110–116.

Schore, A. N. (2003). *Affect Dysregulation and the Disorders of the Self.* New York: Norton.

Schuengel, C., Van IJzendoorn, M., Bakermans-Kranenburg, M. (1999). Frightening maternal behavior linking unresolved loss and disorganized infant attachment. *Journal of Consulting and Clinical Psychology, 67*: 54–63.

Sloman, L., Atkinson, L., Milligan, K., & Liotti, G. (2002). Attachment, social rank, and affect regulation: speculations on an ethological approach to family interaction. *Family Process, 41*: 479–493.

Spangler, G., & Grossmann, K. (1999). Individual and physiological correlates of attachment disorganization in infancy. In: J. Solomon & C. George (Eds.), *Attachment Disorganization* (pp. 95–126). New York: Guilford.

Steele, H., & Steele, M. (2003). Clinical uses of the Adult Attachment Interview. In: M. Cortina & M. Marrone (Eds.), *Attachment Theory and the Psychoanalytic Process* (pp.107–126). London: Whurr.

Steele, K., Van der Hart, O., & Nijenhuis, E. R. (2001). Dependency in the treatment of complex posttraumatic stress disorder and dissociative disorders. *Journal of Trauma & Dissociation*, 2: 79–115.

Teti, D. M., Gelfand, D. M., Messinger, D. S., & Isabella, R. (1995). Maternal depression and the quality of early attachment: an examination of infants, preschoolers and their mothers. *Developmental Psychology*, 34: 361–376.

Van IJzendoorn, M. H., Schuengel, C., & Bakermans-Kranenburg, M. J. (1999). Disorganized attachment in early childhood: meta-analysis of precursors, concomitants and sequelae. *Development and Psychopathology*, 11: 225–250.

Vaslamatzis, G., Coccossis, M., Zervis, C., Panagiotopoulou, V., & Chatziandreu, M. (2004). A psychoanalytically oriented combined treatment approach for severely disturbed borderline patients. *Bulletin of the Menninger Clinic*, 68: 337–349.

Weiss, J. (1993). *How Psychotherapy Works*. New York: Guilford Press.

West, M., Adam, K., Spreng, S., & Rose, S. (2001). Attachment disorganization and dissociative symptoms in clinically treated adolescents. *Canadian Journal of Psychiatry*, 46: 627–631.

CHAPTER FOUR

Shattered shame states and their repair

Judith Lewis Herman

Introduction: shame and the attachment bond

The primate relational systems for attachment, caregiving, mating, social ranking, inclusion, exclusion, and co-operation form a platform upon which complex human social life is built. Under ordinary conditions of peace, I would suggest that shame is one of the primary regulators of social relations. Fear is the primary regulator only in circumstances where social structures for maintaining peace have broken down and social relations are ruled by violence.

As the attachment system was initially conceptualized by Bowlby (1973), fear was considered the primary regulator. Bowlby described anxiety and anger as the infant's emotional responses to separation, and crying, following, and clinging as behavioural responses. As a good Darwinian, he saw the adaptive function of the attachment system in maintaining the infant's proximity to the caretaker, thus affording protection. This basic attachment system is common to human beings and other primates.

On the platform of this attachment bond are built the child's first internal working models of human intimacy. In primary attachment relationships, the child learns to imagine other minds and to be in dialogue with beloved caretakers. Hennighausen and Lyons-Ruth (2005) propose that as humans have evolved "from biologic to dialogic" relational modes, the attachment system has been "partially displaced from its primate base". Emotional sharing and signalling become the primary mode for regulating security of attachment. The infant preferentially seeks out the caregiver who best knows her mind and is most attuned to her emotional signals. She also learns to imagine how others think of her, to become self-conscious.

While major disruptions in the attachment system produce fear, by the second year of life the child reacts to more subtle disruptions with shame. Trevarthen (2005) speaks of "the feeling of shame in failure that threatens loss of relationship and hopeless isolation". Schore (1998) conceptualizes shame as a toddler's response to a disappointed expectation of "sparkling-eyed pleasure" in the maternal gaze. Ordinarily, the child's abashed signals elicit a caring response. The child learns that shame states do not signify complete disruption of attachment bond and that they can be regulated. Through repeated experiences of this kind, the child and caretaker learn to negotiate emotional attunement and mutuality in their relationship.

Where no corrective relational process takes place, pathological variations in the attachment system can develop. In particular, we see disorganized attachment where the primary attachment figure is a source of fear. I would argue that we also see disorganized attachment where the primary attachment figure is a source of unremitting shame. In this case, the child is torn between need for emotional attunement and fear of rejection or ridicule. She forms an internal working model of relationship in which her basic needs are inherently shameful.

We are beginning to see the long-term effects of these "shattered states" in prospective longitudinal studies of high-risk children. Ogawa and associates (1997), in the Minnesota study, found that, as Liotti (1999) has explained, disorganized attachment in infancy was strongly correlated with adolescent dissociation. They also found that having a "psychologically unavailable" caretaker in infancy (as rated by observers in home visits) predicted pathological dissociation in adolescence. A second longitudinal study by Lyons-Ruth (2003) at Harvard Medical School independently reached the same conclusions. Both disorganized attachment behaviour on the part of the child and "maternal disrupted communication" at eighteen months separately predicted dissociation in adolescence.

To unpack what was meant by "maternal disrupted communication", the raters distinguished three styles: hostile, withdrawn, and fearful. I would suggest that all three styles of maternal communication would be likely to produce chronic shame states: the hostile style through criticism and ridicule, the withdrawn and fearful styles through repeated rejection of the child's bids for emotional connection.

Our knowledge of the developmental trajectory of children with disorganized attachment is still rudimentary, but it appears that by age seven many of these children have essentially substituted caregiving or social ranking systems for the damaged attachment system as a way of controlling proximity to a caregiver who does not care (Lyons-Ruth & Jacobvitz, 1999). This can also be conceptualized as an attempt to avoid the constant shame of unrequited love. Both the Minnesota and the Harvard longitudinal studies have also shown us that children who developed disorganized attachment in infancy have later difficulties with peer relationships. They have not learnt to negotiate social co-operation or mutuality.

At the Victims of Violence Program at Cambridge Hospital, where I work, the majority of our adult patients report histories of abuse in childhood. Some were abused by their primary caretaker, but more commonly the abuse was at the hands of someone else. Perhaps the abuser was someone in the family whom the primary caretaker valued more than she valued the child, or perhaps the abuser was an acquaintance outside of the family who had access to the child because the primary caretaker was not paying close attention. In either case, the primary caretaker was not a source of fear, but she was "psychologically unavailable". It is this absence, this breach in the primary attachment relationship, which leaves our patients with the profound conviction that they are unlovable. In treatment, we find again and again that the core issue is shame. Our patients live in a state of chronic humiliation that profoundly distorts their view of self and others. I will speak later of how we try to address these shattered shame states in psychotherapy.

Liotti (2004) speaks of trauma, dissociation, and disorganized attachment as three strands of a single braid. I would like to add a fourth strand to the braid, by focusing on the role of shame in the development of traumatic disorders.

Characteristics of shame

Shame can be likened to fear in many respects. Like fear, it is a "fast-track" physiologic response that, in intense forms, can overwhelm higher cortical functions. Like fear, it is also a social signal, with characteristic facial and postural signs that can be recognized across cultures (Darwin, 1872; Izard, 1971). The gaze aversion, bowed head, and hiding behaviours of shame are similar to appeasement displays of social animals (Keltner & Harker, 1998), and might serve a similar social function among human beings. From an evolutionary point of view, shame might serve an adaptive function as a primary mechanism for regulating the individual's relations both to primary attachment figures and to the social group (Gilbert & McGuire, 1998; Izard, 1977).

Like fear, shame is a biologically stressful experience. In a meta-analysis of 208 laboratory studies, Dickerson and Kemeny (2004) demonstrated that socially embarrassing test conditions (for example, public speaking) reliably produced elevated cortisol and ACTH responses in human subjects. Perhaps because we have not found a reliable way to evoke shame in laboratory animals, however, understanding of the neurobiology of shame is rudimentary compared to the extensive literature on fear. Schore (2003) proposes that shame is mediated by the parasympathetic nervous system and serves as a sudden "brake" on excited arousal states.

More than a century ago, Darwin (1872) described blushing as the most characteristic sign of shame, and questioned "how it has arisen that the consciousness that others are attending to our personal appearance should have led to the capillaries, especially those of the face, instantly becoming filled with blood" (p. 327). This question remains unsolved. A more recent review article (Leary, Britt, Cutlip, & Templeton, 1992) notes that, while some of the available evidence implicates the parasympathetic nervous system, "knowledge of the physiological basis of blushing is meager and clearly ripe for future research" (p. 452).

The subjective experience of shame is of an initial shock and flooding with painful emotion. Shame is a relatively wordless state, in which speech and thought are inhibited. It is also an acutely self-conscious state; the person feels small, ridiculous, and exposed. There is a wish to hide, characteristically expressed by covering the face with the hands. The person wishes to "sink through the floor" or "crawl in a hole and die". Shame is always implicitly a relational experience. According to Lewis (1987b), one of the early pioneers in the study of shame,

> Shame is one's own vicarious experience of the other's scorn. The self-in-the eyes-of-the-other is the focus of awareness . . . The experience of shame often occurs in the form of imagery, of looking or being looked at. Shame may also be played out as an internal colloquy, in which the whole self is condemned. [pp. 15, 18]

Thus, shame represents a complex form of mental representation, in which the person is able to imagine the mind of another.

Developmental origins of shame

Developmentally, shame appears in the second year of life. Erikson (1950) formulates the central conflict of this developmental stage as "Autonomy vs. shame and doubt". Properly speaking no toddler is autonomous; rather, one might formulate the toddler's developmental task as learning to regulate body, affect, desire, and will in attunement with others. Positive resolution of the conflicts of this stage of life creates the foundation for healthy pride and mutuality in relationships, both self-respect and respect for others. Schore (2003) traces the origins of shame to the primary attachment relationship. Separations, which evoke fear and protest in normal toddlers, do not evoke shame; rather, shame can be seen in reunion interactions, when the toddler's excitement is met with indifference or disapproval. To a certain extent, such experiences are inevitable and normal, since no caregiver can be empathically attuned to her child at all times, and sometimes the caretaker must chastise the child. However, under normal circumstances, the child's shame reaction, like the appeasement displays of other primates, evokes a sympathetic response that in turn dispels the feeling of shame. The breach in attachment is thus repaired. Through repetition of this sequence, Schore postulates that the securely attached toddler learns the limits of the caregiver's tolerance and also learns to self-soothe and regulate shame states.

Though shame and guilt are often spoken of interchangeably, and though both can be considered social or moral emotions, the two states are quite distinct. Whereas shame is focused on the global self in relation to others, guilt is focused on a specific action that the person has committed. Shame is an acutely self-conscious state in which the self is "split", imagining the self in the eyes of the other; by contrast, in guilt the self is unified. In shame, the self is passive; in guilt, the self is active. Shame is an acutely painful and disorganizing emotion; guilt might be experienced without intense affect. Shame engenders a desire to hide, escape, or to lash out at the person in whose eyes one feels ashamed. By contrast, guilt engenders a desire to undo the offence, to make amends. Finally, shame is discharged in restored eye contact and shared, good-humoured laughter, while guilt is discharged in an act of reparation (Lewis, 1987a, cf. table on p. 113).

The social functions of shame

Originating in the primary attachment relationship, shame generalizes to become an emotion that serves to regulate peer relationships, social hierarchy, and all the basic forms of social life. Scheff and Retzinger (2001), building on the work of Lynd (1958), Goffman (1967), and Lewis (1971), describe shame as the "master emotion of everyday life". In their conceptualization, shame is the "signal of trouble in a relationship". Shame, for example, serves to regulate social distance. People experience shame both if others are too distant, as in the extreme case of shunning or ostracism, and if others come too close, as in the extreme case where personal boundaries are violated.

Shame also mediates attunement to indices of social value or status. In its milder forms, shame is the result of social slights or ridicule. Mild experiences of shame are a part of ordinary social life. The everyday family of shame emotions includes shyness, self-consciousness, embarrassment, and feeling foolish or ridiculous. Through ordinary experiences of shame, individuals learn the boundaries of socially acceptable behaviour.

In more extreme forms, shame is the reaction to being treated in a degrading manner. The extreme family of shame emotions includes humiliation, self-loathing, and feelings of defilement, disgrace, or dishonour. In hierarchical societies, according to Miller (1997), disgust and contempt are "emotions of status demarcation" that consign to lower status those against whom they are directed. Relationships of dominance and subordination are inherently shaming. The social signals of subordinate status (bowed head, lowered eyes) are ritualized expressions of shame. In slavery, the most extreme form of social subordination, the enslaved person exists in a permanently dishonoured status that Patterson (1982) describes as "social death".

Extreme social subordination is found in relationships of coercive control: in modern-day slavery, which takes the form of forced labor or prostitution (Bales, 2005), in political tyrannies, and in the private familial tyrannies of domestic violence and child abuse. Relationships of coercive control are established and perpetuated by an array of methods that are recognizable across cultures (Amnesty International, 1973). Among these methods, violence and threat of violence instil fear, while other commonly used methods, such as control of bodily functions, social isolation, and degradation, primarily evoke shame.

Extreme or catastrophic experiences of shame are a signal of profound relational disruptions or violations. When methods of coercive control are used within primary attachment relationships, as occurs in the case of child abuse, the developing child learns nothing of ordinary social shame. Rather, the child is overwhelmed with extreme shame states. Fonagy, Target, Gergely, Allen, and Bateman (2003) describe the shame of the abused child as "an intense and destructive sense of self-disgust, verging on self-hatred" (p. 445). They explain that "the shame concerns being treated as a physical object in the very context where special personal recognition is expected" (*ibid.*).

Schore (2003) describes catastrophic shame states as "self-disorganizing". Indeed, it is a characteristic of shame that it can feed upon itself. The shamed person feels ashamed of feeling ashamed, enraged, and ashamed of being enraged. Lewis (1990) describes these self-amplifying, disorganizing shame states as "feeling traps". She proposes that when shame states cannot be resolved, they are expressed as symptoms.

Shame as a predictor of post-traumatic symptoms

Although the literature on this subject is sparse, three recent studies document an association between shame and post-traumatic symptoms. Andrews, Brewin, Rose, and Kirk (2000) interviewed 157 victims of violent crime within one month of the incident and asked directly about shame experiences. At six-month follow-up, shame was the only independent predictor of PTSD symptoms. Talbot, Talbot, and Tu (2004) examined the relationship between shame-proneness and dissociation in a population of ninety-nine hospitalized women with and without histories of childhood abuse. Shame-proneness was measured with a modification of the differential emotions scale (DES-IV; Izard, Libero, Putnam, & Haynes, 1993). Greater shame-proneness was associated with higher levels of dissociation, especially among women who had experienced sexual trauma early in their development. Interestingly, some women who had been abused in childhood were not particularly shame-prone and had dissociative scores within the normal range. The sources of resilience in these women are not well understood and warrant further study. Finally, Dutra, Callahan, Forman, Mendelsohn, and Herman (2008), in a study of 137 trauma survivors seeking out-patient treatment, measured self-reported shame schemas using a modified version of the Young schema questionnaire (YSQ-S; Young & Brown, 1999). Shame schemas were significantly correlated with measures of PTSD and dissociation. Shame schemas were also specifically correlated with self-reported suicidal risk variables, including recent suicide attempts, current suicidal ideation, and current suicidal plans. These data would support the inference that post-traumatic shame states can be life-threatening.

Addressing shame in psychotherapy

Understanding that shame is a normal reaction to disrupted social bonds allows patients to emerge from the "feeling trap" in which they feel ashamed of being ashamed. According to Lewis (1981), addressing shame directly in the psychotherapy relationship facilitates therapeutic work, by normalizing shame reactions and by giving patients a relational framework for containing and understanding them. She writes,

> Adopting the viewpoint that shame is a normal state which accompanies the breaking of affectional bonds allows shame to take its place as a universal, normal human state of being. Analyzing shame reactions in an atmosphere in which their natural function is taken for granted makes analytic work considerably easier. . . . Perhaps the greatest

therapeutic advantage of viewing shame and guilt as affectional bond controls is the emphasis placed on the patients' efforts to restore their lost attachments. [p. 263]

The therapist calls attention to the patient's shame reactions as they happen, noticing the bowed head and averted gaze. The therapist then invites the patient to move out of the shamed position, to lift her head, to make eye contact, and to experience the restorative empathic connection of the treatment relationship. As shame is relieved, often patient and therapist will spontaneously begin to laugh together. Retzinger (1987) explains that shared laughter restores a sense of social connection:

> Shame is a major aspect of the human condition. It serves a fundamental purpose, enabling human beings to monitor their own behavior in relation to others . . . When shame is too great, one feels alienated, disconnected from others, and alone in the world. Laughter serves to reconnect these severed ties, breaking the spiral of shame–rage . . . Without both shame and laughter, complex social life would be impossible. [p. 177]

Numerous verbal, paralinguistic, and non-verbal cues should alert the therapist to shame states. The vocabulary of shame is extensive: words such as "ridiculous, foolish, silly, idiotic, stupid, dumb, humiliated, disrespected, helpless, weak, inept, dependent, small, inferior, unworthy, worthless, trivial, shy, vulnerable, uncomfortable, or embarrassed" can indicate feelings of shame. Paralinguistic cues include confusion of thought, hesitation, soft speech, mumbling, silences, stammering, long pauses, rapid speech, or tensely laughed words. Non-verbal cues include hiding behaviour, such as covering all or parts of the face, gaze aversion, with eyes downcast or averted, hanging head, hunching shoulders, squirming, fidgeting, blushing, biting or licking the lips, biting the tongue, or false smiling (Retzinger, 1995).

Courtois (1988), in her description of therapeutic work with incest survivors, observes that shame might be difficult to address directly because of the way it affects the transference. The patient might have difficulty trusting evidence of her therapist's positive regard, because she expects the therapist to feel the same contempt for her that she has for herself. It might be necessary for the therapist to challenge this distorted perception, gently but directly. Shame also affects the countertransference; as Lewis (1987b) explains, shame is a contagious emotion, and the therapist might avoid addressing shame directly because of her own discomfort.

Cloitre, Cohen, and Koenen (2006), in their manual for treatment of survivors of childhood abuse, devote a chapter to the creation of narratives of shame. They write,

> In the same way that narratives of fear must be titrated so that the client experiences mastery over fear rather than a reinstatement of it, so too narratives of shame should be titrated so that the client experiences dignity rather than humiliation in the telling. [p. 290]

These authors identify numerous reasons for telling about shameful events. They point out that shame perpetuates the bond with the perpetrator; as long as the patient guards her shameful secrets, she might feel that the perpetrator is the only person who knows her intimately. Disclosure in the context of the therapy relationship is a mastery experience that leads to greater self-knowledge, greater self-compassion, and reduced feelings of alienation.

Patients with dissociative disorders have the additional burden of shame and secrecy about their illness itself. In their paper on treatment of dissociative disorders, Turkus and Kahler (2006) write that psychoeducation

> helps to undo the stigmatization and shame associated with being ill. We have heard the words *insane, crazy* and *freak* many times from patients who are traumatized. In fact, patients on our trauma unit have requested that we change the group name to *psycheducation* to eliminate any implication of *psycho*. [p. 246]

Because of the power imbalance between patient and therapist, and because the patient exposes her most intimate thoughts and feelings without reciprocity, the therapy relationship is, to some degree, inherently shaming. For this reason, among others, group psychotherapy might be a particularly valuable treatment modality for traumatized people (Herman, 1992; Herman & Schatzow, 1984; Mendelsohn, Zachary, & Harney, 2007; Talbot et al, 1999). The group members are peers who approach one another on a social plane of equality. Moreover, group members are in a position to give compassionate support as well as to receive it. Thus, they can feel themselves to be of value to the group and deserving of the support they receive. The group becomes a little society within which members experience inclusion, co-operation, and mutuality.

Group treatment must be structured so that group members titrate their exposure and learn to stay present rather than dissociating, both while describing their own experiences and while listening to others. This requires the group leaders to take an active stance, intervening when they notice a group member is disconnected, and modelling the kind of empathic feedback that group members can expect both to give and to receive. The resultant feeling of group acceptance and belonging is a powerful antidote to long-held feelings of shame and stigma (Herman & Schatzow, 1984).

Conclusion

If the thesis of this paper is correct, the role of shame in traumatic disorders and disorders of attachment should be a potentially fruitful area for further study. In particular, future research is needed to develop a fuller understanding of the neurophysiology of shame, to elucidate the role of shame in disorganized attachment and in post-traumatic symptom formation, and to explore the potentially thera-peutic effects of addressing shame as a central issue in the treatment of trauma survivors.

References

Amnesty International (1973). *Report on Torture*. London: Duckworth.

Andrews, B., Brewin, C. R., Rose, S., & Kirk, M. (2000). Predicting PTSD symptoms in victims of violent crime: the role of shame, anger, and childhood abuse. *Journal of Abnormal Psychology, 109*: 69–73.

Bales, K. (2005). *Understanding Global Slavery: A Reader*. Berkeley, CA: University of California Press.

Bowlby, J. (1973). *Attachment and Loss, Vol. 2: Separation: Anxiety and Anger*. New York: Basic Books.

Cloitre, M., Cohen, L. R., & Koenen, K. C. (2006). *Treating Survivors of Childhood Abuse: Psychotherapy for the Interrupted Life*. New York: Guilford Press.

Courtois, C. A. (1988). *Healing the Incest Wound: Adult Survivors in Therapy.* New York: Norton.

Darwin, C. (1872). *The Expression of the Emotions in Man and Animals.* London: John Murray.

Dickerson, S. S., & Kemeny, M. E. (2004). Acute stressors and cortisol responses: a theoretical integration and synthesis of laboratory research. *Psychological Bulletin, 130*: 355–391.

Dutra, L., Callahan, K., Forman, E., Mendelsohn, M., & Herman, J. L. (2008). Core schemas and suicidality in a chronically traumatized population. *Journal of Nervous and Mental Disease, 196*: 71–74.

Erikson, E. H. (1950). *Childhood and Society.* New York: Norton.

Fonagy, P., Target, M., Gergely, G., Allen, J. G., & Bateman, A. W. (2003). The developmental roots of borderline personality disorder in early attachment relationships: a theory and some evidence. *Psychoanalytic Inquiry, 23*: 412–459.

Gilbert, P., & McGuire, M. T. (1998). Shame, status and social roles: psychobiology and evolution. In: P. Gilbert & B. Andrews (Eds.), *Shame: Interpersonal Behavior, Psychopathology and Culture* (pp. 99–125). New York: Oxford University Press.

Goffman, E. (1967). *Interaction Ritual.* New York: Anchor.

Hennighausen, K. H., & Lyons-Ruth, K. (2005). Disorganization of behavioral and attentional strategies toward primary attachment figures: from biologic to dialogic processes. In: C. S. Carter, L. Ahnert, K. E. Grossmann, S. B. Hrdy, M. E. Lamb, S. W. Porges, & N. Sachser (Eds.), *The 92nd Dahlem Workshop Report: Attachment and Bonding: A New Synthesis* (pp. 269–299). Cambridge, MA: MIT Press.

Herman, J. L. (1992). *Trauma and Recovery.* New York: Basic Books.

Herman, J. L., & Schatzow, E. (1984). Time limited group therapy for women with a history of incest. *International Journal of Group Psychotherapy, 34*: 605–615.

Izard, C. E. (1971). *The Face of Emotion.* New York: Appleton-Century-Crofts.

Izard, C. E. (1977). *Human Emotions.* New York: Plenum.

Izard, C. E., Libero, Z., Putnam, P., & Haynes, O. M. (1993). Stability of emotion experiences and their relations to traits of personality. *Journal of Personality and Social Psychology, 64*: 847–860.

Keltner, D., & Harker, L. A. (1998). The forms and functions of the non-verbal signal of shame. In: P. Gilbert & B. Andrews (Eds.), *Shame: Interpersonal Behavior, Psychopathology and Culture* (pp. 75–98). New York: Oxford University Press.

Leary, M. R., Britt, T. W., Cutlip, W. D., & Templeton, J. L. (1992). Social blushing. *Psychological Bulletin, 112*: 446–460.

Lewis, H. B. (1971). *Shame and Guilt in Neurosis*. New York: International Universities Press.

Lewis, H. B. (1981). Shame and guilt in human nature. In: S. Tuttman, C. Kaye, & M. Zimmerman (Eds.), *Object and Self: A Developmental Approach* (pp. 235–265). New York: International Universities Press.

Lewis, H. B. (1987a). Shame and the narcissistic personality. In: D. L. Nathanson (Ed.), *The Many Faces of Shame* (pp. 93–132). New York: Guilford Press.

Lewis, H. B. (1987b). Introduction: shame, the "sleeper" in psychopathology. In: H. B. Lewis (Ed.). *The Role of Shame in Symptom Formation* (pp. 1–28). Hillsdale, NJ: Erlbaum.

Lewis, H. B. (1990). Shame, repression, field dependence, and psychopathology. In: J. L. Singer (Ed.), *Repression and Dissociation: Implications for Personality Theory, Psychopathology and Health* (pp. 233–257). Chicago, IL: University of Chicago Press.

Liotti, G. (1999). Disorganization of attachment as a model for understanding dissociative psychopathology. In: J. Solomon & G. George (Eds.), *Disorganization of Attachment* (pp. 291–317). New York: Guilford Press.

Liotti, G. (2004). Trauma, dissociation, and disorganized attachment: three strands of a single braid. *Psychotherapy: Theory, Research, Practice, Training, 41*: 472–486.

Lynd, H. (1958). *On Shame and the Search for Identity*. New York: Harcourt.

Lyons-Ruth, K. (2003). Dissociation and the parent-infant dialogue: a longitudinal perspective from attachment research. *Journal of the American Psychoanalytic Association, 51*: 883–911.

Lyons-Ruth, K., & Jacobvitz, D. (1999). Attachment disorganization: unresolved loss, relational violence, and lapses in behavioral and attentional strategies. In: J. Cassidy & P. Shaver (Eds.), *Handbook of Attachment: Theory, Research, and Clinical Implications* (pp. 520–554). New York: Guilford Press.

Mendelsohn, M., Zachary, R. S., & Harney, P. A. (2007). Group therapy as an ecological bridge to new community for trauma survivors. In: M. R. Harvey & P. Tummala-Narra (Eds.), *Sources and Expressions of Resiliency in Trauma Survivors* (pp. 227–244). New York: Haworth.

Miller, W. (1997). *The Anatomy of Disgust*. Cambridge, MA: Harvard University Press.

Ogawa J. R., Sroufe, L. A., Weinfield, N. S., Carlson, E. A., & Egeland, B. (1997). Development and the fragmented self: longitudinal study of dissociative symptomatology in a nonclinical sample. *Development and Psychopathology, 9*: 855–879.

Patterson, O. (1982). *Slavery and Social Death: A Comparative Study.* Cambridge, MA: Harvard University Press.

Retzinger, S. M. (1987). Resentment and laughter: video studies of the shame-rage spiral. In: H. B. Lewis (Ed.), *The Role of Shame in Symptom Formation* (pp. 151–181). Hillsdale, NJ: Erlbaum.

Retzinger, S. M. (1995). Identifying shame and anger in discourse. *American Behavioral Scientist, 38*:1104–1113.

Scheff, T. J., & Retzinger, S. M. (2001). Shame as the master emotion of everyday life. *Journal of Mundane Behavior, 1*: 34–59

Schore, A. N. (1998). Early shame experiences and infant brain development. In: P. Gilbert & B. Andrews (Eds.), *Shame: Interpersonal Behavior, Psychopathology and Culture* (pp. 57–77). New York: Oxford.

Schore, A. N. (2003). *Affect Regulation and the Repair of the Self.* New York: Norton.

Talbot, J., Talbot, N., & Tu, X. (2004). Shame-proneness as a diathesis for dissociation in women with histories of childhood sexual abuse. *Journal of Traumatic Stress, 17*: 445–448.

Talbot, N., Houghtalen, R. P., Duberstein, P. R., Cox, C., Giles, D. E., & Wynne, L. C. (1999). Effects of group treatment for women with a history of childhood sexual abuse. *Psychiatric Services, 50*: 686–692.

Trevarthen, C. (2005). Stepping away from the mirror: pride and shame in adventures of companionship: reflections on the nature and emotional needs of infant intersubjectivity. In: C. S. Carter, L. Ahnert, K. E. Grossmann, S. B. Hrdy, M. E. Lamb, S. W. Porges, & N. Sachser (Eds.), *The 92nd Dahlem Workshop Report: Attachment and Bonding: A New Synthesis* (pp. 55–84). Cambridge, MA: MIT Press.

Turkus, J. A., & Kahler, J. A. (2006). Therapeutic interventions in the treatment of dissociative disorders. *Psychiatric Clinics of North America, 29*: 245–262.

Young, J. E., & Brown, G. (1999). *Young Schema Questionnaire: Short Form.* New York: Schema Therapy Institute.

CHAPTER FIVE

"You can kill me with what you say": working with shattered states and the breakdown of inner and outer, self and other, from an attachment-based perspective

Rachel Wingfield Schwartz

I first met Alice three years ago. I opened the door to a twenty-five-year-old woman, who looked fifteen, and who was covered with literally hundreds of deep-set scars on every bit of skin that could be seen. Her face, arms, hands, neck. In the coming months I was to find out that the rest of her body was exactly the same: slashed to pieces, scarred everywhere, particularly deeply around her genitals and stomach. She found it hard to leave the house as everywhere she went people stared and looked shocked at what they could see. I had worked with cutters before, but I had never seen anyone who attacked, ripped, and violated every bit of their skin so repeatedly that the scars had never faded. I found out that this cutting had been happening since Alice was seven years old, and had increased dramatically in its severity since she had been sectioned under the Mental Health Act at the age of fifteen, suffering from anorexia and weighing four and a half stone. When they started force-feeding her, she started taking knives to her throat and genitals and cutting with a depth she never had before. The scars on her wrists and throat were multiple and particularly deep, and quite frightening to see. I could not imagine how she could have survived them, or how she could have borne the pain. Alice would not talk about her pain when I first met her, would not acknowledge any trauma in her history, but her body told her story . . .

Alice was a client who had brought her mental health team repeatedly to the point Liotti describes in this volume: fright without solution. She had been in the mental health system since her teens. After being forced fed, she was put on very heavy doses of multiple medications, including powerful antipsychotic drugs. She remained on this medication for ten years and became addicted to it. She was also given multiple batches of ECT, as well as a range of other interventions, but was offered no talking therapy. Over the years, her diagnosis had frequently changed: an initial diagnosis of anorexia was switched to schizophrenia when she started self-harming, and she was subsequently labelled borderline. When doctors needed to justify a new round of forced antipsychotic medication under section, the diagnosis switched to the new label of choice, "bipolar disorder".

Through the influence of pioneers like Judith Herman, Alice was finally able to find therapy through the Centre for Dissociative Studies. This was possible because of the existence of new diagnoses of complex post-traumatic stress disorder and dissociative identity disorder, which some rare and courageous psychiatrists in the UK are prepared to diagnose, recommending long-term psychotherapy as the treatment of choice. These psychiatrists are, thus, putting themselves on the line professionally in a climate where these diagnoses are still regarded as controversial by many mental health workers.

That day, Alice's mental health team members had reached the end of their tethers. In Alice's absence they asked me: How dare I recommend that Alice needed long-term intensive therapy? How foolish must I be to think any of it would make any difference, and that she would do anything but continually sabotage it and attack me? Didn't I realize Alice had a mental illness? I was doing a great disservice to psychotherapy, and posing a potential danger to Alice, to suggest psychotherapists could work with someone so mentally ill. Only medication could help. I tried to point out that Alice had been given that form of treatment for ten years and had deteriorated. Wasn't something else worth a try, even if it would not be a quick fix?

As Liotti points out, for children with disorganized attachment systems, both options—either approaching towards, or relinquishing, potential attachment figures—are equally frightening. Therefore, these children endure repeated experiences of irresolvable fear. This can make their relationships with therapists and other mental health professionals in adulthood unbearable. Patients then veer from phobia of attachment to clinging dependency, but either choice seems to lead to a blind alley. This creates a relational trap, a "freeze" state, where the person who is perceived as the source of the patient's fear is also simultaneously seen as the attachment figure who should provide the solution.

I tried to explain to the mental health team that this was why we were all feeling so powerless and stuck, angry at Alice's sabotage of any solution offered. But I was speaking a foreign language. They decided to section her again and put her back on antipsychotics and also decided not to fund her therapy.

This experience reinforced powerfully for me how far we still have to go in this country even to begin to make a case for attachment-based therapy as a new approach to treatment for shattered states.

Psychiatrists appear to offer us a model in which things are simple; in which the differences between the real and the symbolic, you and me, imagination and experience, are obvious, as clear-cut as their distinction between madness and sanity, between one psychiatric label or diagnosis and another. We can name this mental state, this human being, as "psychotic", "borderline", "schizophrenic", "bipolar", and so on. We can name this form of distress as "mental illness" and this other form as "normal".

Psychoanalysis has always fundamentally challenged this simplified view of the mind. It offers us an alternative model of the dynamic mind, the mind in conflict, multi-layered, constantly negotiating inner and outer, the boundary between self and other, where you end and I begin; not a mind that we are born with, but a mind which develops only in relationship with others.

Attachment-based psychoanalysis provides us with an understanding that we do not have unified selves, but that our internal worlds are populated by internal working models of self and other, which form our sense of who we are.

So, as a clinician, I will often ask, "What's it like inside your mind when you're alone? Quiet or noisy? Busy or still? Silent or with voices? Full or empty? Are there areas of your mind that you are frightened to get near, or are scared of, that feel unknown or closed off to you?"

Bowlby's work was ground-breaking in enabling our understanding of the populated, social mind—the psyche as part of human society.

He understood our needs for belonging and relationship as crucial to our survival as individuals and as a species. It is particularly fitting that Judith Herman is giving the Bowlby centenary lecture this year, as she represents and takes forward these insights of Bowlby, any acceptance of which we are still having to fight for within our mental health system. Like Bowlby, Judith begins from the starting point of understanding human responses to mental pain as adaptive and relational.

It is not often that any of us has chance to talk on the same platform as someone who is a personal hero and a pioneer. Judith has literally changed the face of understanding around trauma, and brought in a new diagnosis, which I (and, I am sure, many of you) have been able to introduce into work with clients. I know that many people owe their lives to Judith's work, including some people here today, and I feel proud to have her with us for this significant moment in The Bowlby Centre's history.

Those of you who have read *Trauma and Recovery* might recognize that the title of this paper—"You can kill me with what you say"—is a quote taken from that book. These words are spoken by a trauma survivor and quoted by Judith in the book (Herman, 1992, p. 137). The quotation captures the point at which trauma breaks down and shatters the boundaries we draw between inner and outer, self and other, fragmenting our hard-won capacity to test reality, to live in linear time where past, present, and future can be distinguished. Trauma can shatter the crucial, but lifelong and enormous, developmental task of distinguishing self from other, my mind from yours, internal from external.

This morning we have heard two superb papers developing attachment theory, perfect for the centenary year, representing the most significant current theoretical developments. I want to offer you some clinical vignettes and dilemmas to illustrate the theoretical insights offered.

I have chosen to focus on more severe forms of shattered states: the interface with psychiatry. Clients with dissociative identity do not always end up as part as of the mental health system, because it is such a highly effective and creative coping mechanism. However, where dissociative mechanisms have not always been able to protect against fragmented and psychotic states, then many traumatized people end up involved in the psychiatric system, sometimes with repetitive, entangled, and long-term engagements.

The challenges we face in these situations include failures, because we are still developing ways to build successful partnerships with colleagues in the mental health system and to make headway in convincing mental health professionals (including many in our own profession) that we can provide the treatment that can really make a difference to clients presenting with these shattered states. We also face difficulties with clients who have been involved long-term in the psychiatric system, because sometimes we are also dealing with some neurological damage after years of heavy prescribing of antipsychotics and electro-convulsive therapy, which has complicated pre-existing neurological problems laid down by the trauma.

There are many fears surrounding these shattered states. We are constantly up against a need in the mental health system to cling to biological and medical myths, presented as science or certainties, as Brett Kahr has so beautifully described (this volume). These fears include a seeming terror of being sued; of being accused of instigating false memory syndrome; of being taken to court for not accurately assessing risk to self or others. Although we know that patients in shattered states might be more likely to act out in relation to harming themselves, they do sometimes harm others, and health professionals are often scapegoated for this. So, these fears can be understandable. And it is also true that the level of complaints arising from clinical work with this group is higher than from any other, a risk we are all running as psychotherapists when feelings of being betrayed, attacked, or disappointed can be so easily triggered within the transference.

Alice is precisely one of those clients with whom we are told we cannot work; who, in the view of her community mental health team, crosses over that "borderline" into madness from which an engagement in talking therapy can only fail to help her return. Indeed, in their view, it also might well drive her even madder, particularly should we make the fatal error of making a long-term relationship with the client, risking "dependence" (or attachment, as we would term it) and, therefore, catastrophe.

And yes, Alice truly was at the far end of the spectrum of clients who gain access to talking, particularly psychoanalytic, psychotherapy.

Fifteen minutes into a session in July 2005, Alice starts convulsing in her chair and screams, "You just stuck a knife in me and slit my stomach open!" She is clasping her stomach, shaking, terror in her eyes. She is staring at me, but not seeing me.

I am eight months into the work with Alice, and, by this point, I understand what is happening. This is a flashback. I bring her back to the present. I remind her where she is, ground her, and repeat back what she just said to me. She is puzzled and then says, "But it happened. I have this scar. This huge scar across my stomach." She lifts up her jumper to show me. There is a deep scar that she points to.

She tells me then about her experience with a man she met in psychiatric hospital, when she was twenty. Another patient on the mixed ward, he traded sex for joints and other drugs with her, gave her money and a mobile phone, and came to collect her when she was released from her section. He took her back to his flat on a local estate, where he kept her and plied her with drugs for the next six months. During that time he brought his gang colleagues over to have sex with her in exchange for drugs, and to act out what she described as "sado-masochism". "That day they cut right through my stomach," she says. She is terrified and I can feel and smell her terror.

In the moment of reliving the trauma, Alice was not sure who I was, where we were, whether this was ten years ago, or today, whether her stomach was bleeding or the scar had been formed years before.

Eight months previously, how would I have unravelled this statement? I remember the first session with her. She told me, "When I was six I had my ears cut off", and "Only half of my body is here." Sitting in front of me, though, was a young woman with two fully adjoined ears and no missing limbs. She smiled at me. "I only started to be able to see last year. I can see colours. I taught myself to see colours." "I only just found my arm."

I listened hard to what Alice was saying to me and wondered about the meaning behind it. She was communicating some powerful messages about her experience of what seemed to be very early pre-verbal bodily and psychic states, but how could I begin to attune at a level she could take in? How could I digest and metabolize these infantile sensations that were overwhelming her and begin to help us both make sense of what she was trying to communicate to me? I assumed we were a long way from reflective functioning in that session. But I found myself trying a gentle translation of what she was saying. I said, "A small baby finds where its body begins and ends;

that it has a body, that it has arms and legs. That there are separate colours, separate things outside of their body. Separate people. It sounds like you're telling me a part of you is just beginning to grow, to unfreeze and come out of all that confusion a baby lives with."

We were not as far away from mentalization as I had thought. This is one of the things about clients who present with shattered states: the psyche is multi-layered, dissociation and fragmentation can be part of the same internal world as the capacity to mentalize and make meaning. Clients can move in and out of psychotic states. As Bion significantly pointed out, we all can.

Following my comments, Alice said, "Yes. I was born all wrong. My mum's dad had just died. I'm a twin, I have a brother, but my mum only wanted a boy; she says there was a third baby—a triplet—in the womb who died. My sister, she's missing. My other self is missing, like I've lost half my limbs."

For the remainder of the session I spoke to an Alice who could then talk more lucidly about her infancy and early childhood. She told me that her mum was a beautician who was very concerned with appearances, and had had Alice's ears operated on as a small child to make her look "perfect". She said, "I feel my ears were taken away. Those were my ears." She had once again begun to separate internal and external. She told me she had been cutting herself since she was seven years old, and had been sexually abused by a variety of people since she was a small child. As time went on, she continued to move in and out of these states, but could be brought out of psychotic episodes into a more coherent narrative, and they became less frequent.

Initially, Alice's degree of dysregulation and terror of intimacy was so enormous that she was unable to stay and sit still in the room for more than ten minutes. She kept having to leap up to walk around, go outside for cigarettes, sometimes even jump up and down. She found eye contact terrifying, and staying in my presence for the whole session utterly overwhelming. She told me it was more frightening and painful being in the room with me, knowing I was not going to abuse her but not knowing what would happen, than it had been slashing her throat, or being beaten or raped by the gang she had belonged to. Now she can sit and be with me for double sessions, and maintain eye contact.

In the early stages, many words were banned from the room. I was forbidden to use them because the symbolic was still not possible. Use of the word "rape", for example, was experienced, in and of itself, as a violation. This began to shift, first through us agreeing that we would write down scary words on paper, then it became possible for them to be spoken. However, the greatest challenge we faced, and continue to face, was exactly the issue Judith has described. Shame. As the work developed, attachment feelings began to grow. Alice told me she found herself not wanting to leave sessions. Ultimately, and again in writing, she told me she had started to love me. The humiliation of this felt unbearable to her. She had had erotic feelings for women in the past and this had led to some of the more severe self-harm, specifically the attacks on her genitals. As the erotic transference began to kick in, Alice's shame made her start to feel unable to come to sessions. She became convinced I would leave her or reject her. She was terrified of the feelings evoked when we were together, and felt she would have to start cutting again if she allowed these "in love" feelings to be present.

Alice became so steeped in shame, in an obsessive feeling of unrequited love, that we nearly lost the relationship altogether. She refused to continue to see me. I was not even allowed to write to her. She had to reject me first. She wrote a goodbye letter saying that her love for me made it impossible to continue the relationship. Luckily, as she continued her therapy with the clinic, gradually she was able to allow me to say hello and send messages of support through her therapist. The clinic radically used the solution Liotti describes of enabling the team to hold Alice through this period where the transference with one therapist became too intense. It took a year, but she was able to resume her relationship with me again, with more intensity and affection on both sides, and more openness about the past than ever. She almost never revisited states of psychosis. The compulsion to sabotage the relationship continues, however, and this is work in process. But I am proud both of her and of the team for making it possible for me to make a long-term therapeutic attachment with someone on whom everyone else had given up. It is an honour to work with Valerie Sinason. We do not know what the outcome will be. We do know that happy endings are not always possible.

I would also like to share a couple of completed clinical pieces of work with clients in shattered states, which show how the insights Judith Herman and Giovanni Liotti have to offer can help us to navigate our way through some of the feeling traps that client and therapist are inevitably caught in together in the transference–counter-transference constellation.

Matthew

Matthew was referred to me by The Bowlby Centre, presenting himself as depressed following a split with his girlfriend. He was a relatively successful barrister, but said he was feeling anxious at work. He labelled himself as having a bit of a mid-life crisis. "I'm in my early forties, where am I going?"

He described his childhood as "fine". One of five children, he had attended a school where his father was the headteacher and his mother was also a teacher at the school. His dream was to be a footballer; he was considered to be the best player in the school, and was chosen to play for the county. The one memory from his childhood, which he described as "not fine", was that his dad, as headteacher, insisted that he should be dropped from the team, and never gave him an explanation. After school, Matthew had tried sports college and had ended up dropping out, unable to cope. He said he had felt a failure ever since.

In the first session with Matthew, I found myself misattuning to everything he said. I initially took his negative responses to be part of an avoidant/dismissing attachment style. He would come out with an endless stream of statements such as, "Everyone has problems with that"; "I just haven't been lucky, there's no reason for that"; and so on. But I also realized there was something else in the countertransference that I could not really make sense of. I found myself feeling continually pushed away, and every gesture I made towards connection was rejected. After several minutes I became aware that I was struggling to breathe, my heart pounding. I felt literally frozen in terror in the chair. I could see that Matthew himself was pouring with sweat and could not make eye contact with me. We agreed to meet twice a week, and at the end of the session I felt huge relief as I closed the door. At the next session, I felt acute dread as we entered the room. This continued for the next few months. During each session I felt myself looking desperately at the clock, the fifty minutes seeming to last an eternity. Just being able to sit in the room with him and stay there for fifty minutes felt almost unbearable. But the feelings in the room seemed to have no link to the surface content of the session. He would

tell me of his day, details of issues at work, his plans to start swim-
ming, try yoga, move house. He found a way to dismiss or disagree
with any response I gave to anything he said. Even if I were simply
repeating his words to me, he would claim I had misheard them. He
did this calmly, with no anger in his voice.

Leaving him with the silence was even worse, as the dread and
terror in the silence felt unbearable. Even a moment with no words felt
so acutely terrifying on a bodily level that I had to force myself not to
chatter anodynely just to fill the space. I felt stupid, inept; the silence
itself felt like evidence of failure, and the level of the anxiety state
made no sense to me. I felt drenched in it, but with no words to name
it. If there was a pause, he would ask me to say something, or ask
what was the point of him being here. Why wasn't he feeling better?
Any attempt to engage him on this question would be met by: "I'm
OK, my life's just normal, nobody's happy all the time, I don't see why
you're wanting me to feel better."

Stalemate. Every route was a blind alley; I felt frozen, tied in knots,
backed into a corner I could not get out of. I was a useless therapist.
We were locked together in fright and shame (his terror and my
shame) without solution.

Herman says that "Shame is a relatively wordless state, in which
speech and thought are inhibited. It is also an acutely self-conscious
state; the person feels small, ridiculous, and exposed. There is a wish
to hide" (this volume). This is how I felt during every moment of
sitting in the sessions with Matthew.

Any attempt to raise any issue other than what he had been doing
during the week, particularly anything about his family or childhood,
was met with a block, an insistence that it was irrelevant, a reminder
of how normal everything was, how normal his family was, there was
nothing to talk about, and did I really know what I was doing? If I
tried, no matter how gently, to explain the reasons for my raising these
issues, he would flinch as though he had been hit and reply very
defensively in a way which shut the discussion down. Any words I
tried to find for why I might want to know sounded ridiculous, trite,
understandably greeted with scorn for my naïvety.

Judith Herman quotes Helen Bloch Lewis as saying,

> Shame is one's own vicarious experience of the other's scorn. The self-
> in-the-eyes-of-the-other is the focus of awareness . . . The experience of

shame often occurs in the form of imagery, of looking or being looked at. [This volume]

I felt continually self-conscious in the room. Anything I said or did seemed to be an impingement on Matthew, or was in some way experienced as an act of aggression, misattunement, or unintentional rejection. I was repeatedly not *seeing*, getting it wrong. When I tried to talk to him about his high level of anxiety, again he would stonewall me.

Then, in one session, he said he had to ask me something. He just did not understand what I was doing. Why was I throwing him out early after fifty minutes every week? Why did I want rid of him, and why was I charging him for an hour?

I was stunned. I reminded him of our initial discussion in which I had talked to him about the boundaries of the work, including the length of the session. He said he had forgotten this. I said he must have felt puzzled and distressed, thinking I was asking him to leave early every week. He said he assumed I was trying to get rid of him, or perhaps trying to get money out of him that he did not owe me.

I hoped that the clarification of this would help. But then he began pushing at the boundaries one by one. He would arrive early; he would arrive late; he would ask to use the phone to make urgent work calls; he would answer his mobile in the session, and cancel at the last minute.

As Liotti describes, there was no model in Matthew's internal world for mutuality or social co-operation; he had simply blanked out what I had experienced as negotiated agreements around boundaries and every time would deny I had ever talked to him about them. For Matthew, in every interaction one person was dominant and the other subordinate; one person was trying to ridicule or humiliate or reject the other. There was no other kind of relationship.

Judith Herman describes the vocabulary of shame as extensive, including words such as "ridiculous, foolish, silly, idiotic, stupid, dumb, humiliated, disrespected, helpless, weak, inept, small, inferior, unworthy, worthless, trivial, shy, vulnerable, uncomfortable, or embarrassed". I experienced all these states in the countertransference with Matthew. In relation to the paralinguistic and non-verbal cues Judith mentions, Matthew demonstrated them all, including "gaze aversion, hanging head, hunched shoulders, squirming, fidgeting, blushing, biting or licking lips, false smiling" as well as "confusion of thought, mumbling, silences, stammering, rapid speech, tensely laughed words". Everything I said also felt incoherent. Matthew was demonstrating all these signs of intense shame. But why was it so intense, and why was I getting nowhere in helping either of us to understand it or ease it?

I found I had no idea why Matthew continued with the therapy when he seemed to find the sessions so useless. A very powerful part of me wished he would decide not to continue. (I found myself thinking about referring him on, as I was obviously doing him no good. I decided perhaps it was because he needed a male therapist, and started thinking about colleagues I could pass him on to.)

Then, one day when Matthew arrived, he asked to go to the toilet. I was alone in the house. As I sat waiting for him to join me, I felt my terror level even higher than usual. I was literally shaking. I thought to myself, "He's going to come down and rape me."

When Matthew returned, he said he had just been given a present by a client today, a soldier he had got off a rape charge, as a thank you. "He probably did it, though." This felt like one of Stern's now moments. Literally, it felt like "now or never". My feelings of uselessness and shame were momentarily eased by realizing that I could trust the intensity of the countertransference and had to take the risk of putting words to it.

There was an incident that had been mentioned on Matthew's referral form in which he described an epsiode "out of the blue" when his mum had lost her temper and threatened him with a knife when he had brought his first girlfriend home. In the sessions to date, Matthew had never mentioned this and I had found myself unable to either, silenced, as though going anywhere near "secrets" that I knew, or frightening experiences in his past, would destroy us both. This was the Silencer in the room with us:

> Some of the most acute observations on traumatic transference appear in accounts written when the trauma of origin was not yet known. In these accounts a destructive force appears to intrude repeatedly into the relationship between therapist and patient. The terror is as though the patient and therapist convene in the presence of yet another person. The third person is the victimizer, who ... demanded silence and whose command is now being broken. [Herman, 1992, pp. 136–137]

I took a deep breath and said to Matthew, "I can feel so much fear—it's like some kind of terror of violation and attack. It's so powerful today but I can feel it in the room with you so often. Are you frightened I'm going to attack you? Do you want to attack me?"

The risk I took in voicing these countertransference feelings proved to be worth it, as it facilitated work in starting to break the silencing.

Matthew told me that he had not revealed to the referral interviewer or me what had actually happened when he dropped out of college. He said he had had a breakdown; he started having hallucinations and feeling paranoid. He believed that his mum had joined the Mafia in order to conspire against him and that he was being watched everywhere he went. He then started hallucinating that his mother was setting Rottweilers on him, and he kept screaming and collapsing, believing they were attacking him. He had a part- time job at the time, and started having similar hallucinations at work.

The feeling of relief in the session was enormous, and lasted for some time. My sense of dread started to dissipate. The countertransference made total sense. For the first time, rather than feeling useless or isolated in the room, trapped with no solution, we had found the beginnings of an answer.

However, of course, as we know, incidents like this in therapy, although they are breakthroughs, are the beginning, not the end, of a process. This was only one step towards recognizing and making a relationship with someone who had rejected every possibility of being seen, and who I had been repeatedly too frozen to see.

Despite the relief after the session in which Matthew told me about his period of psychosis, the fear began to grow again, and this time it took the form of a fear that remembering and speaking of this psychotic experience would lead him to lose his grip on reality again, that even saying the words would be so contaminating that he would go mad. I still felt there were areas of his mind and secrets he felt terrified to go anywhere near, and that the violence and persecution of his hallucinations communicated something about his internal world that suggested his early history was full of life and death terror. We worked on this incident with his mum, and his shame about his father's dismissal of him from the football team. But the fear and shame started to grow again. Matthew began avoiding sessions as though he felt they would literally contaminate him, and when I was with him I felt viscerally invaded, as if I could smell him and he was too close to me, no matter that he was sitting on the other side of the room. I felt him pulling further away, and I found myself tempted to give up again. My anxiety about saying anything that might trigger his fear of "going mad" left me again feeling silenced, staying away from dangerous areas, and every session became a boring, repetitive litany of his day-to-day routine from which he could not deviate. Again, I was not able to understand what was stopping me from talking to him about this. What was I so frightened of? Why did I feel as if I was colluding in something?

With feelings of dread, I decided I had to feed back this countertransference, and that this time, I had to disclose more of my own fantasies, confusions, fears, and feelings. This would be the only way to break the silence.

Therefore, I told Matthew, "Look, I need to tell you I feel really confused and I don't understand what's happening. Every time we meet I feel we are both terrified of stepping on a landmine; like I'm having to avoid going near something that you don't feel able to talk about. I'm helping keep some kind of secret. Does that make any sense? Do you feel any of that?" He made eye contact, very rare for him, but did not speak. I was encouraged, so I pressed on. "What's confusing me, Matthew, is that these are the feelings I'm used to having in therapy with clients who have been through very traumatic experiences very early in life, experiences they had to hide from themselves and other people. And yet there doesn't seem to be reason why I should be feeling like this when I'm with you. You haven't talked about any of that kind of trauma as a child."

Matthew then said casually, and in an off-hand manner, "Well, there was this paedophile that was arrested in my area when I was a kid. My friend and I used to go and visit him at this place. He lived behind the playing fields. He messed with us, did stuff and I didn't tell anyone. But I don't know what that would have anything to do with anything."

I stared at him in momentary disbelief. Whatever I had expected from my countertransference disclosure, I had not expected something as sudden and dramatic as this. For Matthew at that point, none of this connected up. We had a long road ahead, but at least we were on it, and from that session on the real and effective work of the therapy began.

Ann

Ann came into therapy when she was thirty-eight years old. She had recently been diagnosed as suffering from obsessive–compulsive disorder (OCD). Ann's OCD took the form of intrusive, sexually sadistic, and violent thoughts. Ann had found neither cognitive–behavioural therapy (CBT), nor the medication that had been prescribed for her, helpful. Like most traumatized clients, Ann's history was littered with different mental health problems and diagnostic labels. She lived with her mother, and reported being afraid that her mother would stab or strangle her in the night, or that she was at risk of strangling or stabbing her mum. She said the OCD had been triggered by swearing at her mother in a "sexual" way. Since that time, she had become preoccupied with punishment, as well a terror that she was evil inside and would act out these sexual and violent thoughts.

Ann was a client in a state of chronic humiliation and shame when I first met her. Judith Herman describes shame as a state in which the whole self is condemned: "Thus, shame represents a complex form of mental representation, in which the person is able to imagine the mind of the other" (this volume). In practice, as in this instance, clinically, this can be experienced by the client as akin to feeling that their mind is being colonized by the mind of the shaming other. This colonization is then experienced by the therapist in the countertransference.

From the moment I met Ann, I was drawn into the core of our work together. I opened the front door and Ann entered, shouting, as if in mid-argument with someone, "I have no idea why I've been sent to someone who lives so far away, I asked for someone nearby!" She was angry and distressed and barely registered my presence. Ann said she was going to insist on being given another therapist as I was also too young. I could not possibly have enough experience to know what I was doing.

I responded gently and calmly to Ann's anger, although the feeling in the room was of being with someone who was attacking me with a violent rage. My body felt frozen with fear; at the same time my mind was alert and responsive. I was very struck by this split and by the intensity of the body countertransference. I had been with plenty of angry clients before, but had not experienced this level of numbness in response. It gave me a clue that I was with someone who had needed to use profoundly dissociative defences. The intensity of

the rage also gave me a sense that I was with someone in a very frightened fight/flight state. She expected me to fight her. I knew I needed
to stay calm and respond to the fear, rather than the rage. She seemed
surprised. She had expected a confrontation. Meeting the unexpected
enabled her to shift from her preoccupied state to talk more about why
she had come to therapy. She told me about the extensive memory loss
in relation to her past, and her childhood in particular.

In the next session, Ann began to tell me that the OCD played a
significant role in her current relationship with her mother, mainly in
the service of achieving separation from her mother. For example, she
had to burn anything of hers that her mother had worn. She was
unable to use anything her mother had touched. Ann's sense of intru-
sion and potential threat was clear. She felt she and her mum were
merged. They were regularly seen walking down street arm-in-arm,
Ann unable to let go with one arm, and pinching and hitting her
mother with the other arm. This is a very visual example of the kind
of relational trap Liotti describes in situations of fright without solution.

When she first arrived in therapy, Ann felt she was seen as the local
"mad person", as she wandered round compulsively picking up and
hoarding dying and dead insects and leaves and wearing old clothes
that appeared strange to outsiders. She presented as an ostracized,
stigmatized person, outside of social belonging. At this stage, she was
also preoccupied with issues of control over life and death, and she
had an omnipotent sense of responsibility for any harm or badness in
the world. Travel, and in particular public transport, was a nightmare
for her, as she had to check scrupulously for suspect packages, believing that she would be responsible for many deaths if she missed one.
She also stopped for injured or dying pigeons she had to rescue,
taking them all home and nursing them back to health. During the
first months, she was frequently late for sessions, having stopped to
rescue pigeons and take them to an animal shelter.

Interestingly, the OCD in relation to her journeys to sessions very
soon abated. When she was actually addressing her life, it faded into
the background. She soon got into a routine of coming to therapy
three times a week. The regularity and security of the routine quickly
began to contain her anxiety levels. I needed to adapt to her attachment style, to negotiate with caution her need for, and fear of, proximity. I could sense that she experienced my presence as a threat, and

that the mind of the other was too terrifying too apprehend. However, I felt that she was working very quickly, and her hostility towards me soon disappeared almost entirely, only to reappear again the session before I was going to be away, when she was enraged that I would be abandoning her by taking a break.

This was to be the first of many occasions on which the potential emergence of attachment feelings, or a reminder that I was other than Ann—outside of her control—precipitated shame and then a need to lash out at the therapy. The sessions often felt as though we were walking a tightrope.

If I did or said the "wrong" thing, she told me it would "set off" the OCD and she would have to leave. Any change in the room, colours or clothes that I wore, even the way I was sitting in the chair, might trigger her fear and need to control.

I was also becoming increasingly aware that I was starting to be afraid to tell her things I thought she might not want to hear, particularly holiday dates, and also that I felt anxiety about what her reaction might be if I did not respond to telephone calls from her between sessions. I was feeling increasingly dominated and bullied, and this was reinforced by her new nickname for me, which was "the bitch". She refused to call me by my name.

In sessions, the intensity of Ann's emotions was communicated to me both consciously and unconsciously. The atmosphere in the room was alive with rage or terror. Sometimes, I would feel my heart pounding and my body almost shaking in the seat. I was able to disclose my countertransference as it was happening, which Ann found enormously helpful, recognizing immediately what I was referring to.

Although I often felt Ann was trying to annihilate me in the sessions, I knew it was essential for me to survive her attacks so that two real people could exist in the therapeutic space with neither having to be destroyed, so that she did not hold on to to the belief that the shame and feelings of badness she carried inside would destroy me, too, or that letting me get close to her would increase, rather than diminish, the shame.

A potent example of this came a few months later. Ann told me there was a child inside who desperately wanted to communicate with me, to be comforted and heard. She was ashamed and fearful of the fact that this child was "needy". She told me about a dream in which she was wandering in corridors and a slug appeared. The slug then switched into a cat and attacked and scratched her. "Slugs are intruders," she said, "and the cat looked a bit like your cat, actually." We discussed the fact that Ann felt anyone who got close to her would become "too close" and would intrude or betray her like her mother. Feeling that this had been something of a breakthrough, I found myself lulled into a false sense of security. I could feel myself in the countertransference floating on the ceiling, relaxed and looking down on myself. Then I "came to" and heard Ann saying she would have to stop coming to therapy in September. In fact, she was saying, psychotherapy was probably a load of rubbish. There was no needy child inside; she did not know where she had got that idea.

I was aware in the countertransference that I felt she had suddenly turned on me. I reflected this back to her and said that she was doing to me what the slug and cat had done in her dream: she had found a way in and then attacked me. I wondered if Ann was doing this to me, rejecting me, because she was terrified I would do this to her. She wanted to get in there first. She agreed, and by the time she left we felt close again.

However, my feelings of being colonized and controlled were increasing alongside my finding out more about Ann's history. She revealed, matter of factly, in a dissociated manner, her experience of being used as a child prostitute, pimped by her parents. This had continued into adulthood. Ann began to bring dreams of being dirty inside: dreams of grey rotting maggots inside her, where her organs and guts should be.

Judith Herman describes prostitution as forced labour, or slavery, and points out that relationships of dominance and subordination are inherently shaming (Herman, 1992, pp. 76–77). Herman also reminds us that Allan Schore conceptualizes shame as the toddler's response to a disappointed expectation of "sparkling-eyed pleasure in the maternal gaze" (this volume). Ann's fear of unrequited love, her shame around her feelings for me, seemed to stem from anticipating this disappointment. The solution she had found to avoiding the pain of unrequited love was to hide the emerging self inside. I felt this had happened early in her infancy, and she protected herself from a sense of impending catastrophe by ensuring she could never be seen and, therefore, would never face rejection, never face an absence of recognition, never love without being loved in return.

I felt strongly that Ann's shame needed a mirroring response, a recognition of her specialness. In the countertransference she evoked in me exactly the maternal response she had needed. I felt excited about seeing her, longing to get to know her, to see more. I delighted in her progress, in everything she shared with me. I felt (and still feel) that she was one of the most special people I had ever met. I felt honoured to know her. Although for a long time Ann could not cope with much of this countertransference being verbalized, she could feel its authenticity, and she began to take it in. She began to bring things to show me: pictures, drawings, school essays from childhood, poems she had written, photos of herself as a baby, her cuddly toys. Together, we delighted in them. As Stern describes, the child delights in what she brings, and the parent delights in the child's excitement (Stern, 1985, pp, 132–133).

This brought us closer, and, after weeks of ambivalently approaching and then withdrawing, Ann finally told me she needed to speak about the punishments she had undergone at the hands of her mother as a child. She said she felt soaked in shame. When her mother said Ann had been bad, she would lock her, naked, in the dog kennel, and make her eat dog food on all fours, from a dish on the floor. Ann was not allowed out to go to the toilet, and her mother would punish her further for peeing on the floor. On some occasions, her mother would force her to lick up the pee, and once to eat her own shit. Another time, when Ann had been "disobedient", her mother pissed in her mouth, and made her eat her shit. She told Ann that she could tell she enjoyed it, and that this made her a pervert. I felt intense anger and distress on Ann's behalf and I felt for the first time that she was letting me be a witness and advocate for her. She, in turn, was able to register the authenticity of my response and felt genuinely cared about by me.

In the next session, she brought me a picture she had drawn the night before. She had drawn the two of us standing side by side, a short distance between us. We both looked ahead, but shared a facial expression. We both looked extremely sad. Ann said, "This is what it was like when I told you about my mother. We were both sad." She had experienced us having separate minds, yet sharing the same feelings, a genuinely intersubjective moment.

Ann and I were able to link her mother's abuse of her as a child to her being pimped by her boyfriend later in life as a prostitute. Her shame that she had "let" him do this to her began to abate as we made sense of the fact that a dissociated part of herself that she had split off as a child would "come out" and act out these sadomasochistic episodes, in order to avoid the punishment of being beaten and remaining locked in the kennel. We understood her apparent adult compliance as a survival mechanism, learnt by watching what happened to the children who disobeyed. Judith Herman writes that

> In the same way that narratives of fear must be titrated so that the client experiences mastery over fear rather than a reinstatement of it, so, too, narratives of shame should be titrated so that the client experiences dignity rather than humiliation in the telling. [This volume]

Through this shared understanding, Ann and I were able to revisit the "shame" of her abuse and begin to honour the coping mechanism which had enabled her to survive her childhood.

Ann then felt able to share more of her internal world without fear that I would steal it. She wrote to me and drew pictures. She drew pictures of eyes (hers and mine) and was then finally able to make eye contact with me without shame.

Nevertheless, Ann's fears of punishment and death escalated as she made plans to leave home. She attended our sessions in extremely hostile, dissociated self-states. She tried to play S&M games with me and tried out complex manipulation. For example, she told me that I would trigger her suicide if I were to say or do the "wrong" thing. She then threatened to manufacture a complaint against me, something that would get me struck off. This would mean that even if she could not have me, no one else could either. I could feel her escalating levels of fear and rage in the countertransference with such intensity that, in one session, we experienced a shared hallucination of her holding a knife in her hand. It was an important metaphor for our relationship, as it literally felt that we were poised on a knife-edge. It was never clear which way it would go.

It felt as if Ann could be stuck at this point forever. It only became possible for a shift to occur through an enactment in the transference–countertransference that I came to think of as "the phone call battle". I was, by this point, feeling devoured, in what Valerie Sinason calls the "cannibalistic countertransference". Ann's persecution and abuse of me in the sessions, and her constant pushing of boundaries between sessions, were making me feel victimized. In Kernberg's words, "It is as if the patient's life depends on keeping the therapist under control" (quoted in Herman, 1992, p. 136). "There may also be a displacement of the rage from the perpetrator onto the caregiver" (*ibid.*, p. 137). I realized that I had to liberate myself from the saboteur in the room. Anything else would lock us into a sadomasochistic re-enactment that would feel like a "home from home" for Ann in which relationships were again abusive, only this time I would be the victim. I told Ann that I felt unable to continue the work unless the bullying, and the constant attacks on me and the therapy, stopped. I found my subjectivity, and stood up to her persecutors. She knew I meant it. Having experienced *me* doing this, she was finally enabled to do it, too. She left home, broke contact with those abusing her, and ceased her attacks on the therapy.

Being able to experience me as a separate person who could under-stand her also opened up the possibility for Ann that I could be inti-mate with her. This was startling for Ann. She had begun to take in the maternal mirroring, but as a result of this next developmental leap, with two subjects in the room, the nature of the love and attachment between us changed. We experienced periods of exhilarating intensity and connection between us. This again triggered Ann's unbearable terror of, and shame at, unrequited love, and it felt again as if we were locked in stalemate at every session.

Then, one day, Ann came for her session in acute distress and told me about some biscuits she had discovered that week: organic, choco-late orange biscuits. She started crying, saying that she could not bear it that she now knew they existed. She thought about them all the time, wanted them all the time. What if she could not control the crav-ing? What if they were withdrawn, or the shop sold out? She would never be able to bear it.

By this stage in the therapy, Ann was able to recognize very quickly in the session that this was a response to the intense erotic feelings she had experienced in the room. All her life she had protected herself from ever falling in love, ever risking her love being unrequited. Now she had lost her defence, she feared that she would be utterly dysregulated. She felt it would destroy her, that her feelings were shameful, and that she could never be loved in return when she was so deeply disgusting and shameful inside.

In near despair, I decided to write to Ann. I felt that unless I was willing to make myself vulnerable and exposed in the relationship, the inherent inequality Herman describes would leave Ann locked in shame forever. I wrote to Ann about my feelings that she deserved to be loved, that I did love her. I wrote about how desperately I wanted to reach her, to let her know she mattered, that she did not deserve to feel shame, and how I felt I was failing her by not reaching her. How I felt her mother was there with us, making us both feel ashamed and worthless, but that, nonetheless, this was not succeeding in preventing me from wanting to be close to Ann, and would never make me believe Ann was bad inside.

She wrote back to me: "I seem to have been thinking all the time about (shame). I know this always comes up when I try to get closer to you and it acts as a block. I feel it's unbearable that I'm not allowed to have you.

"It makes me feel like a sort of murderer. I keep resisting the word, but I have to accept it. I feel like the guard of a prison camp inside. Like my mother. Sometimes inside I get thoughts of abusing you or of getting you to abuse me, as a way to escape the deadness. But I know I'm unable to do that anymore, I've changed enough to know that doesn't work or release anything. I look at you and none of the past ways of trying to have relationships will help. I was proud not to feel and now I love you; you are linked to me now inside in a deep way. I guess I should understand it that I want to be alive, and I want you to be. Not for one of us to have to murder the other. Although that brings terrible shame it will have to be borne, and I will have to deny the rules and messages that I do not deserve it".

This experience helped me to realize that shame states can only be overcome by reconnection: this intersubjective moment was experienced by Ann as a reconnection. I realized through this intervention with Ann that there was something in me as a therapist that had needed to let go of my own need for primitive omnipotence, to fully acknowledge that we cannot stop bad things happening to us, we cannot stop people rejecting us or abandoning us. I had to risk that first before Ann could.

I also needed to recognize that what had happened to Ann could just as easily have happened to me. I could have been born into a different family. In different circumstances, I could have been manipulated, humiliated, and abused as Ann had been. I had experienced it with her in the countertransference, and learnt that I, too, was capable of being shamed, and of feeling unable to fight back. I was able to let go of the need we can have to label some people as victims and to believe that somehow they must be weak or to blame for what happens to them.

The final significant moment of meeting in breaking down the secrecy and shame between us came a month later, when Ann had left a session saying she felt shame about her love for me, because I could never share the passion she felt for me. After she left, I wrote a poem. I wrote it for her and to her. In the poem I expressed how I saw her, how much I wanted to reach her and let her know how extraordinary she is; how I wanted to offer her a resting place, for recovery; how I admired and had learnt from her. I am not a great poet, but it was utterly authentic and from the heart. I felt again I needed to take a risk. I sent it to Ann.

This proved to be the turning point: a moment of healing on that agonizingly painful journey to recovery. I want to finish with a quote from a letter I received from Ann about a month ago:

"I was thinking last Tuesday really good things about you. I used to feel so scared if I said or thought nice things about you. Like I'd be punished. But I love you. I can say that now. And I know what I mean to you and that you'll always be there if I need you. Thank you. I'm so glad you know I'm not inadequate, that you know I'm not bad inside. I don't think so either".

I would like to leave you with some words from an interview with Judith Herman:

> The individual can't deal with this alone. That's the take home message that I try to give whenever I teach, and whenever I do my therapeutic work. I don't think patients, survivors, victimized people can recover in isolation. They need other people and they need to take caution in affiliation with others. I don't think therapists can do therapeutic work alone. When we're isolated with this we do give in to despair. Just when you think you've heard everything somebody comes along with a story that just blows you away all over again. So you're dealing with very profound questions of human evil, human cruelty, human sadism. The abuse of power and authority. And the antidote to that is the solidarity of resistance. Nobody can do that alone.

She goes on to say,

The reason I stick with this work is that I'm constantly in awe of the resilience of the people we work with. They really do get better; they really do make new lives for themselves. They find incredibly creative ways to put the pieces of their lives back together—I get to observe the way the patients re-instill hope constantly, in those who are privileged to observe or work with them during this process. [Herman, 2000]

I know myself it is the inspiration I get from the courage of the clients I work with, including those I have talked about today, that gives me the ability to get up and keep fighting the case for us to provide this essential form of therapy. We need to win the argument for long-term attachment based therapy for trauma survivors. We owe it to them. Thank you.

References

Herman, J. (1992). *Trauma and Recovery: From Domestic Abuse to Political Terror*. New York: Basic Books.

Herman, J. (2000). Interview with Harry Kreisler. "Psychological insight and political understanding: the case of trauma and recovery", Conversations with History, Institute of International Studies, UC Berkeley, 21 September.

Stern, D. (1985). *The Interpersonal World of the Infant: A View from Psychoanalysis and Developmental Psychology*. New York: Basic Books.

Reading list

Bloom, S. (1997). *Creating Sanctuary: Toward the Evolution of Sane Societies*. London: Routledge.

Bromberg, P. M. (2001). *Standing in the Spaces: Essays on Clinical Process, Trauma and Dissociation*. New York: Analytic Press.

Buchheim, A., & George, C. (2011). The representational, neurobiological and emotional foundation of attachment disorganization in borderline personality disorder and anxiety disorder. In: J. Solomon & C. George (Eds.), *Disorganization of Attachment and Caregiving* (pp. 343–382). New York: Guilford Press.

Fernando, S. (1999). Race in the construction of dangerousness. Paper presented at the Bowlby Memorial Lecture, CAPP, 1999.

Fletchman Smith, B. (2000). A little girl's story. In: *Mental Slavery: Psychoanalytic Studies of Caribbean People* (Chapter 6, pp. 77–92). London: Rebus Press.

Gerhardt, S. (2004). *Why Love Matters: How Affection Shapes a Baby's Brain*. London, New York: Routledge.

Herman, J. (1992). *Trauma and Recovery: The Aftermath of Violence from Domestic Abuse to Political Terror*. New York: Basic Books.

Herman, J. L. (2000). *Father–Daughter Incest*. Cambridge, MA: Harvard University Press.

Hesse, E. (1996). Discourse, memory and the Adult Attachment Interview: a note with emphasis on the emerging cannot classify category. *Infant Mental Health Journal*, 17: 4–11.

Hesse, E., & Main, M. (2000). Disorganized infant, child and adult attachment: collapse in behavioral and attentional strategies. *Journal of the American Psychoanalytic Association*, 48: 1097–1127.

Hesse, E., Main, M., Abrams, K. Y., & Rifkin, A. (2003). Unresolved states regarding loss or abuse can have "second-generation" effects: disorganized, role-inversion and frightening ideation in the offspring of traumatized non-maltreating parents. In: D. J. Siegel & M. F. Solomon (Eds.), *Healing Trauma: Attachment, Mind, Body and Brain* (pp. 57–106). New York: Norton.

Holmes, J. (2004). Disorganized attachment and Borderline Personality Disorder: a clinical perspective. *Journal of Attachment and Human Development*, 6(2): 181–190.

Howell, E. F. (2005). *The Dissociative Mind*. London: Analytic Press.

Kahr, B. (1993). Ancient infanticide and modern schizophrenia: the clinical uses of psycho-historical research. *Journal of Psychohistory*, 20: 267–273.

Laing, R. D. (1959a). Ontological insecurity. In: *The Divided Self* (Chapter 3, pp. 39–64). Harmondsworth: Penguin, 1990.

Laing, R. D. (1959b). The embodied and unembodied self. In: *The Divided Self* (Chapter 4, pp 65–77). Harmondsworth: Penguin, 1990.

Laing, R. D. (1990). The ghost of the weed garden: a study of a chronic schizophrenic. In: *The Divided Self* (Chapter 11, pp. 178–205). Harmondsworth: Penguin.

Lewis, H. B. (1971). *Shame and Guilt in Neurosis*. New York: International Universities Press.

Liotti, G. (1995). Disorganized/disoriented attachment in the psychotherapy of the dissociative disorders. In: S. Goldberg, R. Muir, & J. Kerr (Eds.), *Attachment Theory: Social, Developmental and Clinical Perspectives* (pp. 343–363). Hillsdale, NJ: Analytic Press.

Liotti, G. (1999) Understanding the dissociative processes: the contribution of attachment theory. *Psychoanalytic Inquiry*, 19: 757–783.

Liotti, G. (2004a). Trauma, dissociation and disorganized attachment: three strands of a single braid. *Psychotherapy: Theory, Research, Practice, Training*, 41: 472–486.

Liotti, G. (2004b). The inner schema of borderline states and its correction during psychotherapy: a cognitive-evolutionary approach. In: P. Gilbert (Ed.), *Evolutionary Theory and Cognitive Psychotherapy* (pp. 137–160). New York: Springer.

Mollon, P. (2001). Schizophrenia and depression: the fragmented self and the thwarted self. In: *Releasing the Self: The Healing Legacy of Heinz Kohut* (Chapter 8, pp. 165–190). London: Whurr.

Ogden, P., Minton, K., & Pain, C. (2006). *Trauma and the Body: A Sensorimotor Approach to Psychotherapy*. London, New York: W. W. Norton.

Read, J. (2004). Poverty, ethnicity and gender. In: J. Read, L. R. Mosher, & R. P. Bentall (Eds.), *Models of Madness: Psychological, Social and Biological Approaches to Schizophrenia* (Chapter 13, pp. 161–194). London: Routledge.

Read, J., Goodman, L., Morrison, A. P., Ross, C. A., & Aderhold, V. (2004). Childhood trauma, loss and stress. In: J. Read, L. R. Mosher, & R. P. Bentall (Eds.), *Models of Madness: Psychological, Social and Biological Approaches to Schizophrenia* (Chapter 16, pp. 222–252). London: Routledge.

Read, J., Van Os, J., Morrison, A. P., & Ross, C. A. (2005). Childhood trauma, psychosis and schizophrenia: a literature review with theoretical and clinical implications. *Acta Psychiatrica Scandinavica, 112*: 330–350.

Roberts, G. (1999). The rehabilitation of rehabilitation: a narrative approach to psychosis. In: G. Roberts & J. Holmes (Eds.), *Healing Stories: Narrative in Psychiatry and Psychotherapy* (Chapter 8, pp. 152–180). Oxford: Oxford University Press.

Searles, H. (1994). *My Work with Borderline Patients*. Northvale, NJ: Jason Aronson.

Searles, H. (1959). The effort to drive the other person crazy: an element in the aetiology and psychotherapy of schizophrenia. In: *Collected Papers on Schizophrenia and Related Subjects* (Chapter 8, pp. 254–283). London: Maresfield Library, 1993.

Searles, H. (1999). *Countertransference and Related Subjects: Selected Papers*. Madison, CT: International Universities Press.

Sinason, V. (2002). *Attachment, Trauma and Multiplicity: Working with Dissociative Identity Disorder*. London: Brunner-Routledge.

Solomon, J., & George, C. (1999). *Attachment Disorganization*. New York: Guilford Press.

Stolorow, R. D., Brandchaft, B., & Atwood, G. E. (1987). Treatment of psychotic states. In: *Psychoanalytic Treatment: An Intersubjective Approach* (Chapter 9, pp. 132–172). Hillsdale, NJ: Analytic Press.

Van der Hart, O., Nijenhuis, E. R. S., & Steele, K. (2006). *The Haunted Self: Structural Dissociation and the Treatment of Chronic Traumatization*. London: Norton.

Van der Kolk, B. A., McFarlane, A. C., & Weisaeth, L. (1996) *Traumatic Stress: the Effects of Overwhelming Experience on Mind, Body, and Society*. New York: Guilford Press.

Vas Dias, S. (2004). Cumulative phobic response to early traumatic attachment: aspects of a developmental psychotherapy in midlife. *Journal of Attachment and Human Development, 6*(2): 163–179.

Werbart, A., & Lindbom-Jakobson, M. (2001). The 'living dead' – survivors of torture and psychosis. In: P. Williams (Ed.), *A Language for Psychosis: Psychoanalysis of Psychotic States*. London: Whurr.

Winnicott, D. W. (1974). Fear of breakdown. *International Review of Psychoanalysis*, 1:103–107.

Zulueta, de F. (1999). Borderline personality disorder as seen from an attachment perspective: a review. *Criminal Behaviour and Mental Health*, 9: 237–253.

Zulueta, de F. (2006). *From Pain to Violence, The Roots of Human Destructiveness*. Chichester: Wiley.

Zulueta, de F. (2006). The treatment of psychological trauma from the perspective of attachment research. *Journal of Family Therapy, 28*(4): 334–351.

Recommended listening

Between Ourselves: CD of the BBC Radio 4 programme broadcast in August 2006 and produced by Karen Gregor. Two women diagnosed with schizophrenia talk with Olivia O'Leary about their traumatic/ abusive childhoods, the experience of hearing voices, their treatment by the psychiatric services, their understanding of their mental illness, and how they cope with this in their everyday lives.

Background information about The Bowlby Centre

Promoting attachment and inclusion

Since 1976, The Bowlby Centre (formerly known as CAPP) has developed as an organization committed to the practice of attachment-based psychoanalytic psychotherapy. The Bowlby Centre is a dynamic, rapidly developing charity which aims both to train attachment-based psychoanalytic psychotherapists and to deliver a psychotherapy service to those who are most marginalized and frequently excluded from long-term psychotherapy.

We provide a four-year, part-time psychotherapy training accredited by the UKCP and operate a psychotherapy referral service for the public, including the low-cost Blues Project. The Bowlby Centre has a wealth of experience in the fields of attachment and loss and particular expertise in working with trauma and abuse. As part of our ongoing commitment to antidiscriminatory practice, we offer a consultation service to the public and private sectors and to individuals and groups in a wide variety of mental health settings.

We are engaged in outreach and special projects, working with care leavers, women experiencing violence and abuse, offenders and ex-offenders, people struggling with addiction to drugs, alcohol, eating difficulties, or self harm. We run short courses on "Attachment and Dissociation", and "The Application of Attachment Theory to Clinical Issues", including learning disabilities. The Bowlby Centre organizes conferences, including the annual John Bowlby Memorial Lecture, and has a series of publications which aim to further thinking and development in the field of attachment.

Bowlby Centre members participate extensively in all aspects of the field, making outstanding theoretical, research, and clinical contributions. Their cutting-edge work is consistently published in the leading journals and monographs.

The Bowlby Centre values

- The Centre believes that mental distress has its origin in failed and inadequate attachment relationships in early life and is best treated in the context of a long-term human relationship.
- Attachment relationships are shaped in the real world and impacted upon by poverty, discrimination, and social inequality. The impact of the social world will be part of the therapy.
- Psychotherapy should be available to all, and from an attachment-based psychoanalytic perspective, especially those discriminated against or described as "unsuitable" for therapy.
- Psychotherapy should be provided with respect, warmth, openness, a readiness to interact and relate, and free from discrimination of any kind.
- Those who have been silenced about their experiences and survival strategies must have their reality acknowledged and not pathologized.
- The Bowlby Centre values inclusiveness, access, diversity, authenticity, and excellence. All participants in our organization share the responsibility for antidiscriminatory practice in relation to race, ethnicity, gender, sexuality, age, (dis)ability, religion, class, educational and learning style.

Patron
Sir Richard Bowlby

Trustees
Dr Elaine Arnold
Dick Blackwell
Dr Heather Geddes

For more information please contact:

The Bowlby Centre
147 Commercial Street
Spitalfields
London E1 6BJ

Telephone 020 7247 9101
Email admin@thebowlbycentre.org.uk
www.thebowlbycentre.org.uk